Nigeria's 2019 Democratic Experience

Nigeria's 2019 Democratic Experience

Edited by
Egodi Uchendu and Olawari D. J. Egbe

DE GRUYTER

ISBN (HARDCOVER) 978-3-11-154059-7
e-ISBN (PDF) 978-3-11-076656-1
e-ISBN (EPUB) 978-3-11-076660-8

Library of Congress Control Number: 2022931107

Bibliographic information published by the Deutsche Nationalbibliothek
The Deutsche Nationalbibliothek lists this publication in the Deutsche Nationalbibliografie;
detailed bibliographic data are available on the Internet at http://dnb.dnb.de.

© 2024 Walter de Gruyter GmbH, Berlin/Boston
This volume is text- and page-identical with the hardback published in 2022.
Cover image: butenkow / iStock / Getty Images Plus

www.degruyter.com

Acknowledgements

The underwhelming feeling generated by Nigeria's 2019 elections prompted this academic exercise, the goal of which is to dissect the sudden retrogression of the nation's democratic journey and to proffer solutions on how it could be fixed.

We acknowledge all the authors who saw the need to engage with this reflection of our 2019 election experiment in order to push forward the nation's democratization plan. We also thank all who supported this exercise by reading the drafts and proffering suggestions for improvement. Our thanks go, as well, to the staff of De Gruyter, Berlin, who processed and published this work.

This study of Nigeria's 2019 general election is not exhaustive. We hope that it will stimulate more reflections on Nigeria's democracy until she gets it right and becomes a stable and exemplary democratic nation with strong and effective institutions.

Foreword

In peripheral states like Nigeria, elections are epic life and death struggles, as various factions and fractions of the local wing of the ruling class employ plethora of methods, including intimidation, thuggery violence, assassination and vote rigging, to capture state power at the federal level, and local power at the state level. The control of state power is critical, because it is the primary instrument for the primitive accumulation of wealth by the ruling faction or fraction of the local wing of the ruling class and their relations. Concomitantly, since politics in Nigeria and other peripheral societies is a zero-sum game, the ruling faction or fraction ensures that the opposition factions or fractions at both the federal and state levels are denied access to the largesse that the control of state power ensures. In sum, despite the political rhetoric, the overarching purpose of the control over power at the federal and state levels is not about transforming the material conditions of ordinary Nigerians, including addressing abject mass poverty, disparities in wealth and income, the high rates of unemployment, and the sordid state of education and health care. Instead, elections serve legitimation purposes: They are designed to convey the impression that the faction or fraction of the local wing of the ruling class that "wins" control of state power was given the opportunity to "govern" by the Nigerian electorate. But, once the ruling faction or fraction "wins" state power at the federal level, and local power at the state level (with few exceptions), the centrepiece of their agendas during their respective tenure of office is to use national and local power to engage in the primitive accumulation of wealth through sundry illegal means, including stealing from the public coffers, bribery, extortion, fraudulent contracts and procurement schemes. In short, since the founding elections that ushered in the "First Republic" on 1st October 1960, elections in Nigeria have been shaped by the competing desires of the various factions and fractions of the local wing of the ruling class to "win" and use state power to accumulate wealth. Against this background, the 2019 elections in Nigeria were no exception.

In this book, "Nigeria's 2019 Democratic Experience," the editors and the contributors have done a masterful job in tackling several of the major issues that shaped the 2019 Nigerian elections: the role of political parties, including the ruling (APC), and the opposition political parties such as the People's Democratic Party (PDP) (the former ruling party and the main opposition party), thuggery and political violence, the role of the Independent National Electoral Commission (INEC), and external interests, including interference. For example, external powers such as the United States and the European Union states were interested in the 2019 election for economic and strategic reasons. For example, with the largest population and economy in Africa, Nigeria provides market for the sale of American and European goods and for investments in the oil and other sectors by metropolitan-based multinational corporations, in light of the competition from China. Similarly, Nigeria is a major producer of oil, which is important for feeding the industrial-manufacturing complexes of the United States and Europe. Similarly, Nigeria is an important bulwark in the struggle against global terrorism, an issue that is of strategic significance to the United States and European states.

Finally, this book makes important contributions to the literature on elections and democratization in Nigeria, Africa, the "Global South," and the world. This is because while the book's focus is on Nigeria, the issues discussed have application to other countries, including the United States, which had a tumultuous 2020 presidential election, including an abortive "constitutional coup" that was anchored by post-election violence.

George Klay Kieh, Jr.

Dean of the Barbara Jordan-Mickey Leland School of Public Affairs & Professor of Political Science, Texas Southern University, USA, and Professor of International Relations, Graduate School, African Methodist Episcopal University, Liberia, and President of the African Studies and Research Forum (ASRF)

Table of Contents

List of Abbreviations —— XI

Map of Nigeria —— XV

Egodi Uchendu
Introduction: Interrogating Democratisation Deficits in Nigeria From the 2019 General Election —— 1

Tunde Agara
Political Parties, Political Opposition and Elections: Towards Consolidating Democracy in Nigeria —— 13

Olawari D. J. Egbe
The Silent Western Votes and the Emergence of the Buhari/APC Presidency —— 33

Olawari D. J. Egbe and David O. Gogo
Ruling and Opposition Parties' Reactions to External Interference in the 2019 Presidential Election —— 55

Patrick Agbedejobi
A Tale of Defective Democracy: De-Democratisation in Nigeria —— 73

John T. Tsuwa and Faeren M. Agaigbe
INEC, the Electoral Process and the Conduct of Elections in 2019 —— 91

Patrick Chukwudike Okpalaeke and Tony Johnson Ekpo
Murdering Their Consciences, 'Right to Vote' and Ethno-Political Conflict in Lagos during the 2019 General Election —— 109

Chikaodili Arinze Orakwue
Thuggery and Election Violence in the 2019 Election —— 131

Nsemba Edward Lenshie, Isa Mohammed and Patience Jacob Kondu
Electoral Politics and Violence in Taraba State —— 149

Obinna Ukaeje
The Security Implications of Election-related Violence in Nigeria and the Way Forward —— 173

Fidelis A. E. Paki
The Challenges of Election Security in Nigeria: A Study of the 2019 General Election —— 195

Uche S. Odozor, Olasupo O. Thompson, Scholastica N. Atata and Stanislaus O. Okonkwo
Beyond the 2019 General Election: Critical Lessons for Nigeria's Democratic Experiment —— 215

Appendix: Timetable and Schedule of Activities for 2019 General Elections —— 235

List of Authors —— 239

List of Abbreviations

AAC	African Action Congress
ACD	Advanced Congress of Democrats
AD	Alliance for Democracy
AFRC	Armed Forces Ruling Council
AG	Action Group
AHRDC	African Humanities Research and Development Circle
ANPP	All Nigeria People's Party
APC	All Progressives Congress
APGA	All Progressives Grand Alliance
APLP	All Peoples Liberation Party
APO	Assistant Presiding Officers
APP	All Peoples Party
ASRF	African Studies and Research Forum
BNYL	Biafra Nations Youth League
BTI	Bertelsmann Transformation Index
BYM	Borno Youth Movement
CAN	Action Congress of Nigeria
CAN	Christian Association of Nigeria
CCP	Coalition for Clean Polls
CDD	Centre for Democracy and Development
CDS	Chief of Defence Staff
CEWS	Conflict Early Warning Signs
CIALS	Committee of Indigenous Association of Lagos State
CJN	Chief Justice of Nigeria
CNC	Congress for National Consensus
CPC	Congress for Progressive Change
CSOs	Civil Society Organisations
CSRS	Centre for Strategic Research and Studies
DAP	Democratic Advance Party
DP	Democracy Promotion
DP	Dynamic Party
DPN	Democratic Party of Nigeria
DSS	Department of State Security
EU	European Union
EA	Electoral Act
EAB	Electoral Act Bill
EAP	Electronic Accreditation Process
ECL	Electoral Logistics Committee
ECN	Electoral Commission of Nigeria
EFCC	Economic and Financial Crimes Commission
EMB	Electoral Management Bodies
EUEOM	European Union Election Observation Mission
FCT	Federal Capital Territory
FDI	Foreign Direct Investment

FEC	Federal Electoral Commission
FEDECO	Federal Electoral Commission
FGDs	Focus Group Discussions
GDM	Grassroot Democratic Movement
GNPP	Great Nigeria Peoples Party
GoG	Gulf of Guinea
GP	Green Party
HoRs	House of Representatives
HRW	Human Rights Watch
ICCES	Inter-agency Consultative Committee on Election Security
INEC	Independent National Electoral Commission
ING	Interim National Government
ING	International Governmental
IRI	International Republican Institute
ITP	Ilorin Talaka Parapo
JP	Justice Party
KII	Key Informant Interviews
LC	Liberal Convention
LGA	Local Government Area
LP	Labour Party
LYM	Lagos Youth Movement
MDF	Midwest Democratic Front
MDJ	Movement for Democracy and Justice
MURIC	Muslim Rights Concern
NAP	Nigeria Advance Party
NASS	National Assembly
NCBWA	National Congress of British West Africa
NCNC	National Council of Nigeria and the Cameroon
NCP	National Conscience Party
NCPN	National Centre Party of Nigeria
NCSSR	Nigerian Civil Society Situation Room
NDC	Niger Delta Congress
NDF	Nigerian Democratic Forum
NDI	National Democratic Institute
NEC	National Electoral Commission
NECON	National Electoral Commission of Nigeria
NEF	Northern Elders Forum
NEPU	Northern Elements Progressive Union
NGF	Northern Governors' Forum
NGOs	Non-governmental Organisations
NHRC	National Human Rights Commission
NIS	Nigeria Immigration Service
NLP	Nigerian Labour Party
NNC	Nigerian National Congress
NNDP	Nigerian National Democratic Party
NPC	Northern People's Congress
nPDP	New People's Democratic Party

NPF	Nigeria Police Force
NPN	National Party of Nigeria
NPP	Nigeria Peoples Party
NRP	National Republican Party
NSCDC	Nigeria Security and Civil Defence Corps
NSP	National Solidarity Party
NST	Nigeria Security Tracker
NTA	Nigeria Television Authority
NTYTR	Not-Too-Young-To-Rule
NYM	Nigerian Youth Movement
NYSC	National Youth Service Corps
ONSA	Office of the National Security Adviser
PDP	People's Democratic Party
PFN	Peoples' Front of Nigeria
PLAC	Policy and Legal Advocacy Centre
PO	Presiding Officers
PRP	Peoples' Redemption Party
PSP	Peoples' Solidarity Party
PVC	Permanent Voters Card
RA	Registration Area
RP	Republican Party
SCR	Smart Card Readers
SDP	Social Democratic Party
SHoA	State House of Assembly
SSS	State Security Services
TNCs	Transnational Corporations
UDP	United Democratic Party
UMBC	United Middle Belt Congress
UNCP	United Nigeria Congress Party
UNDF	United Nations Democracy Fund
UPN	Unity Party of Nigeria
UPP	United Peoples Party
USAFRICOM	U.S. Africa Command
USSR	Union of Soviet Socialist Republics
UYN	Union of Young Nigerians

Map of Nigeria

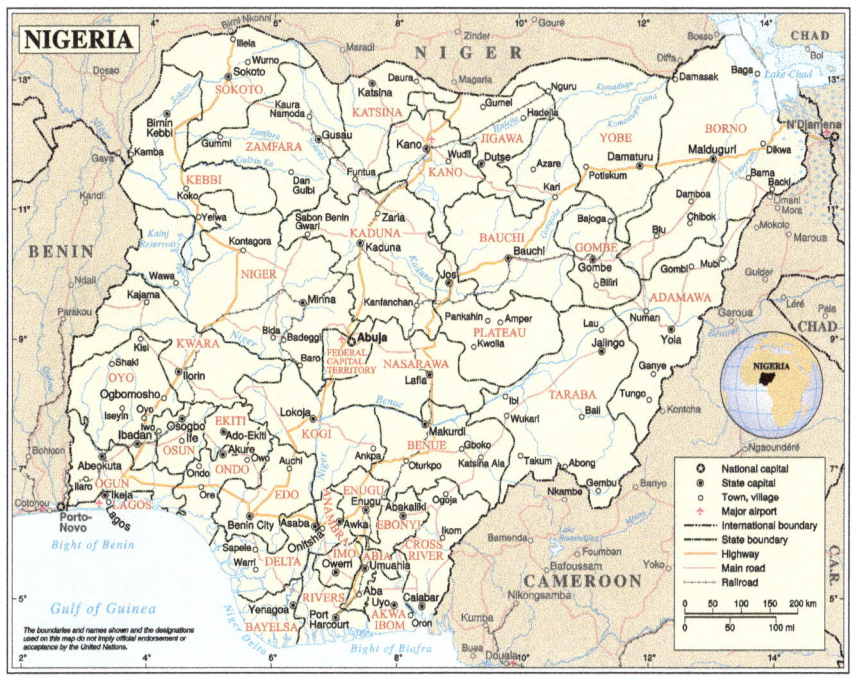

Map 1: Nigeria's 36 States with the Federal Capital Territory. Source: political map of Nigeria. svg.

Egodi Uchendu
Introduction: Interrogating Democratisation Deficits in Nigeria From the 2019 General Election

The idea for *Nigeria's 2019 Democratic Experience* stems from the desire for near perfect, hitch-free elections in Nigeria. The book, therefore, deals with the puzzle: How can national elections – a major ingredient for conferring legitimacy on governments, which until 2019 were run badly in the country – be made right in the present democratic form of government in Nigeria, which began in 1999.

The literature on Nigeria's democratic experiment during her First Republic (1963–1966), Second Republic (1979–1983), Third Republic (1992–1993) and the current Fourth Republic (since 1999) clearly shows that the country's electoral system suffers from concealed North – South differences in the form of religious, ethnic and political infractions. These differences had long existed and surfaces in the politics of the nation especially during electioneering seasons, often resulting in political violence, alongside other electoral maladies.[1] If Nigeria must get it right in her electioneering process, these challenges must be tackled headlong before they force her democracy into autocracy.[2] Presently, this seems a far cry. As a result, Nigeria's current electioneering experience has continually recorded repeated failures just as in all previous democratic experiments since 1963. The fate of the previous three republics may as well befall this Fourth Republic because the mistakes that ended them were wantonly recycled.[3]

The presidential election that heralded Nigeria's Fourth Republic was held on 27 February 1999. It culminated in the emergence of General Olusegun Obasanjo of the People's Democratic Party (PDP) as the president. President Obasanjo served for two consecutive tenures (1999–2003; 2003–2007); and the PDP remained in power until 2015, producing two more successive executive presi-

---
[1] Peter J. Schraeder, *African Politics and Society: A Mosaic in Transformation* (Belmont, CA: Thomson Wadsworth, 2004).
[2] Jan Teorell, *Determinants of Democratisation: Explaining Regime Change in the World, 1972–2006* (Cambridge, Mass: Cambridge University Press, 2010).
[3] Osita Agbu, ed., *Elections and Governance in Nigeria's Fourth Republic* (Dakar: CODESRIA, 2017).

Egodi Uchendu, University of Nigeria, Nsukka

dents – Mr Umaru Yar'Adua (2007–2011) and Dr Goodluck Ebele Jonathan (2011–2015). Whereas the period 1999 to 2010 hardly provided a voice for opposition groups, the years, 2011 to 2015, witnessed extensive political discourses that expanded the political space and strengthened civil society organizations.

In tandem with the ethos of liberal democracy, another round of elections was conducted in 2015. The 2015 general election was a hallmark in the annals of Nigeria's political trajectory for three reasons:

a) A sitting president, Dr Goodluck Jonathan was ousted by an opposition party, the All Progressives Congress (APC).[4] This was the first ever of such in Nigeria's chequered political history.
b) The incorporation of technology in the electoral process.
c) The most important for Nigeria's nascent democracy, President Jonathan conceded defeat and called to congratulate his major opponent General Muhammadu Buhari even before the final votes of the presidential election were counted.

All of these political developments attracted accolades from local and foreign election observers.[5] Thus, the events of the 2015 general election heralded a crucial stage in the nation's democratisation process – a scenario where the major political parties, the PDP and APC, succeeded themselves without political skirmishes. These developments signify democratic consolidation in the country and in Africa, a continent known for second election debacles.[6]

As it turned out, the 2019 election experience was a disappointment. The unruly nature of the electioneering period, the profligacy of political contenders, the degree of hate speech, attacks on the opposition and the media, the mobilisation of voters along ethnic and religious lines, and the desperation for self-succession, among others, demoralized the greater population of Nigeria's eligible voters as well as all others who wished for a progressive growth in the nation's democratic history. Voters were forcefully barred from freely expressing themselves with their votes. The clear underwhelming feeling gendered by the manipulation of votes and voters, electoral and other state institutions, including security agencies, were at the core of this scholarly examination, whose primary

---

[4] APC is a coalition of three main opposition parties – the Congress for Progressive Change (CPC), Action Congress of Nigeria (ACN), All Nigeria People's Party (ANPP) and a faction of the All Progressive Grand Alliance (APGA).
[5] Hakeem Onapajo and Dele Babalola, "Nigeria's 2019 general elections-a shattered hope?" *The Round Table: The Commonwealth Journal of International Affairs* 109, 4 (2020): 363–367.
[6] Ogaba Oche, "Presidential and Gubernatorial Elections in the Fourth Republic," in *Elections and Governance in Nigeria's Fourth Republic*, ed. Osita Agbu (Dakar: CODESRIA, 2017), 124–136.

goal is to analyse what happened in 2019 in order to identify potential lessons that could help subsequent generations of Nigerians to push for a better democratic experience. This review of Nigeria's 2019 election incorporates the story of Nigeria's democracy from its inception; it outlines the paths so far taken, and pinpoints the expanding range of obstacles that continue to confront citizens' efforts towards achieving a solid national democratic profile.

Meanwhile, the disappointing and unanticipated developments in the 2019 election season attracted a babel of critical voices from the media, the academia, the National Assembly, the judiciary, civil society organisations and even international election observers and missions. These various interest groups expressed surprise that Nigeria's political class did not capitalise on the gains of 2015, which earned the country re-echoing accolades from within and outside the shores of the country, to improve on their democratic experience. It is widely acknowledged that although general elections in most countries are saddled with peculiar irregularities, these challenges are commonplace in the Global South. However, they are not unavoidable. The nature and magnitude of electoral irregularities in Nigeria's 2019 general election remain confounding. The following two incidents support the foregoing assertion. The first was President Buhari's refusal to consent to the Electoral Amendment Act for the fourth time in two years. For this, the president remarked that

> passing a new electoral bill this far into the electoral process for the 2019 general elections, which commenced under the 2015 Electoral Act, could create some uncertainty about the applicable legislation to govern the process. Any real or apparent change to the rules this close to the election may provide an opportunity for disruption and confusion in respect of which law governs the electoral process.[7]

President Buhari's decline to assent to the Act was widely interpreted as fear for unfavourable fallouts from the 2019 election especially when the option of electronic transfers of election results was provided in place of the manipulation-prone analogue method of collating, counting and announcing election results. The second incident was the president's hasty removal of the sitting Chief Justice of the Federation, Justice Walter Onnoghen, a Southern Christian.[8] This sack, as believed by a wide spectrum of Nigerians, was also borne our of fear of the crucial roles the Chief Justice would play in the 2019 elections. Justice Tanko Mo-

---

[7] Jude Egbas, "This is why President Buhari refused to sign Electoral Amendment Bill for the 4th time in 2 years," *Pulse*, 10 December 2018, https://www.this-is-why-president-buhari-refused-to-sign-electoral-amendment-bill-for-the-4th/vrc24jm (accessed 7 August 2021).
[8] Bridget Chiedu, "Why Buhari removed me as CJN – Walter Onnoghen speaks," *The Guardian Nigeria*, 19 March 2021.

hammad, a Northern Muslim, replaced Justice Onnoghen without recourse to due process from the Nigeria Judicial Service Council (NJC).[9] Previous general elections were not any different. The political developments before and during the 2019 general election left many irredeemable scenarios, which could be likened to a cancerous wound that is unyielding to medication, including surgery.

While taking the 2019 general election as its point of departure, this book assembled a network of rich scholarship from contrasting perspectives to address several issues on electoral democracy in Nigeria. Those infractions on the 2019 general election include the failure of the political class in Nigeria to deliver on electoral promises,[10] hastily formed parties in 1999 that lacked ideological clarity and relied on a 'must-win mentality' which in turn led them to unorthodox electioneering strategies,[11] electoral violence,[12] election influences such as vote buying and turnout buying,[13] ethno-religious interjections,[14] brazen election insecurity,[15] compromises from officials of the election management organ – Independent National Electoral Commission (INEC), double standards of the judiciary in its pronouncements,[16] external influences[17] and the ill-timed

---

9 Taiwo-Hassan Adebayo, "PROFILE: What You Need To Know About Justice Ibrahim Tanko Muhammad, new Acting Chief Justice of Nigeria," *Premium Times*, 25 January 2019, https://www.premiumtimesng.com/features-and-interviews/308000-profile-what-you-need-to-know-about-justice-ibrahim-tanko-muhammad-new-acting-chief-justice-of-nigeria.html (accessed 30 August 2021).
10 Isaac Shobayo, "Political class has failed Nigeria – Haruna Dabin," *Nigeria Tribune*, 20 June 2021.
11 Oche, "Presidential and Gubernatorial Elections in the Fourth Republic."
12 Sampson Chimene Obiam, "The Nigerian State and Electoral Violence: An Analysis of the 2019 Presidential General Election in Nigeria," *Journal of Humanities and Social Science* 26, 3 (2021): 53–61.
13 Simeon Nichter, "Vote Buying or Turnout Buying? Machine Politics and the Secret Ballot," *American Political Science Review* 102, 1 (2008): 19–31.
14 Dele Babalola, "Ethno-religious Voting in Nigeria: Interrogating Voting Patterns in the 2019 Presidential Election," *The Round Table: The Commonwealth Journal of International Affairs* 109, 4, (2020): 377–385.
15 Noah Echa Attah, "Bullets and Ballots: Exploring Insecurities and the 2019 Elections in Nigeria," *Kujenga Amani*, 15 February 2019, https://kujenga-amani.ssrc.org/2019/02/15/bullets-and-ballots-exploring-insecurities-and-the-2019-elections-in-nigeria/ (accessed 7 August 2021).
16 J. Tochukwu Omenma, Okechukwu O. Ibeanu and Ike E. Onyishi, "Disputed Elections and the Role of the Court in Emerging Democracies in Africa: The Nigerian Example," *Journal of Politics and Democratisation* 2, 1 (2017): 28–55.
17 Edward S. Herman and Frank Broodhead, *Demonstration Elections: U.S.-Staged Elections in The Dominican Republic, Vietnam, and El Salvador* (Boston: South-End Press, 1984).

election results' approval by foreign election observers.[18] In addition to dealing with these core concerns from the 2019 elections in Nigeria, this book also addresses matters arising from previous elections, which had direct and indirect bearing on both the conduct and outcomes of the 2019 elections. Contributing authors therefore present different perceptions of Nigeria's democratic experience. They interrogate INEC's performance and how Nigeria's democracy can be consolidated. They also examine electoral violence as well as local and foreign electoral influences on both the 2015 and 2019 general elections.

Beyond this introduction, chapter two by Tunde Agara on "Political Parties, Political Opposition and Elections: Towards Consolidating Democracy in Nigeria" gives an overview of politics with emphases on the role of political parties and the purpose of elections. Specifically, he lays the background to the development of self-rule and democracy in Nigeria during colonial rule, starting with the formulation of the Clifford's Constitution in 1922. This chapter is important for an understanding of the structure and character of political parties in Nigeria. He shows how the ill-fated Third Republic suffered from the strangulating control of the military government of General Ibrahim Babangida. It was the first time in Nigeria's political history that the Armed Forces Ruling Council (AFRC) decreed political parties into existence, after choosing two out of over 40 interested political associations in the country. The same military government also decreed the selected parties' programmes, funding, ideologies, manifestoes, and structures. The whole idea would appear to aim at breaking the recurring reformatting of old parties, founded along ethnic and religious lines, whose practices derailed the promotion of true democracy in Nigeria leading to the abortion of the first and second republics. But the cumulative effect on Nigeria's democratic development was more negative than positive. Agara concludes with a look at the roles played by different opposition parties during the 2015 and 2019 general elections.

In chapter three, Olawari D. J. Egbe considers "The Silent Western Votes in Presidential Elections: Explaining the Emergence of the Buhari/APC Presidency in 2015 and 2019." He analyses the newly formed All Progressives Congress party and how it became the main opposition party in 2015 with the help of external influences. Egbe emphasizes that external intervention enabled the emergence of President Muhammadu Buhari and enthroned the APC as Nigeria's current ruling party after sixteen years of PDP dominance. From his assessment, the outcome of the 2015 presidential election that produced President Muhammadu Buhari and

---

[18] Judith G. Kelley, *Monitoring Democracy: When International Election Observation Works and Why It Often Fails* (Oxford: Princeton University Press, 2012).

enthroned APC-led government in Nigeria was determined through democracy promotion, tagged here as 'silent Western votes.' At the core of this external interference were President Barack Obama of the United States of America and Prime Minister David Cameron of the United Kingdom, and their respective governments. Egbe argues that the preponderance of democratic autocracies in Africa is a pointer that democracy promotion does not promote democracy, but rather the economic interests of practitioners of democracy promotion. Just like elections alone do not translate into a democracy; democracy cannot be transplanted from one country to another. Developed democracies who try to transplant and export democracy to the rest of the world, do not do in their own nations what they perpetrate abroad, which largely is to install governments or leaders they want in place of those the citizens of the countries they meddle in want.

The fourth chapter, jointly written by Egbe and David O. Gogo on "Ruling and Opposition Parties' Reactions to External Interference in 2019 Presidential Election" is a satire that spotlights the sharply contrasting and deceptive dispositions of the two dominant political parties in Nigeria, the PDP and the APC, over the democracy-promotion foreign policy programme of Western countries in Nigeria. These authors note that the country's two dominant parties, in their separate turns as ruling parties, were uncompromisingly unaccommodating of Western democracy promotion. Still, in their respective dispositions as opposition parties, both parties (the APC during the 2015 general election and the PDP in the 2019 general election) appreciated and condoned democracy promotion as a good development for Nigeria's democracy. President Goodluck Ebele Jonathan and the PDP, had in 2015, accused the governments of President Barack Obama and Prime Minister David Cameron of working to unseat the president.[19] All the while, the APC as the opposition party applauded whatever roles these two governments and their allies played in that presidential election. In the 2019 episode, however, it became the turn of President Muhammadu Buhari and the APC to accuse the West of aligning with the PDP in a grand design to unseat President Buhari.[20] Meanwhile, during that election season, the PDP saw a friend in the West in exactly the same way that APC did in 2015.

---

[19] Goodluck Ebele Jonathan, *My Transition Hours* (Allen, TX: Ezekiel Press, 2018).
[20] John Owen Nwachukwu, "Leave Nigeria alone, face your many troubles–APC tells US, UK, EU," *Daily Post*, 18 February 2019, https://dailypost.ng/2019/02/18/leave-nigeria-alone-face-many-troubles-apc-tells-us-uk-eu/ (accessed 8 May 2019); Tony Ezimakor, "Leave Nigeria Alone: Focus on Brexit, Russia Interference, APC Chieftain Tells US, UK, EU," *The Independent*, 19 February 2019.

In chapter five, Patrick Agbedejobi, writing on "A Tale of Defective Democracy: De-Democratisation in Nigeria" focus on the declining nature of Nigeria's fourth attempt at democratic governance. The author identifies categories of citizens excluded from participating in the electoral exercise either as voters or candidates for political offices. They include the diaspora community, the disabled and the youth. This author further lists the many infractions of the law by the current president, a scenario that exemplifies "unhindered or uncontested illiberal governance where the president or the executive arm of government has absolute powers over other branches of government." He also lists a litany of crimes committed by political office holders in contradiction of the law. With these, he came to the conclusion that Nigeria's democracy was defective; that, in fact, the country is de-democratising thereby resulting in the apparent unpopularity of the current administration.[21]

An examination of the role of INEC was undertaken in chapter six by John T. Tsuwa and Faeren M. Agaigbe. These authors identified a key lapse in the 2019 election, which is: the president's refusal to amend the Electoral Act before the elections. They both note that starting in 1999, it had become an established norm for the Electoral Act to undergo some amendments after every general election. The amendment draws on the lessons from the preceding elections. The preparations for the 2019 elections were not different, and the National Assembly initiated several changes towards the amendment of the Electoral Act. However, the president severally rejected the Amendment Bill. Meanwhile, the proposals put together by the National Assembly contained provisions that would make significant positive impacts on the conduct of elections in Nigeria such as the use of biometric technology to prevent inflation of figures in the register of voters as multiple registrations, a recurring practice in sections of the country, would be rendered technically impossible along with falsifying of votes. The non-approval of the amendment proposals of the Electoral Act Bill (EAB) meant that INEC was constrained to work with the Electoral Act of 2015 with its already identified imperfections. This situation consequently cast a shadow of uncertainty around the 2019 elections. A second major challenge of Nigeria's democratic experience which Tsuwa and Agaigbe interrogates is the failure of INEC to regulate campaigns, monitor the funding of political parties, and both

---

21 Ayodele Ameen, "Military Involvement and the Right to Vote in Nigeria," *Premium Times*, 8 March 2015, https://opinion.premiumtimesng.com/2015/03/08/military-involvement-and-the-right-to-vote-in-nigeria-by-ayodele-ameen/ (accessed 24 December 2018); "BREAKING: After Borno Office, Soldiers Invade Daily Trust's Abuja Office," *Sahara Reporters*, 6 January 2019, http://saharareporters.com/2019/01/06/breaking-after-borno-office-soldiers-invade-daily-trusts-abuja-office.

establish and enforce a code of conduct for political parties and the mainstream media. Other authors in chapters eight, eleven and twelve also touched on the performance of INEC, broadening the discourse on Nigeria's chief electoral organ.

Chapters seven to eleven address ethno-political conflicts that played out during the 2019 elections and issues of election violence and electoral insecurity in Nigeria. Patrick Chukwudike Okpalaeke and Tony Johnson Ekpo in chapter seven, "Murdering Their Consciences, 'Right to Vote' and Ethno-Political Conflict in Lagos: 2019 General Election in Perspective," probes a fundamental lacuna in the 1999 Constitution of Nigeria dealing with the right to vote candidates of choice along with the right to dwell in any part of the country. The authors argue that the franchise of people residing outside their home areas come under threat when they are compelled to vote against their consciences, a happenstance they found recurring in all of Nigeria's democratic dispensations. They identify the Igbo of South-East Nigeria resident in Lagos State as victims of such actions by autochthonous people, whose traditional rulers openly issued death threats on ahead of the 2019 elections. Beyond these, this target group occasionally suffered serial attacks in the process of being compelled to vote along the lines demanded by the traditional leaders of Lagos State.

While democratic consolidation remains elusive in Nigeria, and also in much of Africa, scholarship into electoral discourse in Nigeria has not relented in identifying the causes of Nigeria's democratic malaise and proffering ways of curbing the lag in democratisation. Chikaodili Arinze Orakwue in chapter eight – "Overview of Thuggery and Election Violence in Nigeria: An Interrogation of the 2019 General Election" – shows that politicians and political officeholders have weaponised political violence as a means to secure political office at all cost. She argues that in this so-called 'trade', perpetrated through thuggery, arson, intimidation, banditry, assaults, harassment, kidnappings, assassination, among others, the youth, more than any other category, function as the machinery by which these vices are perpetrated to satisfy the unreasonable desires of those they serve. These, no doubt, have prevented deep-rooted democratisation in Nigeria since 1999. In chapter nine, Nsemba Edward Lenshie, Isa Mohammed and Patience Jacob Kondu took another in-depth look at electoral violence in the context of Taraba State in North-East Nigeria. They note that in Nigeria, generally, electoral violence is inseparable from electoral politics no matter how the democratic process is interpreted as "free," "fair" and "credible." Assessing the situation in Taraba State in 2019, they identify the nature of political competition, patron-clientele politics, polarisation of supporters, and ethnic and religious manipulations as the triggers of unprecedented electoral violence in the state. Arising therefrom, they recommend that reducing the high stakes associated with elections by decentralising political and economic power to local governments will make the local level of governance competitive, attractive and viable, thereby reducing the susceptibility of electoral politics to violence at the state level generally.

It is no hidden fact that elections in Nigeria are violence prone. In fact, election violence has remained a reoccurring phenomenon with security underpinnings that have threatened and ridiculed the country's democracy besides leading to its ascription as a fledgling one. It is this trend of political happenstances that Obinna Ukaeje addressed in chapter ten on "Election-Related Violence in Nigeria and its Security Implications." His historical analysis of Nigeria's elections since colonial times corroborate that elections in Nigeria have remained violent; and this violence is traceable along ethnic, religious and regional lines. Ukaeje thinks that minimizing hate speech during political campaigns can significantly reduce the level of violence experienced. He contends that if all relevant stakeholders in Nigeria's electioneering process, particularly the security agencies and officers of INEC both of which presently constitute obstacles to democratic consolidation in Nigeria, should stop meddling in the electoral process in ways that undermine its peaceful conduct and overall credibility, Nigeria's democratic experience will improve for the better. The author notes that the deployment of the military is unacceptable. This is because military deployment discolours the process by generating tension, voter intimidation and violent conflicts, all of which were witnessed in the 2019 election season. This last point received more attention in chapter eleven by Fidelis A. E. Paki in "The Challenges of Election Security in Nigeria: A Study of the 2019 General Election." Arguing from the premise that after over twenty years of uninterrupted democracy in Nigeria, election security still remains an uphill task, Paki posits that the problem of election insecurity is both burdensome to security agencies and the electorate, majority of who only participate in the process if the atmosphere is peaceful and safe. In other words, electoral insecurity is among the chief reasons for dwindling voter turnout in Nigeria's elections. Paki identifies a number of electoral logistical deficiencies that hinder election security management in Nigeria and maintains that if addressed, election security will be the natural outcome.

To cap it all, Uche S. Odozor, Olasupo O. Thompson, Scholastica N. Atata and Stanislaus O. Okonkwo's chapter – "Beyond the 2019 General Election: Critical Lessons for Nigeria's Democratic Experiment" – summarises the factors undermining a healthy democracy in Nigeria. These authors traced poor electoral outcomes to the actions and inactions of different segments of the Nigerian society. They also debunk the widely held assumption that Nigeria's electoral vices are mistakes, arguing that a mistake is something that happens once from oversight and human limitation. Because it was never intended, there is genuine resolution, effort, and vigilance to prohibit its repetition. However, instead of improving on past mistakes, INEC simply repeats these mistakes. Following this, they list anomalies in both the electoral process and national development agenda that undermine credible democracy in Nigeria. These include: electioneering campaigns that shy away from ways of solving national challenges but dense on defamation of opponents; failure to amend a constitution that is antithetical to liberal democracy; god-fatherism,[22] developmental planning without reliable population data; inability to separate politics and governance; the ruling party's intolerant disposition to criticism; and porous national borders through which foreigners smuggle weapons into Nigeria around election times and citizens of neighbouring nations illegally vote during elections, among others. If there must be a better democratic experience in the years ahead, Nigeria must equally correct these anomalies; and also find a way to reduce the high stakes in politics, which made it the most sought after profession in Nigeria.

In Summary

Democratic consolidation in any nation requires competitiveness and accountability, political pluralism, a virile and vigorous civil society, a political culture of tolerance, cooperation and compromise.[23] The contributors to this volume argue that Nigeria's democratic space remains fledging because it suffers from unbridled political violence, disrespect for the rule of law, a weakened judiciary, a compromised legislature, militarisation of the polity which has institutionalised a culture of violence and intolerance to opposition due to years of military dictatorship and lack of political party ideologies, among others. The contributors collectively agree that in the absence of such critically defining prerequisites for a sustainable democracy, political parties in Nigeria engage in unwholesome

---

[22] "Godfatherism" is a form of patron-client relationship that exists in political circles in which powerful politicians front and sponsor political candidates who become their political sons. This phenomenon has been found to hinder participation, political security and peace in Nigeria's Fourth Republic. These, no doubt, contribute in undermining the consolidation of democracy in the country. See Gbemisola A. Animasawun, "Godfatherism in Nigeria's Fourth Republic: The Pyramid of Violence and Political Insecurity in Ibadan, Oyo-State, Nigeria" (IFRA-Nigeria e-papers, New Series, No. 27, 29 March 2013), *http://www.ifra-nigeria.org/IMG/pdf/godfatherism-nigeria-ibadan.pdf.*

[23] Robert A. Dahl, *Polyarchy: Participation and Opposition* (New Haven: Yale University Press, 1971); Robert A. Dahl, *On Democracy* (New Haven: Yale University Press, 2000); Juan J. Linz and Alfred Stephan, *Problems of Democratic Transition and Consolidation: Southern Europe, Southern America, and Post-Communist Europe* (Baltimore: John Hopkins University Press, 1996).

political strategies including political violence, vote buying and selling, godfatherism and lack of internal democracy to win elections or to stay in power even when they are no longer wanted.[24]

Watchers of democracy in Africa and Nigeria in particular, have expressed mixed feelings to these developments. In the context of Africa, Large and Sisk submit as follows:

> the results of democracy have at times been disappointing. Democracy has been partial; it has failed to deliver hoped-for economic advances and greater social justice; elected governments have lost legitimacy; there has been liberalisation without democratisation; crisis has constrained democracy [...] moreover democracy is not only about elections. It is also about distributive and social justice. If democracy fails to provide for justly distributed socio-economic development, human security is likely to be threatened [...] checks and balances on the use of power and for the protection of rights are essential for a healthy democratic system. The quality of democratic process, including transparent and accountable government and equality before the law is critical.[25]

In the case of Nigeria, Bola Ahmed Tinubu, one of the founding fathers of the All Progressives Congress noted:

> We must not err into thinking that democracy has been anchored in Nigeria or in other countries just because of the conduct of elections and the existence of certain institutions usually found in a democracy. We must be careful not to read too much into the increasing visibility of processes that appear democratic. If we lend too much credence to the outward appearance, we will fail to look critically at the inner workings of government and the substantive quality of its output. We dare not mistake the image of democracy with real democracy any more than we should mistake the image in a mirror with the real person. If so, we will be applauding a form of government that looks like democracy but does not act like it. We will be applauding as Nigeria's political economy becomes a corporatist entity in democrat's clothing.[26]

Similarly, Professor Claude Ake also observed:

> Nigeria [...] democratises with no separation of powers, all powers having been vested in an imperial presidency. There is hardly any rule of law, no plausible system of justice, no transparency. The coercive institutions of the state are above the law, civil society is below it, ordinary people are out of sight, far beyond its protection. The judiciary is disassociated

---

24 Samuel Ngozi Agu, *Nigeria's Claim to Democracy: Conjectures, Refutations and Panacea* (Aba: Ker Expert Books, 2012).
25 Judith Large and Timothy D. Sisk, *Democracy, Conflict and Human Security: Pursuing Peace in the 21st Century* (International Institute for Democracy and Electoral Assistance, IDEA, 2006), 113.
26 Bola Ahmed Tinubu, "Democracy in Nigeria and the Rebirth of Opposition" (paper presented at the Royal Institute of International Affairs, London, 18 July 2013), 3.

> from justice, and the bureaucracy is oppressive and arbitrary. [...] We pretend that we are playing politics when, like mafia families, we are actually waging a violent struggle for a lucrative turf.[27]

Whereas Tinubu's comments were very apt in describing the state of Nigeria's democracy, it is rather more bewildering that Ake's assertions, made in the dark days of military dictatorship, remains apt in Nigeria's Fourth Republic. This, of course, means that no lessons have been learnt or improvements made from previous elections by all stakeholders in Nigeria's electoral experience. Consequently, instead of advancing forward, the winds of reversals have steadily blown to erode whatever gains Nigeria has made in her democratisation plan since 1999. This trend points to these already identified causative factors: a politically unlearned elite, the autocracy of the ruling political party and its government, a clique of docile opposition parties, a weak electoral umpire, a compromised reactive security architecture, a pliable judiciary, a weak civil society, an unyielding encroachment of ethnicity and religion into its politics, a voiceless electorate, and a monetised franchise network where votes are simply articles of trade.[28] These, perhaps, are just few of the problems of Nigeria's democracy that were glaringly manifest in the 2019 election season.

---

27 Claude Ake, *Is Africa Democratising?* (Lagos: Malthouse Press, 1996), 6 and 18.
28 Aduku A. Akubo and Adejo U. Yakubu, Political Parties and Democratic Consolidation in Nigeria's Fourth Republic," *Global Journal of Political Science and Administration* 2, no. 3 (2014): 79–108.

Tunde Agara
Political Parties, Political Opposition and Elections: Towards Consolidating Democracy in Nigeria

Abstract: Based on existing literature, an essential aspect of democratization of any political system is a strong party system. This essential feature of democracy, which allows the participation of members in the process by which they are governed, also allocates to citizens a public office or a place in the sovereign tribunal. The citizen in his political capacity, therefore, becomes a public agent thereby making government not a tool for impulsiveness but the instrument of collective deliberation. This chapter argues that any form of exclusion from participation becomes a subtle form of suppression. This participation that accords a citizen the vesture of a public agent is achieved through partaking in periodic elections that determine who governs. As part of its trajectory, the chapter turns its attention to the fact that elections allow for the recognition of opposition parties and opposite views, which have become an important mainstay of every democratic format. Thus, the existence and recognition of opposition parties, which need not be clamorous, very often provide the electorates alternatives from which to choose. The chapter posits that the presence of opposition parties not only confirms the claim to democratization but also institutionalizes one of the strong points of democracy which is tolerance of opposing views. The chapter will therefore follow a historical pathway to trace the development of the opposition party system in Nigeria from 1960. Incidentally, opposition parties have not fared well in Nigerian politics partly because there is no clear ideological difference among existing parties and also partly because the opposition has not recognized the importance and impact it should have on the democratization process. The institution of an opposition political party system that should act as a safety valve for the possible excesses of the party in power has failed, enabling any party in power to act with impunity which further impairs the consolidation of the country's democracy.

Keywords: democracy, political parties, political opposition and elections

---

Tunde Agara, Ambrose Alli University, Ekpoma

https://doi.org/10.1515/9783110766561-006

Introduction

An important feature that justifies the claim to practising democracy of the Western liberal type is the existence of political parties, one party or a coalition of parties in power and another party or a coalition of parties in opposition. As important and significant as political parties are in any political system, it suffers from a definitional crisis. A way to meander around the complex and confusing array of definitions is to organise them into three groups of research questions such as: (a) What does a party do? (b) What motivations underlie a party's behaviour? (c) How does a party operate and why does it operate the way it does?

Definitions, which address the question of what a party does, can be divided into two categories. First are the normative definitions which address questions such as what parties can or should do; and descriptive definitions which focus either on party traits, such as the collective nature of parties, or on the various aspects of a party's activity, like selection of candidates and participation in elections, among others. Academic convention dictates that we start with Burke's definition that emphasises the primacy of ideology or interests.[1] Burke defines a political party as a body of men united for promoting, by their joint endeavours, the national interest upon some particular principle in which they are all united.[2] While this definition does not take into account the vital aspects of political structures and decision-making with which politics is concerned; however, to the extent that Burke sees a party as being solely motivated by 'principle' rather than by some mix of policy influence, vote-maximisation or office-maximisation, the definition falls into the normative category. From this perspective, a party can be considered 'good', whereas a political faction, which is motivated by other interests – especially personal ambition – may be considered 'bad'. Another implication of Burke's definition is that there must be something wrong with a party or governmental system when the party in power fails to behave in accordance with the values it advances or promises the populace or as stated in its party manifesto when seeking power. In reality, there may be numerous reasons, such as group pressures and public opinion, for a party to move away from the policy aims it professes. Thus, Burke's definition highlights the pitfalls of approaching parties in normative terms by focusing on what a party can or should be, instead of what parties actually do.

---

1 E. Burke, "Thoughts on the Cause of the Present Discontents," in *The Writings and Speeches of Edmund Burke*, ed. P. Langford (Oxford: Clarendon Press, 1981).
2 Burke, "Thoughts on the Cause of the Present Discontents," 317.

Madison's definition falls into the descriptive category. He defined a political faction (which at that time was not distinguished from a political party) as "a number of citizens, whether amounting to a majority or minority of the whole, who are united and actuated by some common impulse of passion, or of interest, adverse to the rights of other citizens, or to the permanent and aggregate interests of the community."[3] Madison's definition is important in that it associated a political party with the idea of being in 'adversity' with other groups which implies some degree of, or a potential for, competition over the direction of government. The underlying premises of Madison's definition, which is, the collective character of a political party and its electoral focus, were used partly by MacIver[4] and Chambers[5] or fully by Epstein[6] as the foundation of their definitions of a political party. For instance, Epstein defined a political party as "any group, however loosely organised, seeking to elect governmental officeholders under a given label. Hence having a label (which may or may not be on the ballot) rather than an organization is the crucial defining element."[7] Epstein views parties as the only true linkage between society and government. The premise underlying this view is that democracy is best served by the majoritarian principle. This perspective, termed "responsible" or "party government," views parties as articulators of demands, aggregators of interests and educators of the electorate. The objective for responsible parties is the implementation of clearly defined policies, with elections serving only as the means to this end.

Many scholars have called attention to the role of parties in the manifestations of social divisions in the political process; and in the process of policy formation have also adopted a similar perspective to Epstein. This has led to the labelling of some parties as 'workers' parties,' 'bourgeois parties,' 'peoples' parties,' 'mass parties' and 'peasant[8] parties'; labels used to describe the prevalent social composition of a party's electorate, membership, policy, and sometimes even a party's behaviour. Neumann provides a good example of this perspective when he defines a political party generally as:

> the articulate organisation of society's active political agents, those who are concerned with the control of governmental power and who compete for popular support with another group or groups holding divergent views. As such, it is the great intermediary which

---

3 J. Madison, *The Federalist* (New York: Modern Library, 1787), 54.
4 R. M. MacIver, *The Modem State* (Oxford: Oxford University Press, 1964).
5 W. N. Chambers, *Political Parties in a New Nation* (Oxford: Oxford University Press, 1963).
6 L. D. Epstein, *Political Parties in Western Democracies* (New Brunswick, N.J.: Transaction Books, 1980).
7 Epstein, *Political Parties in Western Democracies*, 9.
8 This translates to "talakawa" in Hausa language.

links social forces and ideologies to official governmental institutions and relates them to political action within the larger political community.⁹

From this definition, one can derive a common ground for all parties, which is, the partnership of individuals in a particular organisation, taking part in electoral contests and participating in the decision-making process, or at least the attempt at, and a chance for, such a mobilisation of action. This ever-present readiness alone, Neumann argues, makes them political in a genuine sense, for only in their fight for control and in their conscious influence on political forces, do parties gain meaning and importance. Thus, for any grouping or organisation to qualify as a political party, it must openly claim to link the public to political power by placing the representatives of their organisations in positions where they may exercise that power on behalf of that public. Alternative formulations, which follow Neumann's orientation, are Eldersveld who defines it as "a structural system seeking to translate or convert (or to be converted by) social and economic interests into political power directly."¹⁰ Power, according to Eldersveld is characterised by a "reciprocal deference structure" due to the party's need to "cope with widely varying local milieu of opinion, tradition and social structure [...] [that] encourages the recognition and acceptance of local leadership, local strategy, [and] local power."¹¹

In this sense, a political party plays an intermediary role for groups representing multiple social interests for the achievement of direct control over government. The weak point in this perspective of a 'party as an agent' orientation is that it leads to seeing competitions and conflicts between opposition and party as modes of interaction between representatives of different social interests. It also tends to represent divergences in the sociological profile and composition of the party leadership, parliamentary group, members and electorate as being caused by 'distortions' in the representation of social interests. Further, it ignores the fundamental process through which factors internal to the process of party competition can produce or sustain party differentiation.¹² In other words, it ignores the parties ability to shape voters' preferences because of their control over the political agenda, their control over the 'rules of the game,' their ability to use state power to try to produce favourable changes in the social structure, and

---

9 S. Neumann, "Toward a Comparative Study of Political Parties," in *Comparative Politics: A Reader*, eds. H. Eckstein and D. E. Apter (New York: The Free Press, 1963), 351–67.
10 S. J. Eldersveld, *Political Parties: A Behavioral Analysis* (Chicago: Rand McNally, 1964), 6.
11 Eldersveld, *Political Parties*, 9.
12 P. Dunleavy, *Democracy, Bureaucracy and Public Choice* (Hemel Hempstead: Harvester Wheatsheaf, 1991).

their ability to intervene to alter their relative social and economic positions in order to strengthen their support among a target category. Thus, the 'party as an agent' orientation underestimates the ability of parties and candidates to use state power in order to tip the scales of electoral competition decisively towards the party in government.

Descriptive definitions that address what parties do can also be identified once the process of candidate nomination is understood as part of a party's role. By indicating that parties must be able to nominate candidates, such formulations restore the distinction between parties and their factional sub-groups in that whereas, factions, interest groups and financial contributors may propose the candidates, it is the party that obtains their election. Definitions, which fall within this framework are Riggs to whom a party is "any organisation which nominates candidates for elections to a legislature,"[13] and LaPalombara and Weiner who argue that to be labelled a political party, an organisation must set up local units, seek electoral support from the general public, play a part in political recruitment and be "committed to the capture or maintenance of power, either alone or in coalition with others."[14] In addition, Sartori advances the characterisation of a party as a group that "presents at elections, and is capable of placing, through elections, candidates for public office."[15] For Sartori, the electoral process wherein a party competes under its official label is taken as a discriminatory tool between parties and interest groups. Thus, the occurrence of an election suffices to distinguish the single party from those political groups that do not have recourse to electoral rituals. A conclusion that can be derived from the descriptive definitions is that political parties form a distinctive group. They are unique in that they are a combination of collective team and "common impulse of passion or of interest." They are also significantly oriented towards elections and they engage in the process of candidate nomination.[16]

If political parties are made up of, and created by, groups of individuals, what then are the goals, which underlie party behaviour? Two broad categories of definitions fall within this framework of analysis: the first relates to the ideo-

---

13 F. Riggs, "Comparative Politics and the Study of Political Parties: A Structural Approach," in *Approaches to the Study of Party Organization*, ed. W. J. Crotty (Boston: Allyn and Bacon, 1968), 45–104.
14 J. La Palombara and M. Weiner, "The Origin and Development of Political Parties," in *Political Parties and Political Development*, eds. J. La Palombara and M.Weiner (Princeton, N.J.: Princeton University Press, 1966), 3–42.
15 G. Sartori, *Parties and Party Systems: A Framework for Analysis, Volume I* (Cambridge: Cambridge University Press, 1976), 64.
16 Sartori, *Parties and Party Systems*.

logical aims of the party, while the second refers to those aims that all political parties are supposed to have. According to Gross, "a political party is an organized group, an association, oriented toward political goals, which attempts by its actions to maintain the status quo or to change the existing social, economic and political conditions by means of influencing achievement or conquest of political power."[17] This definition is based on two presuppositions, namely, that parties are groups that pursue goals, and that a party's ideology is the best indicator of its goals. For the second category of definitions, rational choice theorists have developed a set of theories wherein the party is defined according to its stipulated objective. For instance, Strom has distinguished between: (a) vote-seeking; (b) office-seeking; and (c) policy-seeking parties.[18] Concerning the vote-seeking approach, Downs defined a political party as 'a team of men seeking to control the government apparatus by gaining office in a duly constituted election. By *team*, we mean a coalition whose members agree on all their goals instead of on just part of them."[19]

Downs' definition suggests that a party is monolith with an absolute consensus about the preference ordering of the alternative strategies and policies of that party. It is assumed that each member of a party share similar or common goals. Thus, a party can be regarded as a unitary actor, a decision-making agent separated from voters and other actors, such as interest groups. Going by the assumption that parties are concerned only with the rewards of office, Downs argues that "parties formulate policies in order to win elections, rather than win elections in order to formulate policies."[20] This implies that each party seeks to receive more votes than others. The more votes a party gets, the higher its bargaining power in the coalition negotiation, especially in multi-party systems, and hence the higher its chances to gain office and formulate policies which would contribute to its re-election. Thus, the Downsian conception of parties is not only as vote-seekers but also as vote-maximisers.

For the office-seeking approach, Riker[21] and Leiserson[22] identify parties as maximisers of their control over political office. Both agree that the yearning for office by political parties exhibit a desire to control some sort of fixed

---

17 Feliks Gross, "Sociological Analysis of a Political Party," *Il Politico* 32, no. 4 (1967): 702.
18 K. Strom, "A Behavioural Model of Competitive Political Parties," *American Journal of Political Science* 34, no. 2 (1990): 565–98.
19 A. Downs, *An Economic Theory of Democracy* (New York: Harper and Row, 1957), 25.
20 Downs, *An Economic Theory of Democracy*, 28.
21 W. H. Riker, *The Theory of Political Coalitions* (New Haven: Yale University Press, 1962).
22 M. Leiserson, "Factions and Coalitions in One-Party Japan," *American Political Science Review* 62 (1968): 770–787.

prize, a prize captured by the winning coalition and divided among its members. The capture and control of elected office is operationalised in terms of government portfolios or ministries, and coalition bargaining is thus viewed as a competitive process, which determines how these portfolios will be allocated. Strom enlarges the scope of 'office benefits' to include private goods bestowed on recipients of politically discretionary governmental and sub-governmental appointments.[23] Seeking office implies therefore a consistent pursuit of such goods over and above their electoral or policy value. Finally, the works of Chappell and Keech,[24] Hanson and Stuart[25] and Axelrod[26] are illustrative of the policy-seeking perspective of political parties. These works view parties as groups that maximise their effect on public policy. According to Strom, party joins or supports a government with the opinion of effecting policy change in its favour.[27] This supposition has a fundamental impact on the entire process of electoral competition and coalition bargaining because most policy outputs are public goods that apply to all, whether or not the actors concerned have participated in the policy process; whether or not, indeed, they are in cabinet.[28]

The last academic trajectory in defining political parties has to do with their mode of operation, which distinguishes them from other organisations in society. These definitions focus on parties as 'institutions,' implying durable and recurring patterned ways of doing things; and differences between parties are therefore explained in terms of their mode of internal management. According to McDonald, the issue of party management can be conceptually divided into two categories.[29] The first category refers to the party way of running the government, that is, the way it ensures binding decisions and allocation of resources. This mode directs attention to the ways by which the party parliamentary group, the extra-parliamentary organisation and the party sub-groups adapt themselves to being a part of a governing machine. The second category refers to the party managers' way of running a party. This mode relates to the ways

---

[23] Strom, "A Behavioural Model of Competitive Political Parties," 567.
[24] H. W. Chappell and W. R. Keech, "Policy Motivation and Party Differences in a Dynamic Spatial Model of Party Competition," *American Political Science Review* 80, 2 (1986): 881–899.
[25] I. Hanson and C. Stuart, "Voting Competitions with Interested Politicians: Platforms Do Not Converge to the Preferences of the Median Voter," *Public Choice* 44, 3 (1984): 431–441.
[26] A. Axelrod, *Conflict of Interests: A Theory of Divergent Goals with Applications to Politics* (Chicago: Markham, 1970).
[27] Strom, "A Behavioural Model of Competitive Political Parties."
[28] M. Laver and N. Schofield, *Multiparty Government: The Politics of Coalition in Europe* (Oxford: Oxford University Press, 1990), 47.
[29] N. A. McDonald, *The Study of Political Parties* (New York: Random House, 1955).

by which party officers deal with constitutional, procedural and behavioural problems within the party.

A definition that focuses on the mode of party management, that is, the way party managers run a party, is Holcombe's. He views parties as a kind of *process* involving the coordination of factional interests, the presentation of a leading personality element, and the sublimation and merging of interests.[30] According to this view, factions continuously shape the opportunities faced by the party, as well as its structure and character. As Holcombe has noted, parties are more than their leaders. Leadership seems to be the most important factor in the original organisation of political parties, but when a party becomes a going concern, its character is determined in some measure by its followers. However, for the opposition parties, the opportunities are always conditioned by the membership of the factions from which the opposition is organised and which determine its character. It is easier for the major opposition party to leave the pioneer work on behalf of new principles to the minor parties. The latter are not embarrassed by the necessity of coordinating such a variety of special interests as the major parties.[31]

The stress of the interplay of these elements suggests what might be regarded as an institutional approach to the definition of political parties. This is emphasised by the suggestion that a party's character is determined by the conditions, which make for durability in the factions' relations in a party. To understand these conditions one should address the modes of internal management across different parties. Discussions about party management as the crucial defining element of political parties require, among other things, an appreciation of four organisational problems faced by party managers. The first is the presence of individuals and groups within the party whose interests must somehow be adjusted and coordinated. The second is the existence of differences among individuals and subgroups in terms of involvement and information regarding party activity, which may lead to differences in their behaviour. The third is the need to apply discipline and authority by the party leadership if the aims of the party are to be achieved. The fourth is the establishment and maintenance of conditions, however loose they are, whereby the authority of representatives and officials is limited and made to conform to the preferences of the party supporters. These problems can be found in parties irrespective of political ideology and constitutional settings. While they are present in other types

---

[30] A. N. Holcombe, *Our More Perfect Union: From Eighteenth-Century Principles to Twentieth-Century Practice* (Cambridge, Mass.: Harvard University Press, 1950).
[31] Holcombe, *Our More Perfect Union*, 102–103.

of organisation, in the political realm these problems are of particular significance because they bear directly upon party competition, the key component of the liberal democratic order. As Michels notes: "it is an organization which gives birth to the dominion of the elected over the electors, of the mandatories over the mandators, of the delegates over the delegators. Who says organisation, says oligarchy."[32]

This rest of this chapter shall be divided into two sections. The first section traces the development of political parties in Nigeria from the colonial to post-independence period. The second section looks at the role of opposition parties in the consolidation of democracy. While we shall conclude by positing that succession politics may be a major discerning characteristic of political parties and democracy in Nigeria; our major concern is that, despite its negative impacts on our democracy, should this phenomenon be allowed in the 2023 general election?

Emergence of Political Parties in Nigeria

The formation of the early political parties coincided with the rise of nationalism. Both were engendered by the Clifford's Constitution of 1922. Preceding the Constitution was the National Congress of British West Africa (NCBWA), founded in 1920, so that people of African descent could participate in their own governance. The elective principle clause in the Clifford Constitution was the immediate factor that impelled the formation of political parties. In response to this constitution, Herbert Macaulay formed the Nigerian National Democratic Party (NNDP) in 1923 as a platform to contest the three elective positions for Lagos colony. Under his leadership, the party won these elective positions in 1923, 1928 and 1933 until the Nigerian Youth Movement (NYM) challenged its monopoly in 1938. The NYM was a nationalist movement, which evolved out of the former Lagos Youth Movement (LYM) in 1934. LYM itself evolved from the Union of Young Nigerians (UYN) formed just after the 1923 elections into the legislative house. Its leadership consisted of a crop of young and highly educated Nigerians such as Dr J. C. Vaughan, Ayo Williams, Nnamdi Azikiwe, S. Akinsanya, H. O. Davies and Ernest Ikoli. Conflict between the Igbo and the Yoruba over nominations led to the departure of the Igbo led by Nnamdi Azikiwe. It is instructive, therefore, to note that as early as the 1920s and 1930s what was to later characterize

---

[32] R. Michels, *Political Parties: A Sociological Study of the Oligarchy Tendencies of Modern Democracy* (New York, The Free Press, 1962).

and become one of the major features of the political system and political parties in Nigeria – ethnic politics and intolerance – had started to emerge.

Nnamdi Azikiwe with other Igbo left NYM to join the newly formed National Council of Nigeria and the Cameroon (NCNC) in 1944. Herbert Macaulay, a Yoruba, became the president while Azikiwe, an Igbo, became the general secretary of the party. However, with the death of Macaulay in 1946, Azikiwe became the party president. Although the party had a predominantly Igbo base it remained the only true Nigerian party until 1950, once again affirming the fact that the ethnic base of the present political parties can be traced to this period. Between 1950 and 1960, other political parties emerged such as the Action Group (AG) whose origin can be traced to the collapse of the NYM. Between 1941 and 1944, it had become certain that NYM could not be salvaged. Chief Obafemi Awolowo then formed the "Egbe Omo Oduduwa," a Pan Yoruba cultural group, in 1945 from former NYM's embers. The Action Group Party metamorphosed from this cultural group in 1951 with the aims of forcing a reform of the Native Authority System, opposing the NCNC and capturing power in the Western Region under the electoral system produced by Richards Constitution. Its ideological stance and programmes were essentially welfarist and populist.

The second major party of this period was the Northern Peoples Congress (NPC) which was founded in 1949 and, which like the AG emerged from a cultural association of the Northern peoples called the "Jam'iyya Mutanen Arewa" formed earlier in 1949. Its leadership consisted of young intellectuals such as Dr Umaru Dikko, M. Yahaya Gusau, Aminu Kano and Abubakar Imam. The party inherited the primary aim of the cultural group, which was to emancipate northern youths from ignorance, idleness and feudal injustice as perpetuated by the northern feudal oligarchy. It however soon lost this aim as the leadership was hijacked from the few progressive elements in the party. A new leadership emerged in the persons of Sir Ahmadu Bello, the Sarduana of Sokoto, with Abubakar Tafawa Balewa as the deputy and Ibrahim Imam as the secretary general. Like the AG among the Yoruba, the NPC did not do anything to hide its regional and ethnic concerns as only persons of northern origin were considered for membership. This period saw the consolidation of ethnic politics in Nigeria.

Another discernible characteristic of Nigerian political parties emerged at this time and this was the phenomenon of breakaway groups. This phenomenon manifested itself in the form of party members breaking away to form other parties as a result of incompatibility, contradictory views, ideological standpoint, intolerance, failure to arrive at a compromise or a consensus or even personality clashes. In rather quick succession, the three major parties experienced this breakaway. Chief Akintola broke away from the AG and formed the United Peoples Party (UPP). In March 1964, Chief Akintola formed the Nigerian National

Democratic Party (NNDP) whose membership was made up of former members of UPP and NCNC. The inability of the NPC to accommodate some radical members who sought for a people-oriented welfare programme and the demolition of the feudal ideology along with its hegemonic hold on the masses became a problem. These radical members, led by Aminu Kano, formed the Northern Elements Progressive Union (NEPU). In 1951, NCNC expelled some of its members for "unparty" activities. The expelled led by Professor Eyo Ita, Dr Udoma and Jaja Nwachuku formed the National Independent Party (NIP) in 1953.

Apart from those mentioned above, other parties of minor character also emerged. These could be grouped into two types: those that represented and articulated minority ethnic views and those in opposition in their respective regions. The first type comprised the United Middle Belt Congress (UMBC) led by J. S. Tarka with its ethnic base among the Tiv of the Middle Belt, now North Central Nigeria, and the Niger Delta Congress (NDC) led by Chief Dappa Dipriye with its base among the ethnic minority groups in the Delta region. The second type comprised the Borno Youth Movement (BYM) based in the Northeast and led by Alhaji Ibrahim Waziri; the Ilorin Talaka Parapo (ITP) based in the present Kwara State and founded by Josiah Olawoyin; the Dynamic Party (DP) led by Dr Chike Obi, and the Republican Party (RP) both based in Eastern Nigeria and the Midwest Democratic Front (MDF) in the Midwest Region.

With the military purge in January 1966, party politics of the First Republic went into oblivion until September 1978 when it was restored following the lifting of the ban on party politics. This second democratisation process was kick-started with the drafting of a new constitution, which opted for the adoption of an American-style presidency and separation of powers. Out of about 53 political associations that emerged to contest the 1979 elections, the Federal Electoral Commission (FEDECO) tasked with managing elections registered only five. However, a sixth party was later added to contest the 1983 elections. These parties were the National Party of Nigeria (NPN), the Nigeria Peoples Party (NPP), the Great Nigeria Peoples Party (GNPP), the Peoples' Redemption Party (PRP), the Unity Party of Nigeria (UPN) and the Nigeria Advance Party (NAP). Two major features of these parties, probably with the exception of NAP, can be discerned. The first was that they were patent offshoots of the former political parties of the First Republic. This reflected the beginning of succession politics. The second was that the ethnic cloak was still visibly present and memberships of these parties were mainly drawn from the discredited politicians of the First Republic.

On 25 August 1985, General Ibrahim Babaginda assumed office as the President and Commander-in-Chief of the Armed Forces of Nigeria. By May 1989, he lifted the ban on politics and over 40 political associations emerged almost overnight, 13 of these sought for registration following the stringent guidelines on party formation laid down by the National Electoral Commission (NEC), which replaced FEDECO. Some of the parties that emerged were the Peoples' Solidarity Party (PSP), Peoples' Front of Nigeria (PFN), Liberal Convention (LC), Nigerian Labour Party (NLP) and Nigerian National Congress (NNC). The National Electoral Commission (NEC) refused to register any of the parties but instead submitted a draft of the report of the political bureau inaugurated on 30 September 1987 to organize a public debate regarding the political future of the country. The Armed Forces Ruling Council (AFRC) accepted the report of the bureau and for the first time in Nigeria's political history decreed into existence two political parties – the Social Democratic Party (SDP) and the National Republican Party (NRP). The parties' programmes, funding, ideologies, manifestoes, and structures were also decreed alongside their existence. In sum, the two parties were government-sponsored in all respects. First, the government determined the modus operandi and ideology for the two parties. In this respect, the SDP was a "little to the left" while the NRC was a "little to the right." Second, their funding was derived from the government who also built secretariats all over the country for both parties and appointed their key staff from among serving civil servants. Third, every member of the party was a 'joiner' not a 'founder.'

Going by the membership list of the SDP and NRC it can be stated by extension that a marriage of convenience was contrived between former opposing political parties and individuals. For example, among the bulk of SDP members can be identified former members of the old AG, NCNC, NEPU, UPN, GNPP, NPP and PRP. The party was led by Babagana Kingibe from 1990 to 1992, and later by Chief Anthony Anenih. True to its decreed ideology, the party espoused progressive, populist and welfarist ideas. The NRC led by ultra-rights and conservatives like Tom Ikimi and later Dr Kusamotu fielded Alhaji Tofa as its presidential candidate. Furthermore, the NRC's party pedigree can be traced to conservative parties such as NPN, NNDP and NPC.

The Babaginda political experiment did not materialize into concrete democracy partly because it was so intended. However, the political unrest and agitations that followed the annulment of the 12 June 1993 elections forced Babaginda to step aside. An interim national government (ING) was inaugurated under Chief Ernest Shonekan, which was promptly disposed by General Sanni Abacha on 17 November 1993. By December 1995, the establishment of yet another election management organ, the National Electoral Commission of Nigeria (NECON), consequently lifted the ban on political parties. On 30 September 1996, Abacha's umpire, Chief Dagogo-Jack announced the registration of five political parties out of the lot that had sought for registration without resolving the 12 June 1993 debacle. These five registered parties, which Chief Bola Ige sarcastically referred to as 'the five fingers of a leprous hand' were the United Nigeria Congress Party

(UNCP), the Democratic Party of Nigeria (DPN), the Grassroot Democratic Movement (GDM), the Congress for National Consensus (CNC) and the National Centre Party of Nigeria (NCPN).

The demise of Abacha did not terminate the transition to the Third Republic, which continued with the rise to power of General Abdusalami Abubakar who succeeded Abacha on 8 June 1998. This change culminated in the appointment of a retired Supreme Court judge, Ephraim Akpata, as the new transition umpire to head the new Independent National Electoral Commission (INEC). The provisionally registered parties were the All Peoples Party (APP), Peoples Democratic Party (PDP), Alliance for Democracy (AD), Movement for Democracy and Justice (MDJ), United Peoples Party (UPP), Peoples Redemption Party (PRP), National Solidarity Party (NSP), Democratic Advance Party (DAP) and United Democratic Party (UDP). The outcome of the 5 December 1998 local government election resulted in six of the parties being deregistered, leaving only AD, PDP and APP to contest the remaining elections. Nonetheless, more political parties were to be registered later by INEC, which brought the total to 40. Notable among these new parties were the All Progressives Grand Alliance (APGA), the National Conscience Party (NCP) led by Chief Gani Fawehinmi, the All Nigeria Peoples Party (ANPP), the new name adopted by the former APP, the Movement for Democracy and Justice (MDJ) led by Alhaji M.D. Yusuf, a former Inspector-General of Police, the Peoples Redemption Party (PRP) led by Alhaji Balarabe Musa, the Green Party (GP) led by Olisa Agbakoba, the All Peoples Liberation Party (APLP) and the Justice Party (JP) led by Reverend Chris Okotie. The number of parties continued growing as new ones emerged during every election period.

Elections, Opposition Parties and the Consolidation of Democracy

The comparative literature on democratisation, particularly during Africa's "third wave" emphasises the primacy of elections.[33] Elections are central to competitive politics. Ideally, they guarantee political participation and competition, which in turn are pivotal to democratic transition and consolidation. Elections are also central to the institutionalisation of orderly succession in a democratic setting, creating a legal administrative framework for handling inter-elite rivalries.

---

33 S. Lindberg, *Democracy and Elections in Africa* (Baltimore: Johns Hopkins University Press, 2006).

They also provide opportunity for popular backing for new rulers.[34] The general opinion about elections is that they are an important element for the institutionalisation of popular participation, competition and legitimacy, which are the three major foundations of democracy. Although elections are an important element in the process of democratisation, it is also important to note that they are not a guarantee for sustainable democratic transition and consolidation because they can be used to institutionalise authoritarian rule.[35]

In its strictest sense, there can be no democracy without election. Ample examples have shown that some countries with authoritarian leaders simply transformed to civilian regimes without elections and without regards to democratic ethos. This cannot be regarded as democracy. It is against this backdrop that Huntington points out that a political system is democratic "to the extent that its most powerful collective decision-makers are selected through fair, honest and periodic elections in which candidates freely compete for votes, and in which virtually all the adult population are eligible to vote."[36] In its proper sense, election can be described as a process of selecting the officers or representatives of an organisation or group by the vote of its qualified members.[37] Elections provide the medium through which the different interest groups within the bourgeois nation state can stake and resolve their claims to power through peaceful means.[38] They, therefore, determine the proper way of ensuring that responsible leaders take over the mantle of leadership. In terms of origin, modern-style elections are alien to African political systems where elections to royal thrones were through royal bloodlines. Meanwhile, in the western model leaders are chosen through modern-style elections. Following political decolonisation in Nigeria from 1945, there was an extension of the electoral franchise and the scope of representative institutions, which go with the election process. The fact, however, remains that in African societies elections had often been conducted in a way that gives a poor reflection of the popular will, which leads to violence.

---

[34] A. Hughes and R. May, "The Politics of Succession in Black Africa," *Third World Quarterly* 10, no. 1 (1988).
[35] E. Scheiner, *Democracy without Competition in Japan: Opposition Failure in a One-Party Dominant State* (Cambridge: Cambridge University Press 2006).
[36] S. P. Huntington, *The Third Wave: Democratization in the Late Twentieth Century* (Norman, OK: University of Oklahoma Press, 1991).
[37] O. B. C. Nwolise, "Electoral Violence and Nigeria's 2007 Elections," *Journal of African Elections* 6, no. 2 (2007).
[38] F. Iyayi, "Elections, INEC and the Problems of Election Mindset in Nigeria," in *Proceedings and communiqué of the INEC National Forum on Nigeria's 2007 General Elections: The Critical Challenges Ahead* (Abuja, 2007).

Opposition parties are essential mainly because their existence is an indicator of the levels of competition and quality of the democratic process in the society. The role of opposition party becomes crucial and important in an electoral democracy especially within a federal system where minorities and ethnic groups need such an avenue for voicing their opinions about the policies and behaviour of the ruling party. The existence of an opposition party gives vent to the fact that divergent views are tolerated and there is political accommodation for all within a heterogeneous system suffused with more differences than similarities, as it is the case in Nigeria. The ability of opposition parties to challenge ruling regimes is integral to representative democracy. A viable opposition is important not just because competitive elections are a necessary condition of most definitions of democracy,[39] but because opposition is in fact a critical check on a country's rulers. Writing in the Schumpeterian tradition, scholars such as Downs[40] and Schlesinger[41] propose that in order to be elected, parties are drawn to reflect the people's will. In competing with each other for votes, parties are in fact vying to better represent the public. Where one party is dominant, there is little competition, and, as a result, the dominant party need not be very responsive. Party competition forces political elites and voters alike to consider alterations to the existing political agenda; examine alternative ideological, cultural, or policy ideas; and re-evaluate which societal groups should be represented by the government and how. Most of all, the presence of a viable opposition and party competition provides the ultimate check against unrestrained power. As long as a party fears loss of office, it will be much less likely to act arbitrarily. However, if, as Schattschneider suggests, democracy needs parties in order to function, a system made up of nonresponsive parties suggests problems in democracy's functioning because democracy is based on competition."[42] A one-party democracy is not supposed to happen.

In addition to the normal functions that all political parties play in every society, Kiiza has also submitted that opposition parties promote national conversation and push democratic discussion to a higher level of political development and maturity.[43] They hold the government and the ruling party accountable for their policies by promoting national conversation on issues that are salient

---

39 J. A. Schumpeter, *Capitalism, Socialism and Democracy* (London: Allen and Unwin, 1954).
40 Downs, *An Economic Theory of Democracy.*
41 J. A. Schlesinger, *Political Parties and the Winning of Office* (Michigan: University of Michigan Press, 1991).
42 E. E. Schattschneider, *The Semi-Sovereign People: A Realistic View of Democracy in America* (New York: Holt, Rinehart and Winston, 1960).
43 J. Kiiza, *The Role of Opposition Parties in a Democracy* (2005), www.fes-tanzania.org.

and important. As a 'shadow government,' opposition parties present alternatives to the incumbent government and party by providing the people with alternative ideas of how government should be run and the policies that should be made. By constituting their own 'shadow cabinet.' opposition parties provide a veritable training ground for future leaders and members of cabinet. The existence of opposition parties strengthens the culture of democracy and tolerance of opposition by promoting open debates and discussions of issues, policies and government's action or inaction.

The above discussion provides us with a basis on which the Nigerian democratic process can be evaluated, especially in relation to the role of a virile opposition party. In the First Republic, the AG provided a very strong opposition to the ruling coalition of the NPC and NCNC. The opposition was based on both ideological and ethnic differences. During the Second Republic, under Shagari's government, UPN again provided a strong opposition party to the ruling NPN and the basis of opposition was predicated more on an ideological level. Of course other parties, like NEPU with its welfarist (*talakawa*) orientation, also provided some degree of opposition to the bourgeois-dominated ruling NPN. With the coming in 1999 of the democratic dispensation that constituted the Fourth Republic, the longest so far in Nigeria's democratic history, the element of a strong virile opposition has been watered down more so because there is no distinct ideological difference between the parties. Only the AD has offered some level of opposition, which at best was limited to ineffectual occasional outbursts and press releases. The political terrain in Nigeria has not witnessed again the robust political play as offered by the First Republic party system. The populace was not offered an alternative to the ruling PDP and this may have accounted in part for the PDP's dominance for 16 years coupled with massive riggings and corruption of the electoral process.

Given the docility and almost non-existence of any serious opposition party in Nigerian politics, can one really talk of democratic consolidation? Linz and Stepan have argued that democracy is consolidated when its tenets become internalised behaviourally, attitudinally and constitutionally.[44] Behaviourally, a democracy can be said to be consolidated when no political actor or group of actors attempt to achieve their personal objectives by creating a non-democratic regime or by seceding from the state. Attitudinally, a democracy is consolidated when the majority, no matter the level of opposition or dissatisfaction against the

---

[44] J. J. Linz and A. Stephan, *Problems of Democratic Transition and Consolidation, Southern Europe, Southern America, and Post-Communist Europe* (Baltimore: John Hopkins University Press, 1996).

incumbent government, still holds on to the belief in democratic institutions and procedures as the best way to govern a nation. Constitutionally, a democracy is consolidated when both governmental and non-governmental forces are all agreed that conflict should be settled within the parameter and bounds set down by laws, procedures and institutions established by the constitution.

Linz and Stepan further specified five conditions that must be in place before a democracy can be consolidated. These are:

a) The existence of a virile and free civil society. Within this context, civil society provides the general public the necessary arena to articulate values, create associations and advance various interests.
b) There must be an independent or autonomous political society in which every political actor or group has legitimate rights and can compete for power within laid down rules.
c) All major political actors of the state must be subjected to the rule of law that not only guarantees and protects individual freedom, but also ensures that elected government officials are subject to transparency and accountability.
d) There must be in place a state bureaucracy, which is empowered and allotted the responsibility to protect the rights of citizens and deliver basic services.
e) Finally, an institutionalised economic society must exist; an economic society made up of norms, regulations, policies and institutions that can sustain a mixed economic system.

When assessed against Huntington's 'two turn over test' recipe and indicator of democratic consolidation,[45] which posits that a democracy can be said to be consolidated if the party or group that takes over power in the initial election loses the subsequent election and peacefully hands over power to the in-coming winner, the democratic experiment in Nigeria cannot really be said to be consolidated. Since 1999, the PDP turned Nigeria into a one-party state by rigging and meddling with the electoral process and the election results. Now, the APC is set to repeat the same process and experience.

There is a need to break away from the 'frontier' character of periodic elections.[46] This façade, which only entrenched the PDP, and lately the APC, as the ruling party, substantially weakened the opposition delete entirely and at the same time discredits them as bearers of the hopes and aspirations of the people for change. The opposition party has not enjoyed a level playing ground with the

---

45 Huntington, *The Third Wave: Democratization*.
46 R. Joseph, "Progress and Retreat in Africa: Challenges of a Frontier Region," *Journal of Democracy* 19, no. 2 (2008).

incumbent party against whom they are contesting. Using every state apparatus and institution to either harass them or fractionise them, the prospects and life in the opposition party does not look so promising. This led to the extinction of the only existing viable opposition party, the AD, after the 2003 elections. The extinction of AD occasioned mass defection and carpet-crossing of members from the opposition to the ruling party, a move calculated to include them in the largesse that emanate from controlling power. This scenario actually reinforces Dudley's observations that in Nigeria:

> The shortest cut to affluence is through politics. Politics means money and money means politics. [...] To be a member of the government party means open avenue to government patronage, contract deals and the like. But once having known the profitability of having power, the party (and the individual members) naturally uses the same governmental machinery to stay in power. The leadership becomes a self-recruiting oligarchy and no self-recruiting (oligarchy) has been known to tolerate opposition to it.[47]

Conclusion

Competition is critical to democracy. Fundamental to democracy is the principle that all leaders are ultimately accountable to the people. Within modern democracy, this process works through representatives who, themselves, are accountable to citizens through regular elections. To overcome collective action and social choice problems, representatives organize in political parties, which makes parties also accountable to the public.[48] When parties enter the government, as Manin, Przeworski and Stokes note, they "are 'accountable" if voters can discern whether governments are acting in their interest and sanction them appropriately, so that those incumbents who act in the best interest of citizens win re-election and those who do not lose them.[49] One would assume that incumbent leaders who get re-elected are those deemed by voters to be working in the latter's best interest. The presence of a governing party that continues to get re-elected when it is *unpopular* indicates a failure of accountability and an effective (or defective) opposition party system. In a country where the ruling party is unpopu-

---

47 B. J. Dudley, "Explaining Political Instability in New States," *Journal of Modern African Studies* 11, no. 3 (1973): 357–359.
48 J. H. Aldrich, *Why Parties? The Origin and Transformation of Party Politics in America* (Chicago: University of Chicago Press, 1995).
49 B. Manin, A. Przeworski and S. C. Stokes, "Elections and Representation," in *Democracy, Accountability, and Representation*, eds. Adam Przeworski, Susan C. Stokes and Bernard Manin (New York: Cambridge University Press, 1999).

lar, a lack of party competition is not merely a puzzle, it is also a problem of accountability and a virile opposition system and, therefore, very much a problem for democracy and its consolidation.

Olawari D. J. Egbe
The Silent Western Votes and the Emergence of the Buhari/APC Presidency

Abstract: Has democracy promotion as a Western foreign policy improved elections and good governance in Africa? Was democracy promotion of any significant effect on the 2015 presidential election in Nigeria? This chapter argues that elections alone do not make a democracy; but constitute the means to legitimate acquisition of political offices in a democracy. If democracy is not domiciled in elections, but rather in what takes place between elections; nations undergoing elections, and voters, must never be cajoled by international pressures into installing democratic autocracies. While the resultant issues from Nigeria's 2015 general elections are still unresolved, the conduct of the President Muhammadu Buhari's government since after the 2015 elections still stares Nigerians in the face. For example, the issues generated by the 2019 presidential election are traceable to Western democracy-promotion agenda in Nigeria. The link between the 2015 and–2019 presidential elections remains that the latter (2019) is the brainchild of the former election. If not for Western democracy promotion that produced President Muhammadu Buhari and the APC government in 2015, the story would not have been the same in the 2019 presidential election. Thus, the attendant regrets are the outcomes of Western democracy promotion. This chapter investigates the influence of the silent Western votes in the 2015 presidential elections in Nigeria and concludes that the outcome of the 2015 presidential election in Nigeria was strongly influenced by Washington DC and fellow world capitals in London and Paris, among others. The results are testimony that Nigeria must be weary of external influences in future presidential elections.

Keywords: Nigeria, elections, silent votes, Western nations

Introduction

One spectre that has plagued African democracies and their democratisation processes is Western democracy promotion plan. Specifically, this chapter interrogates the following questions: Why would external powers intervene in the elections of other states? How has democracy promotion improved the conduct of presidential elections in Nigeria's Fourth Republic? Why is force deployed in

Olawari D. J. Egbe, Niger Delta University

democracy promotion as it is in the Middle East?[1] Moreover, is liberal democracy transplantable?

While these questions seek answers, there was the July 2016 United States' (U.S.) Senate Congressional inquiry into Russia's involvement in her 2016 presidential election that brought Donald Trump to the White House. The Senate Congressional inquiry seeks to determine the culpability of Russia in influencing the outcome of the 2016 presidential election and to specifically ascertain if Donald Trump was aware of Russia's involvement and profited from it. But why would the U.S. Senate be making a congressional inquiry into the meddlesomeness of another state into her elections? Maybe Russia's alleged involvement in the 2016 U.S. presidential election is Russia's peculiar form of democracy promotion. Why is the U.S. keenly agitated by Russia's exercise of democracy promotion on her?[2] Moreover, is it not the hallmark of U.S. democracy promotion agenda in the so called Third Wave of democratisation?[3]

Furthermore, what is the purpose of democracy promotion if it is not centrally targeted at enthroning democracies in the Global South even at the detriment of the citizenry by installing democratic autocracies?[4] The preponderance of democratic autocracies in Africa is a pointer that democracy promotion does not promote democracy; but instead promotes the economic interests of practitioners of democracy promotion.[5]

The 2015 presidential election in Nigeria had come and gone but the ensuing issues thereof have refused to settle. The blame is laid on the altar of democracy promotion – an agenda essentially aimed at the democratisation of countries of the Global South and usually undertaken by different subtle strategies such as deliberate propaganda, financial inducement of one political party against the other(s), deliberate favouring of one candidate at the expense of another, playing

---

[1] Steven E. Finkel, Anibal Perez-Linan and Mitchell A. Seliogson, "The Effects of U.S. Foreign Assistance on Democracy Building, 1990–2003," *World Politics* 59, no. 3 (2007): 404–439.
[2] Lincol A. Mitchell, *The Democracy Promotion Paradox* (Washington DC: Brookings Institution Press, 2016).
[3] Samuel P. Huntington, *The Third Wave: Democratisation in the Late Twentieth Century* (Norman: University of Oklahoma Press, 1991).
[4] Andreas Schedler, "Elections without Democracy," *Journal of Democracy* 13, no. 2 (2002): 36–50; Andreas Schedler, ed., *Electoral Authoritarianism: The Dynamics of Unfree Competition* (Boulder: Lynne Rienner, 2006); Steven Levitsky and Lucan A. Way, "The Rise of Competitive Authoritarianism," *Journal of Democracy* 13, no. 2 (2002): 51–65; Larry Diamond, "Elections without Democracy: Thinking about Hybrid Regimes," *Journal of Democracy* 13, no. 2 (2002): 21–35.
[5] Ruvimbo Natalie Mavhiki, "Does Democracy Promotion Promote Democracy? The Zimbabwean Case" (M. A. thesis, the Lingnan University, Hong Kong, 2016).

security, ethnic, religious cards, etcetera. This tactic of democracy promotion is what this chapter classifies as Western 'silent votes'.

From all indications, the U.S. and her compatriots in democracy promotion, such as the European Union, Britain and France appear to see the conduct of elections alone as democracy.[6] More so, that liberal democracy in its impressive rise in the U.S. is not easily transplantable.[7] However, democracy is not this narrow but far deeper. And it is the deeper picture of democracy that developed democracies conduct their governance at home but perpetrate abroad that which is unjust, which they do not do at home such as installing governments or leaders they want in place of those the citizens want.[8] A deeper picture of democracy is the fact that democracy is what actually takes place in-between elections.[9] For example, the All Progressives Congress (hereafter APC) and its presidential candidate, then Major General Muhammadu Buhari, during the 2015 presidential election, flew the twin kites of insecurity and anticorruption crusades to the West with the claims that as an upcoming government, they would combat these two hydras. To this effect, Buhari noted in his 26 February 2015 speech at the Royal Institute of International Affairs, London:

> Permit me to close this discussion on a personal note. I have heard and read references to me as a former dictator in many respected British newspapers including the well-regarded *Economist*. Let me say without sounding defensive that dictatorship goes with military rule, though some might be less dictatorial than others. I take responsibility for whatever happened under my watch... I cannot change the past. But I can change the present and the future... So before you is a former military ruler and a converted democrat who is ready to operate under democratic norms and is subjecting himself to the rigours of democratic elections for the fourth time.[10]

The Barack Obama and David Cameron governments acted naively in assuming that Muhammadu Buhari was a better candidate to support in the 2015 presiden-

---

6 William Blum, *Rogue State: A Guide to the World's Only Superpower* (London: Zed Books, 2003); William Blum, *America's Deadliest Export Democracy: The Trust about U.S. Foreign Policy and Everything Else* (London: Zed Books, 2013).
7 Paul R. Pillar, *Why America Misunderstands the World: National Experience and Roots of Misperception* (New York: Columbia University Press, 2016).
8 Lincoln A. Mitchell, *The Democracy Promotion Paradox* (Washington DC: Brookings Institution Press, 2016); Shmuel Nili, "Injustice Abroad, Authority at Home? Democracy, Systemic Effects, and Global Wrongs," *American Journal of Political Science* 62, no.1 (2018): 72–83.
9 Peter Esaiasson and Hanne Marthe Narud, *Between-Election Democracy: The Representative Relationship After Election Day* (Colchester: ECPR Press, 2013).
10 Muhammadu Buhari, "Prospects for democratic consolidation in Africa: Nigeria's transition" (London: Chatham House, February 2015), 1–6.

tial election in Nigeria. Six years on, the question is: What democratic ethos such as the rule of law, separation of powers, and constitutionalism, has the Buhari-led government demonstrated? These democratic indicators distinguish the democratic tenets of governments in-between elections. Assessments indicate that Nigerians in the last six years are yet to fully appreciate these democratic tenets. The road to this conclusion proceeds as follows: the next section undertakes a conceptual clarification of the democracy promotion agenda of the West. The section after that examines the silent votes of the West as the determinants of the electoral outcome of the 2015 presidential election in Nigeria, while the last section concludes the chapter.

Democracy Promotion: Meaning, Trajectory, Conduct and Critique

Democracy promotion or democracy assistance is awash with a burgeoning literature on account of the interests, anxieties and heartaches it provokes.[11] Huber says "democracy promotion is...all those foreign policy activities which aim at fostering the transition to, consolidation of, or improvement of democracy in other states and their societies."[12] For Bush, democracy promotion is "any attempt by a state or states to encourage another country to democratise, either via a transition from autocracy or the consolidation of a new or unstable democracy."[13]

Schmitter and Brouwer more elaborately defined democracy promotion as "consisting of all overt and voluntary activities adopted, supported, and implemented by (public or private) foreign actors explicitly designed to contribute to the political liberalisation of autocratic regimes and the subsequent democratisation of autocratic regimes in specific recipient countries."[14] They pinpoint that democracy promotion excludes covert activities of external actors in the form of sublime diplomatic efforts or activities of secret services. This argument, however, is not tenable in all domains of democracy promotion, especially in Africa

---

[11] Michael McFaul, "Democracy Promotion as a World Value," *The Washington Quarterly* 28, no. 1 (2004): 147–163.
[12] Daniela Huber, *Democracy Promotion and Foreign Policy: Identity and Interests in US, EU and non-Western Democracies* (New York: Palgrave Macmillan, 2015).
[13] Sarah Sunn Bush, *The Taming of Democracy Assistance: Why Democracy Promotion Does Not Confront Dictators* (Cambridge: Cambridge University Press, 2015), 6.
[14] Phillippe C. Schmitter and Imco Brouwer, "Conceptualising, Researching and Evaluating Democracy Promotion and Protection" (EUI Working Paper, SPS No. 99/9, 1999), 13.

and the Middle East where overt (direct military intervention) and covert (the deployment of intelligent networks) methods are optimally put to use by the U.S.[15]

Democracy promotion is traceable to the years after the Cold War when the U.S. found itself in considerable strategic difficulties as it was left with no formidable enemy like the Soviet Union to contend with.[16] This, of course, corroborated a 1988 promise to the U.S. by Georgi Arbatov, a top Soviet foreign policy officer, when he said: the Soviet Union was "going to do a terrible thing to you; we are going to deprive you of an enemy."[17] Indeed, by this singular global security reconfiguration, the U.S. had a number of scenarios: first, no enemy to contend with; second, subsisting as the sole surviving superpower; third, compelled to abandon the policy of containment; and fourth, to embrace democracy promotion as its foreign policy agenda,[18] a path the U.S. took on account of seeing herself as a model other states should emulate.[19]

This period equally coincided with the era of Third Wave democratisation in Southern and Eastern Europe, Latin America and parts of Africa, from 1974 to 1991.[20] Contrary to the hitherto superpower support for autocratic regimes in Africa that promoted multiple intractable conflicts across the continent at the termination of the Cold War (such as the Angolan Crisis and the Darfur Crisis in

---

[15] Robert Pinkney, *Democracy in the Third World* (Boulder, Colorado: Lynne Rienner, Inc., 2003); Lincoln A. Mitchell, *The Democracy Promotion Paradox* (Washington D C: Brookings Institution Press, 2016).

[16] Tony Smith, *America's Mission: The United States and the Worldwide Struggle for Democracy in the Twentieth Century* (Princeton, NJ: Princeton University Press, 2012); Tudor A. Onea, *U.S. Foreign Policy in the Post-Cold War Era: Restraint Versus Assertiveness from George H. W. Bush to Barack Obama* (New York: Palgrave Macmillan, 2013).

[17] Onea, *U.S. Foreign policy*, 1.

[18] Onea, *U.S. Foreign policy*.

[19] Michael W. Fowler, "A Brief Survey of Democracy Promotion in U.S. Foreign Policy," *Democracy and Security* 11, no. 3 (2015): 227–247.

[20] Ziauddin Sardar, "The Future of Democracy and Human Rights," *Futures* 28, no. 9 (1996): 839–859; Lise Rakner, Alina Rocha Menocal and Verena Fritz, "Democratisation's Third Wave and the Challenges of Democratic Deepening: Assessing International Democracy Assistance and Lessons Learned" (London: Overseas Development Institute, Working Paper 1, 2007); Tanza A. Borzel and Thomas Risse, "Venus Approaching Mars? The European Union's Approaches to Democracy Promotion in Comparative Perspective," in *Prompting Democracy and the Rule of Law: American and European Strategies,* eds. Amichai Magen, Thomas Risse and Michael A. McFaul (New York: Palgrave Macmillan, 2009), 34–60; Bush, *The Taming of Democracy Assistance.*

Sudan, amongst others), dictatorial regimes in the Third World were compelled to accept liberal democracy.[21]

Wherever it is so promoted, liberal democracy requires states to conduct elections, accord their citizens full democratic participation, and show a modicum of human rights and observance of rule of law as conditions for receiving foreign assistance in the form of economic aid, military assistance and training, and humanitarian support, among others.[22] For example, as compensation for democracy promotion acceptance, in October 2001, Tony Blair offered to cancel much of the debt of the Global South, insisted on the practice of free trade and military training assistance to African soldiers.[23] However, whereas these conditions seem superlatively attractive in ensuring that hitherto intractable conflicts in Africa became easily resolved by reason of superpower withdrawal of external military support to the different warring leaders, liberal democracy remains the greatest undoing to Africa as it served more of external interests.[24]

The U.S. identifies threats to her national security as coming from autocratic regimes in the Middle East (referred to as 'Axis of Evil') and from Hobbesian territories where terrorists find safe haven.[25] Therefore, the U.S. identifies democracy promotion as the best means of projecting the values of political and economic freedom to Hobbesian territories.[26] Democracy promotion is conducted on three fronts namely: coercive, utilitarian and identitive measures. First, coercive democracy promotion is undertaken by means of force especially by military intervention or the deployment of sublime, subtle covert force. Utilitarian explanation in the use of coercive democracy promotion is that such interventions – example the U.S.-led invasion of Iraq in 2003 – are motivated by democracy

---

[21] Dionysis Markakis, *U.S. Democracy Promotion in the Middle East: The Pursuit of Hegemony* (New York: Routledge, 2016).
[22] Danielle Resnick and Nicolas van de Walle, eds., *Democratic trajectories in Africa: Unravelling the impact of foreign aid* (Oxford: Oxford University Press, 2013).
[23] Pinkney, *Democracy in the Third World*.
[24] Johannes Bubeck and Nikolay Marinov, "Process or Candidate: The International Community and the Demand for Electoral Integrity," *American Political Science Review* 111, no. 3 (2017): 535–554.
[25] James Traub, *The Freedom Agenda: Why America Must Spread Democracy Just Not the Way George Bush Did* (New York: Farrar, Straus and Giroux, 2008); Michael Cox, Timothy J. Lynch and Nicolas Bouchet, eds., *U.S. Foreign Policy and Democracy Promotion: From Theodore Roosevelt to Barack Obama* (New York: Routledge, 2013).
[26] Amichai Magen and Michael A. McFaul, "Introduction: American and European Strategies to Promote Democracy-Shared Values, Common Challenges, Divergent Tools," in *Promoting Democracy and the Rule of Law: American European Strategies,* eds. Amichai Magen, Thomas Risse and Michael A. McFaul (New York: Palgrave MacMillan, 2019), 1–33.

advancement. Bilateral explanation says coercive democracy promotion occurs when a democratic government requests an intervention similar to the French intervention in Mali in 2013. Multilaterally, coercive democracy promotion is best seen at the instance of the United Nations Security Council authorisation of Libya's invasion in 2011.[27] Critics of coercive democracy promotion pinpoint that among other reasons, it is mostly concerned with regime change; that it is highly motivated by economic incentives (for example, oil and gas in Iraq); it is not a peaceful or democratic foreign policy measure;[28] and that it also hurts democracy at home and abroad in countries that promote democracy.[29]

Second, utilitarian democracy promotion mounts pressure, by means of conditions, on a given regime to open up the political space for democratisation or allow an external democracy promoter to directly undertake democracy promotion. In utilitarian democracy promotion framework, unilateral measures are undertaken negatively such as through 'the stick approach,' which entails curtailing or outright cancelation of incentives like economic, military and humanitarian aid to the state in question.[30] Contrariwise, the positive measure – the carrot approach – bolsters the economic and political muscles of a state to fast track it towards democratisation. A good example of a unilateral endeavour is the European Union's enlargement programme, which opens up its membership to democratising states. An example of bilateral utilitarian democracy promotion was undertaken by means of "commonly steered E.U. Task Forces with Arab Spring states."[31] While multilaterally, democracy promotion is carried out through such measures as the United Nations Democracy Fund.[32]

Third, identitive democracy promotion is a non-financial measure. Instead, it attains its goals by means of persuading values through speech acts, which are utterances that are not only expected to state something but to actually do something.[33] Thus, in identitive democracy promotion, the logic resides in arguing and the use of speech. Unilaterally, speech acts either name or shame violation of basic democratic ethos; condemns the lack of progress at democratisation or

---

27 Huber, *Democracy Promotion and Foreign Policy*.
28 Mlada Bukovansky, "Liberal States, International Order, and Legitimacy: An Appeal for Persuasion over Prescription," *International Politics* 44, no. 2 (2007): 175–193; Huber, *Democracy Promotion and Foreign Policy*.
29 Lawrence Whitehead, "Losing the Force? The 'Dark Side' of Democratisation after Iraq," *Democratisation* 16, no. 2 (2009): 215–242.
30 Huber, *Democracy Promotion and Foreign Policy*.
31 Huber, *Democracy Promotion and Foreign Policy*, 27.
32 Huber, *Democracy Promotion and Foreign Policy*.
33 Huber, *Democracy Promotion and Foreign Policy*.

laud ongoing democratisation pace in a state. For example, Nelson Mandela's speech in 1995 condemning the killing of Ken Saro Wiwa and eight other Ogoni environmental rights' activists by the Sani Abacha government in Nigeria was a speech act. Furthermore, the action in suspending Nigeria from the Commonwealth of Nations in 1995 on account of the execution of Ken Saro Wiwa and his fellow environmental activists' was an identitive democracy promotion action. Bilateral and multilateral identitive democracy promotions entail bilateral and multilateral exchanges on issues of democracy, which oftentimes are not in the public realm.[34]

Critics of democracy promotion are unconvinced of U.S. intentions.[35] Blum refers to democracy promotion as the West's deadliest export to the Global South.[36] For Bush, democracy promotion does not tame military dictators but in overt or covert measures work with autocratic regimes that serve U.S. economic aspirations, especially in the Middle East.[37] Thus, a recurring argument on how democracy promotion is presently deployed is that it is laden with economic motives; an agenda attained by equating liberal democracy with free market capitalism and as a goal fiercely pursued by means of military force for profit motives.[38]

Noam Chomsky unequivocally noted that the guardians of world order are Janus-faced in promoting democracy in one sense, while blocking it in another sense.[39] For example, for the U.S. and Britain, democracy promotion serves a number of political and economic interests. First, as a strategy for enabling unpopular governments in the Global South to secure legitimacy, and help to keep the citizenry quiescent and distanced from the decision-making process;[40] second, an economic strategy to exploit the Global South to satisfy the economic needs of the capitalist West; and third, as a source of raw materials also to the West. Chomsky contend that the U.S. achieve this feat by exploiting:

---

34 Huber, *Democracy Promotion and Foreign Policy.*
35 Walter Gam Nkwi, "Western Democracy in Africa as a Failed Project: Which Way Forward?" *East-West Journal of Humanities* 4 (2013): 111–125; Blum, *Rogue State.*
36 Blum, *America's Deadliest Export Democracy.*
37 Bush, *The Taming of Democracy Assistance.*
38 Noam Chomsky, *Deterring Democracy* (London: Vintage, 1992); S. Krasner, "America's Role in the World: The Costs of Walking Away" (Washington DC: United States Institute of Peace, 2011); Nicole Bibbins Sedaca and Nicolas Bouchet, "Holding Steady? U.S. Democracy Promotion in a Changing World," (London: Chatham House, February 2014).
39 Chomsky, *Deterring Democracy.*
40 Barry Gills and Joel Rocamora, "Low Intensity Democracy," *Third World Quarterly* 13, no. 3 (1992): 501–523.

virtual monopoly in the security market [...] as a lever to gain funds and economic concessions. [...] The U.S. has cornered the West's security market and others lack the political will [...] to challenge the U.S. in this market. The U.S. will therefore be the world's rent-a-cops and will be able to charge handsomely for the service.[41]

Interestingly, if the U.S. can exert such level of influence to extract profit from fellow democracy promoters, then governments in the Global South remain easily cajoled into submission and chiefly function to police their working classes and their superfluous population, whereas Transnational Corporations (TNCs) will have no-holds-barred access to resources and monopolise new technology to serve Western interests.

Samir Amin points to the misplaced equation of liberal democracy to free market (capitalism) where the market is basically a euphemism for capitalism, which in itself considered the basis of global development.[42] Amin concludes that democracy promoters have come to consider democratisation as the natural by-product of the worldwide market that is dependent on the logic that capitalism equals democracy, and democracy equals capitalism.[43] By implication, in the new world order, all states are expected to be democratic to enthrone the new ideological agenda of global capitalism. The ascendancy of this façade of democracy is only meant to cloak emerging forms of authoritarianism and repression, which will legitimise a deeper subordination to global capital.[44]

Andre Gunder Frank's chapter on democracy promotion was simply captioned "Marketing Democracy in an Undemocratic Market."[45] He opines that democracy promotion is a façade that has been invented to replace development on account of the colossal failure of development as a model of advancement in the Global South. As Frank notes further, democracy in the Global South "may well become a flag – or the fig-leaf – for continued exploitation and oppression of the South by the North."[46] He therefore concludes that a government by the people, of the people and for the people is infeasible in the Global South in as much as the economic possibilities of people's participation are limited and

---

41 Naom Chomsky, "The Struggle for Democracy in the New World Order," in *Low Intensity Democracy: Political Power in the New World Order*, eds. Barry Gills, Joel Rocamora and Richard Ashby Wilson (London: Pluto Press, 1993), 80–99.
42 Samir Amin, "The Issue of Democracy in the Contemporary Third World," in *Low Intensity Democracy*, 59–79.
43 Amin, "The Issue of Democracy," 60.
44 Gills and Rocamora, "Low Intensity Democracy," 501–523.
45 Andre Gunder Frank, "Marketing Democracy in an Undemocratic Market," in *Low Intensity Democracy*, 35–58.
46 Frank, "Marketing Democracy, 35.

constrained by their participation in the world economy controlled by the global North.[47]

Interestingly, in the democracy promotion enterprise "everyone applaud democracy, those who in practice oppose it applaud most loudly."[48] Wherever democracy is promoted, it is not for the benefit of where it is superficially seen to be promoted, but for the self-serving interests of the propagators–the West alone. In this respect, Bubeck and Marinov[49] conclude that the partisanship noticed in U.S. democracy promotion render the effort ineffective. Nigeria's 2015 presidential election manifested these self-centred, pecuniary agenda of the West whose sole motive was regime change.

The Silent Western Votes in the 2015 Presidential Election

Events leading to the 2015 presidential election in Nigeria witnessed an unprecedented activism from the United States Embassy in Nigeria. Uncritical political watchers explained United States' interest in the 2015 presidential election as a desire for hitch-free presidential election. However, a considered assessment of the U.S. embassy activism was interpreted as diplomatically unusual, especially the undiplomatic appearance at the 2015 presidential collation centre of the most senior U.S. diplomat, Ambassador James F. Entwistle.[50] Curiously, what would the ambassador be doing in the 2015 presidential election collation centre while results were still being counted? This section discusses the silent western votes in the 2015 presidential election in Nigeria.

The Silent Identity Votes

Except by deliberate choice, man is helpless in determining his race, colour, ethnicity, language and, above all, his religion. These inheritances are birth determinants and therefore ought not to be the determinants of one's suitability to

---

47 Frank, "Marketing Democracy.
48 Gills and Rocamora, "Low Intensity Democracy," 503.
49 Bubeck and Marinov, "Process or Candidate," 550.
50 Simon Ateba, "Entwistle, U.S. Ambassador Who Broke Diplomatic Protocol During 2015 Elections, Leaves Nigeria," https://www.Entwistle%2C+U.S.+Ambassador+Who+Broke+Diplomatic+Protocol+During+2015+Elections%2C+Leaves+Nigeria (accessed 12 July 2019).

an elective office. Unfortunately, instead of meritocracy gaining ascendancy, ethnicity continues to witness revival, intensification and unrelenting persistence in issues of politics.[51] In Nigeria, the aforementioned birth markers play dominant roles in national elections.[52] Religious differences portend real threat to peaceful elections in Nigeria because citizens are strongly attached to religious identities. Both the People's Democratic Party (PDP) and the All Progressives Congress (APC) fiercely aroused these sentiments to gain electoral ascendancy over each other in 2015 and 2019 respectively.[53] In the 2015 presidential election, the elements of identity – birth circumstances – of the main contending presidential candidates, Goodluck Ebele Jonathan and Muhammadu Buhari, were manipulated by the West to influence the electoral outcome.

Thus, the first card played was the religion card, which features widely in national and global politics.[54] Whereas, the manipulation of religion is a recurring practice in Nigeria's chequered political history, the Northern Elders Forum (NEF) seemed to have played it out of proportion in 2015. In October 2013, the NEF declared that "the North magnanimously conceded power to the South in 1999 and that there is no going back on the presidency returning to the North in 2015."[55] Manglos and Weinreb show that 76% of Christians and 91% of Muslims consider religion more important to them than their identity as Nigerians or Africans.[56] Auge noted that the structure of political competition is greatly influ-

---

51 David T. Mason, "Ethnicity and Politics," in *Encyclopaedia of Government and Politics*, vol. 1., eds. Mary Hawkesworth and Maurice Kogan (London: Routledge, 1992), 568–586.
52 Sunday M. A. Aloko and Usman Abdullahi, "Ethnicity, Religion and the Future of Nigerian Democracy," *Scientific Research Journal* 2, no. 11 (2014): 12–18; Matthew E. Egharevba, "The State and the Problems of Democracy in Nigeria," *Nigerian Sociological Review* 2, no. 1 (2005): 74–82; John Tor Tsuwa and Elijah Terdoo Ikpanor, eds., *The 2015 General Elections in Nigeria: Emerging Issues* (Abuja: Donafrique Publishers, 2017); Robin Lovin, "Religion and Politics," in *Encyclopaedia of Government and Politics*, Vol.1, eds., Mary Hawkesworth and Maurice Kogan (London: Routledge, 1992), 521–533; Insa Nolte, Nathaniel Danjibo and Abubakar Oladeji, *Religion, Politics and Governance in Nigeria – Religions and Development Research Programme No. 39* (Birmingham: University of Birmingham Press, 2009); Okechukwu Oko, *Key Problems for Democracy in Nigeria: Credible Elections, Corruption, Security, Governance and Political Parties* (New York: Edwin Mellern Press, 2010).
53 International Crisis Group (ICG), "Nigeria's Dangerous 2015 Elections: Limiting the Violence" (Africa Report No. 220, 2014).
54 Gertjan Dijkink, "When Geopolitics and Religion Fuse: A Historical Perspective," *Geopolitics* 11 (2006): 192–208; P. Mandaville, "How Do Religious Beliefs Affect Politics?" in *Global Politics: A New Introduction*, eds. Jenny Edkins and Maja Zehfuss (New York: Routledge, 2014), 108–131.
55 International Crisis Group, "Nigeria's Dangerous 2015 Elections," 3.
56 Nicolette D. Manglos and Alexander A. Weinreb, "Religion and Interest in Politics in Sub-Saharan Africa," *Social Forces* 92, no. 1 (2013): 195–219.

enced by religion, which directly impact voter perceptions.⁵⁷ The enormity of the religion card is that "87% of Nigerians consider religion to be 'very important in their life' and 31% say they could support only leaders from their own religious group... The parties, therefore, have an incentive to play this card by using divisive rhetoric in a bid to secure the loyalty of their respective electorates."⁵⁸ It is in such contexts that critical watchers of Nigeria's democratic space assert that the PDP's declaration that the APC, whose two main leaders, Muhammadu Buhari and Bola Tinubu were both Muslims, was the equivalent of the Muslim Brotherhood of Nigeria, aptly illustrates the enduring influence of religion in Nigeria's presidential elections.

Barack Obama who was widely quoted as saying that he became a Christian by choice used this religious identity card. His assertion implies that by his childhood upbringing he was a Muslim. Moreover, his hidden middle name 'Hussein' made both admirers and others to call him the hidden Muslim. In his Cairo speech on 4 June 2009, Obama remarked: "I am a Christian, but my father came from a Kenyan family that includes generations of Muslims. As a boy, I spent several years in Indonesia and heard the call of the *azaan* at the break of dawn and the fall of dusk. As a young man, I worked in Chicago communities where many found dignity and peace in their Muslim faith."⁵⁹ Strategically, therefore, the two contending presidential aspirants in the 2015 presidential elections, Goodluck Ebele Jonathan (Christian) and Muhammadu Buhari (Muslim) fell into his religious calculations, as Barak Obama made no secret of his support for Buhari who shared the same faith with him.

Furthermore, the role played by the twenty-year-old Pakistani Nobel Peace laureate, Malala Yousafzai, in the case of the kidnapped Chibok schoolgirls is equally worthy of mention as indication of religion having an impact on the outcome of Nigeria's 2015 presidential election. She stated:

> Nigerian leaders and the international community can and must do much more to resolve this crisis and change their weak response to date. If these girls were the children of politically or financially powerful parents, much more would be done to free them. But they

---

57 Benjamin Auge, "Africa in Question No.19: Nigeria's 2015 Presidential Election: Deciphering a High-Risk Operation" (IFRI, Sub-Sahara Africa Programme, 2015), 4.
58 Auge, "Africa in Question No.19."
59 Barack Obama, "Obama's speech in Cairo University," 4 June 2009, paragraph 5, https://www.nytimes.com/2009/06/04/us/politics/04obama.text.html (accessed 20 June 2019).

come from an impoverished area of north-east Nigeria and sadly little has changed since they were kidnapped.⁶⁰

Whereas Malala Yousafzai was actively involved on the state of the kidnapped Chibok schoolgirls and her open condemnation of the Goodluck Jonathan government's efforts at recovering the Chibok schoolgirls, Malala Yousafzai was silent on the occasion of the Dapchi school girls under Muhammadu Buhari's administration and in particular the continued kidnap of the remaining Christian Dapchi school girl, Leah Sharibu. Malala Yousafzai has never spoken a word on the unending kidnap of Leah Sharibu. The ruling APC government is silent as well. What explains this deliberate silence if not for the religious faith of the girl in question? The emphasis is that religion and not concern for the education of the Chibok schoolgirls informed Malala Yousafzai's assertion about the Jonathan government on the Chibok schoolgirl's kidnap impasse.

Secondly, ethnicity as an identity factor also played out in determining the outcome of the 2015 presidential election in Nigeria, and was as well used by the West. At the commencement of the Fourth Republic in 1999, the PDP adopted a zoning formula that alternates the presidency of Nigeria between North and South; an arrangement seen by most Nigerians as undemocratic.⁶¹ The North's resolve to ensure a return of a northern president was resolute. No stone was left unturned. The avowed commitment of NEF for a return of the presidency to the North was carried through by a number of measures to be outlined below.

First, NEF summoned several meetings on just this subject – the return of Nigeria's presidency to the North. Some of the resolutions signed by Mohammed Sharif at their 16 August 2014 meeting reads as follows:

a) Resolution No. 2: All avenues must be explored towards enthroning a president of northern extraction in the forthcoming 2015 election,
b) Resolution No. 3: A committee will be put in place to liaise with the INEC Chairman and some States Resident Electoral Commissioners in order to favour the North in the creation of additional polling units,
c) Resolution No. 6: The committee must ensure that strict adherence to eligibility is observed in the South-South and South-East in the continuous voter registration exercise with the support of INEC,
d) Resolution No. 7: 34 legal luminaries, 14 of whom are notable Senior Advocates will be constituted to challenge the incumbent in court once he de-

---

60 Lee Debarros, "Malala Yousafzai criticises 'weak' effort to free girls kidnapped by Boko Haram, *The Guardian* (U.K.), 2015, https://www.theguardian.com/world/2015/feb/08/malala-yousafzai-criticises-efforts-free-nigerian-girls-boko-haram (accessed 4 June 2019).
61 Auge, "Africa in Question No.19."

clares to run for the presidency in 2015 with the view to diverting and frustrating his attention,

e) Resolution No. 8: A committee will be put in place to liaise with senior northern judges in order to obtain favourable court rulings in the suits to be filed against President Jonathan's eligibility to contest the 2015 presidential election, and,

f) Resolution No. 9: The standing committee should liaise with northern Governors towards raising funds for these purposes.[62]

Second, Resolution No. 3 above called for the creation of additional polling units to deliberately favour the North. A NEF meeting held with Attahiru Jega, the INEC chairman, on 20 August 2014 restated the need to install a northern president on the platform of the APC through the instrumentality of the INEC. The NEF demand was attained by creating additional polling units that increased the total polling units in Nigeria from 119,973 to 150,000. Three states benefitted from this exercise: Lagos State got additional 2,870 polling units totalling 11,565 polling units; Kano State got 2,878 additional polling units bringing the state total to 7,485, and Katsina State got additional 1,339 polling units bringing that state's total to 3,818.[63] In Kano and Katsina States especially, the creation of more polling units were used mostly for the registration of under-aged voters.[64] These three states were APC strongholds.

In affirmation of NEF's determination to enthrone a northern president, Paul Unongo, Deputy Leader of NEF, would later declare that President Jonathan did not lose the 2015 presidential election. He posited as follows:

> From the onset, we made it clear that we are a political organisation concerned with global politics, and we articulated our views on the politics that had gone on and the one that had to go on. We felt that if a northerner was made the President of the Republic, he would know our pains, he would feel our pains and he would take action and stop the murderous campaign that was decimating the population of the North. So, we said that in the next elections, we would lead Nigeria, particularly the North, not to consider any other party except a political party that chose a northerner as its presidential candidate. We resolved that we would all work to have that candidate elected and we did so. We carried our campaigns across the whole of Nigeria. We carried our campaign without fear or intimidation to the international community. We went to the United States and confronted the United States administration and explained our position to them. And all these were done in the context

---

62 Danusa Ocholi, "Will Jega Survive? *Verbatim* 4, no. 4 (2015): 18.
63 Soni Daniel, "2015: INEC creates more 30,027 polling units," *Vanguard*, 20 August 2014, https://www.vanguardngr.com/2014/08/2015-inec-creates-30027-polling-units/ (accessed 15 December 2020).
64 Daniel, "2015: INEC creates more 30,027 polling units."

of our firm belief that when the North is united, Nigeria becomes united. That when Nigeria has a crisis and the North is together, the Nigerian crisis can be better solved. And this Kano was the very place we came and issued that document called 'the Kano Declaration'.[65]

This harmful regional politics was the tool used by the Barack Obama administration in bringing about regime change in Nigeria's 2015 presidential election. For example, the Obama government invited to the U.S. twelve sitting northern governors and a deputy governor to discuss measures to curtail the spread of Boko Haram. Dr Mu'azu Bangangida Aliyu, then Chairman of Northern Governors' Forum (NGF), who attended the meeting, noted that the discourse on Boko Haram was superficial; rather the real motive for the invitation was a regime change in Nigeria "for which the Americans had resolved not to support Jonathan. They just wanted to size us up for the level of commitment to regime change."[66]

The Silent Security Votes

The question of insecurity in North-East Nigeria under the occupation of the Boko Haram sect worked against the Jonathan government.[67] A number of persons and political parties, especially the opposition party, the APC, profited therefrom as insecurity became one of their cardinal campaign manifestoes. With a policy stance on regime change in Nigeria, the U.S. capitalised on the insecurity situation in North-East Nigeria to actualise her intentions. The Obama administration was particularly Janus-faced in a number of respects that raises the following concerns.[68] (i) Why did the Obama administration refuse to sell arms to Nigeria claiming that the Leahy Amendment debars it from selling arms to Nigeria on account of gross human rights violations perpetrated by Nigerian military troops in countering insurgency in the North-East? (ii) Why would

---

65 "Paul Unongo: Jonathan Didn't Lose 2015 Elections; We Northern Elders Plotted His Removal in Kano, White House in USA, 21 May 2017, *Channels News* (Nigeria), https://timepostng.blogspot.com/2017/05/bombshell-jonathan-didnt-lose-2015.html (accessed 12 June 2019).
66 Olusegun Adeniyi, *Against the Run of Play: How an Incumbent President was Defeated in Nigeria* (Lagos: Kachifo Ltd, 2017), 183.
67 John Campbell, "U.S. to Counter Nigeria's Boko Haram" (The Council on Foreign Relations, Special Report No.70, 2014).
68 James Simpson, "Obama Accused of Obstructing Battle against Boko Haram to Promote Axelrod's Nigerian Muslim Client," 24 March 2015, http://www.aim.org/aim-column/obama-accused-of-obstructing-battle-against-boko-haram-to-promote-axelrods-nigerian-muslim-client/ (accessed 12 June 2019).

the Obama administration diplomatically persuade other countries – Britain, France, Israel and even South Africa – not to sell arms to Nigeria? (iii) Why did the Obama administration deny Nigerian authorities vital security information on Boko Haram that was at its disposal? (iv) Why did the Obama administration stop the purchase of Nigeria's crude petroleum, the mainstay of the Nigerian economy? How would the Nigerian government undertake such a herculean counter-insurgency expedition without arms and a zero purchase of Nigeria's crude oil? Meanwhile, while the U.S. was under no obligation to buy Nigeria's crude petroleum, Nigeria was, and remains, a strategic military partner to the U.S. in sub-Saharan Africa and had cleaned-up for the U.S. quite a number of security concerns such as the Liberia's civil war. Thus, a partner of Nigeria's military standing ought not to have been treated by the U.S. the way the Obama administration did. (v) What was Obama's erstwhile senior adviser, David Axelrod, doing in Buhari's campaign organisation? These concerns compelled Simpson to rhetorically ask:

> And guess who's assisting Buhari with his campaign? None other than the consulting firm AKPD, founded by David Axelrod. You might remember him [...] the force behind President Obama's election victories in 2008 and 2012. He served as Obama's Senior Advisor until 2011. A well-placed Nigerian interviewed for this report who asked to remain unidentified says that influential Nigerians within and outside the government believe Obama deliberately undermined the war effort and sabotaged the Nigerian economy to make President Jonathan appear weak and ineffectual, and thus bolster the electoral prospects for AKPD's client, Buhari. [...] The Obama administration has said it is barred from supplying weapons to Nigeria by the so-called Leahy Amendment which forbids foreign states that have committed 'gross human rights violations' from receiving military aid. However, this did not stop the U.S. from sending Special Forces to Uganda – another country accused of such violations – to assist in capturing Lord Resistance Army leader Joseph Kony. Nor did it prevent Obama from supporting al-Qaeda-linked rebel groups in Libya, who later went on to attack the Benghazi mission, and have now joined ISIS.[69]

Interestingly, insecurity in North-East Nigeria has not become any better under President Buhari and his ruling APC government.

---

69 Simpson, "Obama Accused of Obstructing Battle."

The Silent Votes Arising from the Same Sex Prohibition Law in Nigeria

The great 'sin' supposedly committed by the Goodluck Jonathan administration in the eyes of the U.S. and other Western governments remains the signing into law of the same-sex prohibition law. This became another reason for casting a silent vote against him during the 2015 presidential election in Nigeria.[70] Expectedly, Nigeria-U.S. relations deteriorated to an all-time low. But why would Nigeria-U.S. diplomatic relations be adversely impacted whereas U.S. relations with a number of states such as Germany, Hungary, France and Romania are defined through constitutional provisions where the subject of marriage is treated as solely heterosexual? Why is U.S. diplomatic relations with France still normal, when the French government declined to endorse same-sex marriage and also after that government's attempt to enact same-sex legislation in 2013 was greeted with massive demonstrations by persons who interpreted the legislation as denial of children with a mother and father?

While President Barack Obama government was mounting pressure on Nigeria and other African governments to legitimise same-sex marriage, the same government did not institute legal pressure on such institutions as the European Court of Justice, the European Court of Human Rights, the United Nations Human Rights Committee, the French Constitutional Court, the Italian Constitutional Court, the German Federal Constitutional Court and the New Zealand Court of Appeal, amongst others, to amend their respective interpretations of same-sex marriage. All of the aforementioned institutions reject same-sex marriage as a constitutional or human rights issue. For example, the United Nations Human Rights Committee recognize as marriage "only the union between a man and a woman wishing to marry each other." It also holds "that a mere refusal to provide for marriage between homosexual couples did not breach the Covenant."[71]

If the concerns expressed by Durham et al[72] above is anything to go by, acceptance of same-sex couples and relationships should be left with public opinion of the country in question to determine by means of voting rather than being

---

[70] Bolaji Abdulalhi, *On a Platter of Gold: How Jonathan Won and Lost Nigeria* (Lagos: Kachifo Ltd, 2017).
[71] W. Cole Durham, Jr., Robert T. Smith and William C. Duncan, "A Comparative Analysis of Laws Pertaining to Same-Sex Unions," *SSRN* (2014): 15, https://www.A+Comparative+Analysis+of+Laws+Pertaining+to+Same-Sex+Unions (accessed 24 May 2019).
[72] Durham, Jr., Smith and Duncan, "A Comparative Analysis of Laws."

determined through judicial rulings as happened in the U.S. Supreme Court in the Obergefell v. Hodges case (26 June 2015).[73] Maybe overwhelmed by the U.S. Supreme Court ruling in Obergefell v. Hodges, the Obama administration went haywire in compelling other sovereign states to introduce same-sex legislations or dissuading states from enacting same-sex prohibition laws, which, of course, attracted severe sanctions in cases of noncompliance. As a result, President Goodluck Jonathan became a victim of regime change in the 2015 presidential election.

The Silent Votes of Western Media

While the noble roles of the media are widely acknowledged,[74] the conduct of a number of foreign media in the 2015 presidential election in Nigeria was bizarre.[75] The partisanship displayed by the U.K based *The Economist* leaves much to be desired. In its 5 February 2015 edition, the magazine with a caption, "Nigeria's Election, The Least Awful: Former Dictator is a Better Choice than a Failed President," stated thus:

> as Africa's biggest economy stages its most important election since the restoration of civilian rule in 1999, and perhaps since the civil war four decades ago, Nigerians must pick between the incumbent, Goodluck Jonathan, who has proved an utter failure, and the opposition leader, Muhammadu Buhari, a former military dictator with blood on his hands. The candidates stand as symbols of a broken political system that makes all Nigeria's problems even more intractable. [...] We are relieved not to have a vote in this election. But were we offered one we would – with a heavy heart – choose Mr Buhari. Mr Jonathan risks presiding over Nigeria's bloody fragmentation; if Mr Buhari can save Nigeria, history might even be kind to him. Start with Mr Jonathan, whose party has run the country since 1999 and

---

73 Evan Gerstmann, *Same-Sex Marriage and the Constitution* (New York: Cambridge University Press, 2003); Faith Olanrewaju, Felix Chidozie and Adekunle Olanrewaju, "International Politics of Gay Rights and Nigeria-U.S. Diplomatic Relations," *European Scientific Journal* 11, no. 4 (2015): 504–520.
74 Hajo G. Boomgaarden, Rens Vliegenthart and Claes H. de Vreese, "A Worldwide Presidential Election: The Impact of the Media on Candidate and Campaign Evaluations," *International Journal of Public Opinion Research* 24, no.1 (2012): 42–61; Hillary I. Ekemam, "The International Politics Imperative of Nigeria's 2015 Presidential Election: The Role of the Media," *International Journal of Information Research and Review* 3, no. 4 (2016): 2140–2145.
75 Mojeed Adekunle Animashaun, "Nigeria 2015 Presidential Election: The Votes, the Fears and the Regime Change," *Journal of African Elections* 14, no. 2 (2014): 186–211.

who stumbled in to the presidency on the death of his predecessor in 2010; the PDP's reign has been a sorry one.[76]

The Economist continued:

> Mr. Jonathan has shown little willingness to tackle endemic corruption. When the governor of the central bank reported that $20 billion had been stolen, his reward was to be sacked. [...] He has shown little enthusiasm for tackling insecurity and even less competence. Buhari is a sandal-wearing ascetic with a record of fighting corruption. Few nowadays question his commitment to democracy or expect him to turn autocratic: he has repeatedly stood for election and accepted the outcome when he lost. He would probably do a better job of running the country, and in particular of tackling Boko Haram. As a northerner and Muslim, he will have greater legitimacy among villagers whose help he will need to isolate the insurgents. As a military man, he is more likely to win the respect of a demoralised army.[77]

Following this publication, Goodluck Jonathan, a sitting president of Nigeria had a reason to engage in altercations with the magazine stating loudly in an address that he did not need their support.[78] President Goodluck Jonathan further described the *Economist's* publication as a "baseless, jaundiced and malicious vilification."[79]

The partisan roles also played by two other U.K newspapers, *The Observer* and *The Guardian of London* were as well ignoble.[80] On 18 January 2015, the editorial column of *The Observer*[81] criticised the Jonathan government for lacking a workable strategy to combat insurgency in North-East Nigeria and that his government failed to tell Nigerians how to contain the spate of bombings and kidnappings that were commonplace in that region. However, in contrast, the paper rained glowing praises on General Buhari, noting among others that "Buhari earned a reputation for strong leadership and intolerance of corruption during his brief period in power in 1983–1985." *The Guardian of London* in its own

---

76 "Nigeria's election, the least awful: A former dictator is a better choice than a failed president," *The Economist*, 5 February 2015, https://www.economist.com/leaders/2015/02/05/the-least-awful.
77 "Nigeria's election, the least awful," paragraphs 2 and 3.
78 Goodluck E. Jonathan, "I Don't Need Your Support, Jonathan Tells Economist Magazine," *Premium Times*, 7 February 2015, https://www.premiumtimesng.com/.../176404-dont-need-support-jonathan-tells-economist (accessed 4 May 2019).
79 Jonathan, "I Don't Need Your Support."
80 Animashaun, "Nigeria 2015 Presidential Election," 194.
81 Animashaun, "Nigeria 2015 Presidential Election," 194.

editorial of 16 January 2015 noted that the two presidential candidates were flawed leaders unworthy of the presidency of Nigeria. It continued:

> President Jonathan stands accused of inertness and procrastination in dealing with Boko Haram, and of ineffective performance in office generally. General Muhammadu Buhari, his rival, has a reputation as one of the more honest and well-intentioned of the country's military rulers, but not one of the most astute.[82]

The emphasis is that these foreign media organisations with enormous coverage and readership, along with David Axelrod's AKPD that reputedly secured Barak Obama's electoral victories in both 2008 and 2012, greatly influenced Nigerian voters in the 2015 presidential election.[83]

Conclusion

As noted in this chapter, democracy promotion is simply the silent votes cast by Western countries in the elections of Global South countries; and these adversely impact on electoral outcomes in the latter.[84] Besides this primary conclusion, other insights emerged as well from this chapter's analysis. They include the fact that the Obama administration helped to enthrone Muhammadu Buhari as the president of Nigeria in the 2015 presidential election. Since coming into power, the Buhari government fits best as a democratic autocracy where human rights are violated. His widely acclaimed anticorruption crusade has been lopsided, and the much-anticipated decimation of the Boko Haram sect remains a ruse. The change that was hugely proclaimed and expected from 2015 onwards has been nothing but a mirage.[85] The totality of Buhari's actions as president negates his commitments and the promises he made during his acceptance speech in April 2015 where he promised Nigerians: "you shall be able to go to bed knowing that you are safe and that your constitutional rights remain in safe hands. You shall be able to voice your opinion without fear of reprisal or victimisation."[86]

---

[82] Animashaun, "Nigeria 2015 Presidential Election," 195.
[83] Ekemam, "The International Politics Imperative of Nigeria's 2015 Presidential Election," 2140– 2145.
[84] Andreas Schedler, ed., *Electoral Authoritarianism: The Dynamics of Unfree Competition* (Boulder, CO: Lynne Rienner, 2006).
[85] Animashaun, "Nigeria 2015 Presidential Election."
[86] "Acceptance Speech by General Muhammadu Buhari, GCFR, President-Elect of Nigeria, *Vanguard*, 1 April 2015.

It should be noted that Nigeria is in great danger under democracy promotion. This is because democracy promotion remains blind to the how of election conduct,[87] not to mention that the predominant ethos of liberal democracy also remains alien to non-Western cultures except with modifications.[88] The fact that liberal democracy is not meeting economic expectations has caused disillusionment,[89] leading scholars to advance an African variant of democracy.[90]

There are countervailing interests in propagating democracy in Nigeria and indeed much of Africa. However, as the West is forcing some nations along this path, it is simultaneously blind to others like the autocratic regimes of Omar Bongo (Gabon), Paul Biya (Cameroon), Jose Eduardo dos Santos (Angola) and Teodoro Obiang Nguema Mbasogo (Equatorial Guinea) because of the economic benefits they derive from these nations, which includes crude petroleum in Equatorial Guinea.[91] Thus, U.S. relation with Equatorial Guinea is simply devoid of pressure to institutionalise liberal democracy.[92]

Democracy promotion in several ways undermines the sovereignty of states and sanctity of the office of presidents as the following instances illustrate. First, it is diplomatically established that for the sake of due diligence and respect for the sovereignty of any state into its final stages in compilation of official results, no staff of a foreign mission be allowed entrance into the presidential collation centre. Yet, Ambassador James F. Entwistle of the U.S. committed this diplomatic blunder.[93] Second, altercations between President Jonathan and the U.S. and U.K foreign missions were unsavoury to say the least.[94] President Jonathan's insis-

---

87 Bubeck and Marinov, "Process or Candidate," 535–554.
88 Tanza A. Borzel, and Thomas Risse, "Venus Approaching Mars? The European Union's Approaches to Democracy Promotion in Comparative Perspective," in *Promoting Democracy and the Rule of Law: American and European Strategies*, eds. Amichai Magen, Thomas Risse and Michael A. McFaul (New York: Palgrave Macmillan, 2009), 34–60; Robert Pinkney, *Democracy in the Third World* (Boulder, Colorado: Lynne Rienner, 2003); Elliot P. Skinner, "African Political Cultures and the Problems of Government," *African Studies Quarterly* 2, no. 3 (1998): 17–25.
89 Sardar, "The Future of Democracy and Human Rights," 839–859; Michael J. Sodaro, Nathan J. Brown, and Dean Walter Collinwood, *Comparative Politics: A Global Introduction* (New York: McGraw-Hill, 2001).
90 Claude Ake, "The Unique Case of African Democracy," *International Affairs* 69, no. 2 (1993): 239–244; Claude Ake, *The Feasibility of Democracy in Africa* (Dakar: CODESRIA Books, 2000).
91 Thomas Carothers, "Democracy Policy Under Obama: Revitalisation or Retreat?" (Washington DC: Carnegie Endowment for International Peace, 2012).
92 Carothers, "Democracy Policy Under Obama."
93 Ateba, "Entwistle, U.S. Ambassador Who Broke Diplomatic Protocol.2
94 Wale Odunsi, "UK Replies Jonathan, Says Nigerians Choose Buhari in 2015," *Daily Post*, 29 April 2017, https://dailypost.ng (accessed 12 June 2019).

tence that President Obama spearheaded a conspiracy with the U.K and France to unseat him in 2015 attracted an avalanche of newspaper headlines and official statements such as the following: "Your people, not Obama voted you out, U.S. tells Jonathan," and "U.K response to Jonathan with the headline, we had no hand in your defeat."[95] Russel Brooks, erstwhile U.S. embassy spokesperson, said "the US advocated a free, fair and transparent election. The election outcome was an expression of the will of the Nigerian people."[96] These exchanges denigrate the office of the president of any country, and the U.S. would never have tolerated such in its own soil. Thus, Western democracy promotion falls short of leading to the deepening of democracy as most African states have oscillated from a de facto one-party state to a competitive electoral democracy and then to electoral autocratic democracies.

---

[95] "Your People, Not Obama Voted You Out, U.S. Tells Jonathan," 27 April 2017, www.ripplesnigeria.com (accessed 12 June 2019).

[96] "Your People, Not Obama Voted You Out."

Olawari D. J. Egbe and David O. Gogo
Ruling and Opposition Parties' Reactions to External Interference in the 2019 Presidential Election

Abstract: At the close of the Cold War, Democracy Promotion (DP) by the Global North became pervasive in the Global South. Expectedly, world capitals – Washington DC, London, Paris, among others – have played influential roles in presidential elections in the Global South. Their influential roles are regarded as 'silent votes'. They are external political interferences in domestic electioneering matters and often determine electoral outcomes judging from their power to influence voters, ruling and opposition parties, civil society organisations and others. This chapter examines the reactions of Nigeria's ruling and opposition parties to such external interferences during Nigeria's presidential elections. It considers the implications on public trust in one of the institutions of representative democracy – the political party. Since 1999, political parties have presented a Janus-faced approach to external interferences during electioneering periods. Whereas the ruling party expresses dissatisfaction and reservations, the opposition party applauds and profit from such external interferences. This scenario is typical of the manner the Peoples' Democratic Party (PDP) and the All Progressives Congress (APC) reacted to external influences in the 2015 and 2019 presidential elections respectively. Relying on secondary sources, supported by "the institutional performance model," the authors conclude that African democracies should not totally interpret external influences as entirely disruptive as they help to strengthen and widen the democratic space. Instead, we recommend that if the political class is uncomfortable with external influences, it should be introspective and get used to strengthening national democracy watch institutions or collaborate with continental democracy watch institutions like the Electoral Institute for Sustainable Democracy in Africa to woo and secure legitimacy rather than seeking legitimacy from Western democracy watch institutions like the Royal Institute of International Affairs, London.

Keywords: Nigeria, presidential elections, the West, democracy promotion, silent votes, political parties

Olawari D. J. Egbe and David O. Gogo, Niger Delta University

https://doi.org/10.1515/9783110766561-008

Introduction

Save for Nigeria's First Republic, all transitions to democracy were supervised by the military on account of the incessant military regimes in Nigeria.[1] Expectedly, therefore, the military government of General Abdulsalami Abubakar worked to enthrone Nigeria's Fourth Republic in 1999 with deliberate assiduity and an unalloyed commitment to citizens' yearnings for democracy, which had a clear message of intent – 'we are tired of military rule.'[2] Although Nigeria's Fourth Republic is still in its democratisation process, the ensuing political developments, either in the positive or negative domains, deserve to be studied. In Nigeria's democratic space, the political arena remains dominated by two political parties – the PDP that controlled governance from 1999 to 2015 and the APC that took over power in 2015. The dominance of these parties had strong impacts on Nigeria's presidential elections.[3]

Major Western actors in global electoral politics frequently intervene in the electoral process of developing countries. This interference is referred to in this chapter variously as "silent Western votes," "democracy promotion," "electoral intervention," or "foreign interests". Electoral interventions or better still promotion of liberal democracy by Western states, especially the United States, the European Union, Britain, and France,[4] are specifically undertaken for two reasons: interventions in favour of a particular candidate and party (the "who" of elections) and interventions in favour of the democratic process (the "how" of elections).[5] For example, while during Nigeria's 2015 presidential election, external interventions were clearly in favour of Major General Muhammadu Buhari the presidential candidate of the APC; in the 2019 presidential election, the external interests supported a free and fair democratic process which made the APC feel

---

[1] Anthonia Ahonsi-Yakubu, "Political Transitions, Crime and Insecurity in Nigeria," *Africa Development* 26, no.1 and 2 (2001): 73–98.
[2] Egbunam E. Amadife, "Liberalisation and Democratisation in Nigeria: The International and Domestic Challenge," *Journal of Black Studies* 29, no. 5 (1999): 619–645.
[3] Bidemi G. Badmus, "The Contents and Discontents of Party Politics and Democratic Experiment in Nigeria," *International Journal of Research in Business Management and Studies* 1, no.1 (2017): 23–39.
[4] Beate Jahn, "Rethinking Democracy Promotion," *Review of International Studies* 38, no. 4 (2012): 685–705.
[5] Johannes Bubeck, and Nikolay Marinov, "Process or Candidate: The International Community and the Demand for Electoral Integrity," *American Political Science Review* 111, no. 3 (2017): 535–554.

that external interests tilted towards the PDP and its presidential candidate, Alhaji Atiku Abubakar.

Besides the two generic reasons given above, interventions by advanced democracies in Nigeria's presidential elections were also for several specific strategic reasons. First, Nigeria occupies strategic economic and military positions in Africa and beyond. Nigeria is a major economic actor in oil and gas politics in the Gulf of Guinea as well as a military powerhouse in Africa. Therefore, Western nations would want to partner with Nigeria and whoever governs it.[6] Second, Western nations espouse a commitment to enthrone democracy globally with the belief that 'undemocratic spaces' are breeding grounds for terror and terrorism. In pursuit of this agenda, they deploy subtle measures to enthrone democracy among developing countries.

While these strategic reasons may seem laudable, external interventions in favour of the democratic process (the "how" of elections), is commonly hotly contested by political parties in nations venturing into presidential elections. In Nigeria, for instance, the two major political parties in their utterances displayed enormous dislike for foreign interference in the country's presidential elections. As shown in the previous chapter, the APC profited from interference from the governments of the United States under President Barrack Obama and Britain under David Cameron during the 2015 presidential elections. Thus, Muhammadu Buhari, delivering a speech at the Royal Institute of International Affairs, London, stated: "so, let me say upfront that the global interest in Nigeria's landmark election is not misplaced at all and indeed should be commended, for this is an election that has serious import for the world. I urge the international community to continue to focus on Nigeria at this very critical moment."[7] Then came the 2019 presidential election, President Buhari and his government began to critically and unequivocally condemn the West, particularly the U.S. and Britain, for interfering in the internal affairs of Nigeria. It then becomes clear that silent Western votes are indications that international diplomacy and politics are a combination of the propagation of foreign and corporate interests and of the interests of politicians contesting presidential elections.

This chapter evaluates PDP and APC's reactions to the democracy promotion agenda of the West during the 2015 and 2019 presidential elections. It also con-

---

6 Tim Murithi, "The Evolution of Africa's International Relations," in *Handbook of Africa's International Relations*, ed. T. Murithi (London: Routledge, 2014), 1–7; Ben Smith, Daniel Harari, Jon Lunn, Louisa Brooke-Holland, Matthew Ward and Rob Page, "Nigeria 2015: Analysis of election issues and future prospects" (Research Paper 15/02, House of Commons Library, 2015).
7 Muhammadu Buhari, "Prospects for Democratic Consolidation in Africa: Nigeria's Transition" (London: Chatham House, February 2015).

siders the implications of democracy promotion on public trust in political parties, which constitute a key institution of representative democracy. The chapter is split into four sections. After this introduction, section II examines the operations of the "institutional performance model," the theoretical framework for this chapter. Section III then discusses the issues that generated diverse reactions, from the PDP and the APC, to foreign interests in Nigeria's presidential elections; and lastly, the conclusion.

The Institutional Performance Model

The political party, one of the central institutions of representative government, is hunted by the spectre of eroding public trust. This trend is commonplace in developed and developing democracies alike;[8] that the Trilateral Commission, in discussing the crisis of democracy, concluded that "dissatisfaction with, and lack of confidence in the functioning of the institutions of democratic government have thus now become widespread."[9] Scholars have sought plausible theoretical explanations for this crisis and those identified include theories of trust and confidence.

The theories of public trust and confidence espouse three explanatory models: "social-psychological explanations," "social and cultural model," and "institutional performance model." The "social-psychological explanations" model explains trust and confidence as personality types or traits (such as trust in oneself and others, feelings of inner goodness, and early life experiences) that influence aspects of behaviour.[10] The "social and cultural model" posits that life experiences gender in citizens trust and cooperation, interpersonal relations and civic mindedness, which in turn cause people to invest their trust in

---

[8] Arthur H. Miller, "Political Issues and Trust in Government, 1964–1970," *American Political Science Review* 68 (1974): 951–972; Russell J. Dalton, "Political Support In Advanced Industrial Countries," in *Critical Citizens: Global Support for Democratic Government*, ed. Pippa Norris (Oxford: Oxford University Press, 1999), 1–23; Virginia A. Chanley, Thomas J. Rudolph and Wendy M. Rahn, "The Origins and Consequences of Public Trust in Government: A Time Series Analysis," *The Public Opinion Quarterly* 64, no. 3 (2000): 239–256.

[9] Michel Crozier, Samuel P. Huntington and Joji Watanuki, *The Crisis of Democracy* (New York: University Press, 1975), 158.

[10] Gordon W. Allport, "*Pattern and Growth in Personality* (New York: Holt, Rinehart and Winston, 1961); Raymond B. Cattell, *The Scientific Analysis of Personality* (Baltimore: Penguin Books, 1965).

institutions.[11] The "institutional performance model," which serves as the core theoretical handle of this chapter, "focuses on the actual performance of government as the key to understanding citizen's confidence in government."[12] The "institutional performance model" also counters the former two models, asserting instead that trust and confidence are neither issues of personality traits nor the direct outcomes of social conditions. Rather, because all citizens are exposed to government actions "confidence in political institutions is likely to be randomly distributed among various personality types and different cultural and social types." It went further to state that "government institutions that perform well are likely to elicit the confidence of citizens; while those that perform badly or ineffectively generate feelings of distrust and low confidence."[13]

Trust and confidence in public institutions as derivatives from this model have the following three implications. First, the general public assesses the performance quality of the government or political institutions and reacts accordingly. Second, questions of public confidence provide possible measurement of public life. Third, there are implications for public policy. For example, if there is loss of confidence in public institutions, the remedy lies in either the political class promising less (that is lowering public expectations) or promising more by improving institutional performance. In the context of Nigeria, Vergee, Kwaja and Onubogu note:

> The first-ever peaceful transition of power in 2015 raised expectations for government performance. Many Nigerians feel their hopes have not been met... the electorate is sufficiently disappointed that voter apathy will be greater in 2019 than in 2015, with the unifying narrative of change that helped elect the APC in 2015 much less compelling as a factor in mobilising the electorate, and perceptions that another defeat of the presidential incumbent is less likely to happen in 2019.[14]

The next section looks at the reactions of the PDP and APC to the silent Western votes in the 2015 and 2019 presidential elections.

---

[11] Kenneth Newton, "Social Capital and Democracy," *American Behavioral Scientist* 40, no. 5 (1997): 575–586.
[12] Kenneth Newton and Pippa Norris, "Confidence in Public Institutions: Faith, Culture or Performance?" (paper presented at the annual meeting of the American Political Science, Atlanta, 1–5 September 1999), 7.
[13] Newton and Norris, "Confidence in Public Institutions," 7.
[14] Aly Vergee, Chris Kwaja, and Oge Onubogu, "Nigeria's 2019 elections: Change, continuity and the risks to peace" (Washington DC: United States Institute of Peace Special Report 429, 2018), 5.

PDP and APC's Reactions to Silent Western Votes in Nigeria's Presidential Elections

The outcome of the 2015 presidential election was adjudged nationally and internationally as reflecting the wishes of Nigerians. This assessment was on account of a number of first-occurrence factors in Nigeria's political trajectory. For the first time an incumbent president conceded defeat prior to an official declaration of election results and even called to congratulate the opposition presidential candidate. Second, for the first time, a ruling political party was voted out of office at the presidential polls. And third, for the first-time, external interests in Nigeria's presidential election moved beyond the mere involvement of international observer missions to a high politics domain where foreign governments (especially that of Barack Obama and David Cameron) demonstrated covert and overt activism in the 2015 presidential election.

While Nigerians appreciated these three instances, the two major political parties in the country, the PDP and the APC, reacted to the third instance in similar ways capable of causing waning public trust and confidence in these two political parties. As ruling political parties, in 2015 and 2019 respectively, they both expressed dissatisfaction and reservations about foreign involvement in Nigeria's presidential elections. Both parties interpreted democracy promotion as an unwelcome interference in the internal affairs of Nigeria. If these two parties exhibited similar dislike for democracy promotion, no political party in Nigeria should wear the toga of 'holier than thou'. The sanctimonious claims of the ruling Buhari-led APC government are tantamount to the pot calling the kettle black. The rest of this section examines similar reactions of the PDP and the APC on several issues bordering on democracy promotion in Nigeria's 2015 and 2019 presidential elections.

United States' Embassy Activisms

In the 2015 presidential election, the PDP accused the U.S. Embassy in Nigeria of activism beyond their accredited mandate. Party members wondered aloud over what the then U.S. Ambassador, James F. Entwistle, was doing in the election collation centre. To them, the ambassador broke diplomatic protocols by visiting the presidential election collation centre in Abuja during the 2015 polls. This action was not heard of before and, therefore, was considered as disrespect for the sovereignty of Nigeria by a U.S. diplomat. On his part, Ambassador James F. Entwistle claimed that he acted on the suspicion that President Goodluck Jonathan was intending to rig the presidential election.¹⁵ Meanwhile, before the election, James F. Entwistle had forwarded to the citizens the following message from his principal, President Barack Obama:

> With elections across Nigeria right around the corner, I'd like to share with each of you a personal message from President Obama to the Nigerian people... So many of you are already doing your part to ensure that all who want to vote, can vote, without fear. The President and the American people appreciate the great work you're doing in your communities to help support democracy and peace, and to build a stronger, more prosperous Nigeria. [...] How you participate in this election – and how your leaders respect its outcome – is important not just for Nigerians, but also for the entire continent of Africa and the global community... What do these elections mean to you? How will you contribute to a successful election as a leader in your community? What do you hope to see for the future of Nigeria?¹⁶

Ambassador James F. Entwistle followed up by organising a meeting between Presidents Goodluck Jonathan and Muhammadu Buhari in Lagos rather than Abuja, an action also described as totally disrespectful to the sitting president.¹⁷ In addition, the U.S. Secretary of State, John Kerry, made a diplomatically inappropriate visit to Nigeria on the verge of the 2015 presidential election. President Goodluck Jonathan responded with the remark: "Mr. Kerry's brief visit is a departure from the U.S. policy that disallows its senior officials from visiting countries about to hold elections, to avoid the perception of supporting one candidate against another."¹⁸

In celebration of a successful democracy promotion in Nigeria, the U.S. sent a special delegation to the inauguration of President Muhammadu Buhari on 29 May 2015. The team comprised John Kerry, U.S. Secretary of State, James F. Entwistle, U.S. Ambassador to the Federal Republic of Nigeria, Linda Thomas-Greenfield, Assistant Secretary of State for African Affairs, Department of State, General David M. Rodriguez, Commander, U.S. Africa Command (USAFRICOM), Grant T. Harris, Special Assistant to the President and Senior Director for African Affairs, National Security Council and Mr. Hakeem Olajuwon, NBA Legend and U.S. Olympics Gold Medalist.¹⁹

---

15 Simon Ateba, "Entwistle, U.S. Ambassador Who Broke Diplomatic Protocol During 2015 Elections, Leaves Nigeria," https://www.Entwistle%2C+U.S.+Ambassador+Who+Broke+Diplomatic+Protocol+During+2015+Elections%2C+Leaves+Nigeria (accessed 12 July 2019).
16 "Moving forward: When Nigeria Decides, Nigeria Wins. A News Letter of the U.S. Mission in Nigeria," *Crossroads* 21, no. 4 (April/May 2015), 5.
17 Ateba, "Entwistle, U.S. Ambassador Who Broke Diplomatic Protocol."
18 Goodluck E. Jonathan, *My Transition Hours* (Allen, TX: Ezekiel Books, 2018), 65.
19 U.S. Mission Nigeria, "President Obama Announces Presidential Delegation to Nigeria to Attend the Inauguration of His Excellency Muhammadu Buhari, President-elect of the Fed,"

Whereas the PDP complained of undue foreign missions' activism, the APC was comfortable with the entire scenario to the degree that its presidential candidate in his address in Chatham House, London, both welcomed external interest in the election and even urged the international community to continue to focus on Nigeria at such moments.[20] In his capacity as the new president, Muhammadu Buhari minced no words in commending foreign interests in the 2015 presidential election. According to him:

> The U.S. support before, during and after the 2015 elections was vital to Nigeria's stability and I will never forget the role they played in the stability of Nigeria. We were lucky to have had an INEC Chairman who was competent and courageous. Mr. Ambassador, you occupied a position at a very strategic time in Nigeria's history and I hope our historians will record this because it meant so much for our stability. I hope you write a book on your experience in Nigeria. The commitment of U.S. in supporting Nigeria has been unprecedented.[21]

Whereas Ambassador James F. Entwistle simultaneously poured accolades on President Buhari, Attahiru Jega, the Independent National Electoral Commission (INEC) chairman, and INEC as the electoral umpire, no reference was made to the historic role the out-going president, Goodluck Jonathan, played in the 2015 election because it was the original agenda of the U.S. to ensure regime change in Aso Rock, Nigeria's seat of power.

However, in the course of the 2019 presidential election, the APC sang quite a different song. The APC interpreted foreign interests in that election as interference in Nigeria's internal affairs. First, the Executive Governor of Kaduna State, Nasir el-Rufai, who also was the gubernatorial candidate of the APC in Kaduna State, condemned, threatened international observers' and interpreted their statements to be based on non-information. He described them as "most irresponsible" noting:

> I'm happy that the Presidency responded to them. As Nigerians, we must understand that these guys can sit pretty in their countries and say things but when crisis breaks, we are here. We are the victims; our wives and children are the victims. We must unite and say no to violence in this country. We are waiting for the person that will come and intervene. They will go back in body bags, because nobody will come to Nigeria and tell us how to run our

---

https://www.U.S.+Mission+Nigeria%2C+President+Obama+Announces+Presidential+Delegation+to+Nigeria+to+Attend+the+Inauguration+of+His+Excellency+Muhammadu+Buhari%2C+President-elect+of+the+Fed (accessed 10 October 2020).

20 Buhari, "Prospects for Democratic Consolidation in Africa."
21 Simon Ateba "Entwistle, U.S. Ambassador Who Broke Diplomatic Protocol," 2.

country. We've got that independence and we are trying to run our country as decently as possible.[22]

The main opposition party, the PDP, reacted to Nasir el-Rufai's comment made on Nigeria Television Authority (NTA). Its National Publicity Secretary, Mr. Kola Ologbondiyan, said at a press conference in Abuja that the party would be left with no option but to consider a review of its being signatory to the Peace Accord if no action was taken over el-Rufai's unsavoury comments.[23] Meanwhile, Steven Chukwu, the Director of Publicity for the Nigerian Democratic Forum (NDF), raised an alarm over plots by the United States, the United Kingdom and the European Union to impose a presidential candidate on the people of Nigeria through the backdoor. The NDF press statement reads:

> These countries have been in the business of issuing coordinating statements that are intended to criminalise the incumbent President, His Excellency, Muhammadu Buhari, who incidentally is the candidate of the All Progressives Congress (APC). These countries have stepped beyond all known diplomatic bounds to the extent that they want to decide how Nigeria runs its domestic affairs, including how to run the judiciary and even what to do about its fight against corruption. The outpouring of condemnations from patriotic Nigerians forced the PDP, U.S., U.K. and E.U. to beat a hasty retreat to re-strategise. We have confirmation that their incentive will not allow them give up the plot to force their desired outcome on the elections even when this is a glaring violation of all known laws. The driving force for their support of Atiku Abubakar is worrisome and calls for any Nigerian that desires to still have a country after the elections to stand up against the re-colonisation of Nigeria.[24]

Rescheduling of Presidential Elections in 2015 and 2019

The rescheduling of presidential elections in 2015 and 2019 respectively attracted intense external pressure on the Nigerian government. The two major political

---

22 Adelani Adepegba, Oladimeji Ramon and Success Nwogu, "2019 polls: PDP slams el-Rufai for issuing death threat to foreigners," https://www.2019+polls%3A+PDP+slams+elRufai+for+is-suing+death+threat+to+foreigners (accessed 12 May 2019).
23 Ojobo Ode Atuluku, "Nigeria's 2019 elections: So many choices, so difficult to choose," https://www.Nigeria%E2%80%99s+2019+elections%3A+So+many+choices%2C+so+difficult+to+choose (accessed 12 September 2019).
24 Ameh Comrade Godwin, "2019: US, EU, UK others warned against imposing presidential candidate on Nigerians, 14 February 2019," https://www.2019%3A+US%2C+EU%2C+UK+others+warned+against+imposing+presidential+candidate+on+Nigerians%2C+February+142019 (accessed 20 May 2019).

parties, the PDP and APC reacted in a similar manner. Both parties interpreted foreign interests in their rescheduled presidential elections as interference in the internal affairs of Nigeria. Just like the PDP complained bitterly over U.S. and British interests in the rescheduled 2015 presidential election, the APC equally expressed discomfort over U.S. interests in the postponement of the 2019 presidential election. In 2015, Muhammadu Buhari clearly welcomed foreign interests in the rescheduled election with the comment:

> given increasing global linkages, it is in our collective interests that the postponed elections should hold on the rescheduled dates; that they should be free and fair; that their outcomes should be respected by all parties; and that any form of extension, under whichever guise, is unconstitutional and will not be tolerated.[25]

Meanwhile, President Jonathan was highly incensed at U.S. concern on the rescheduled presidential election. In retrospect, President Goodluck Jonathan stated:

> President Obama sent his Secretary of State to Nigeria, a sovereign nation, to protest the rescheduling of the election. John Kerry arrived in Nigeria on Sunday January 25, 2015 and said it is important that these elections happen on time as scheduled. [...] How can the U.S. Secretary of State know what is more important for Nigeria than Nigeria's own government? How could they have expected us to conduct elections when Boko Haram controlled part of the North-East and were killing and maiming Nigerians? Not even the assurance of the sanctity of the May 29, 2015 handover date could calm them down [...] the foreign pressure on the issue of election rescheduling was intense [...] the meeting of Council of State where the decision to reschedule the election was taken were almost all the living former Heads of State of this country. That should have convinced John Kerry of the good intentions of the government. He cannot claim to love and defend Nigeria more than all our former Heads of State present at the meeting.[26]

Like the 2015 presidential election, INEC had logistical reasons to postpone the 2019 presidential election. As usual, African observer missions, comprising of eminent African personalities,[27] expressed their reservations on the postponement:

---

25 Buhari, "Prospects for Democratic Consolidation."
26 Jonathan. *My Transition Hours*, 64–67.
27 These include Ellen Johnson-Sirleaf, former President of Liberia and then Chairman of the Economic Community of West African States (ECOWAS); Hailemariam Desalegn, former Prime Minister of Ethiopia who led the African Union; Jakaya Kikwete, former President of Tanzania who led the Commonwealth; Rupiah Banda, former President of Zambia, that led the Electoral Institute for Sustainable Democracy in Africa; Mohamed Ibn Chambas, the Director of African

We, the heads of the international election observation missions and the UN present in Nigeria, have taken note of the decision of INEC to postpone the 2019 general elections due to logistical and operational challenges. We urge INEC to use this time to finalise all preparations and ensure that the new election dates are strictly adhered to.[28]

In addition, the U.S., the U.K. and the E.U. and their respective embassies and offices issued separate statements supporting the position of the observer missions in calling for free, fair and credible elections.

Like the PDP in 2015, the ruling APC became Janus-faced in 2019. The subsisting Minister of Foreign Affairs, Geoffrey Onyeama, called on INEC to ensure a seamless conduct of the rescheduled presidential election. He wondered why after years of preparations, INEC could not deliver as promised. INEC's election postponement instigated reactions from the party's high hierarchy. The president acted disappointed and described the postponement as unpardonable.[29] Next, a segment of the APC leadership poured countless accusations on INEC and threatened diplomats for making comments which, according to APC loyalists, were capable of undermining the integrity of the election besides suggesting external meddling in the domestic matters of the nation.

Disputes over Foreign Observer Reports

The European Union, the International Republican Institute (IRI) and National Democratic Institute (NDI) are the regular election observer missions in African elections. Nonetheless, the election monitoring reports submitted by these internationally acclaimed observer groups have been contested by both the PDP and APC. In 2015 the PDP questioned the final reports on the presidential election from these foreign observer missions, but the APC, as the opposition party, welcomed the reports describing them as indeed reflective of the true position on ground. However, following the 2019 presidential election, the APC as the ruling party vigorously protested the final reports of foreign election observer missions

---

Political Affairs and the UN Special Representative of the Secretary-General for West Africa and the Sahel and Boubakar Adamou of Organisation Islamic Cooperation.

28 "U.K, U.S. speak on postponement of Nigeria general elections," 17 February 2019, https://www.U.K%2C+U.S.+speak+on+postponement+of+Nigeria+general+elections (accessed 7 July 2019).

29 "Nigeria Will Not Allow Foreign Interference in Its Affairs, Presidency Tells UK, US, EU," https://www.Nigeria+Will+Not+Allow+Foreign+Interference+in+Its+Affairs%2C+Presidency+Tells+UK%2C+US%2C+EU%E2%80%9D (accessed 6 May 2019).

such as the version reproduced below. At a press conference in Abuja, the EU Chief Observer, Maria Arena, and her deputy, Hannah Roberts noted:

> The EU observed 94 collation centres. In almost all, the results forms and smart card readers were not packed in tamper-evident envelopes as required. Numerical discrepancies and anomalies on polling unit results forms were identified and were mostly corrected by collation officers on the spot, but without a clear system of record-keeping. Leading parties were at fault in not reining in acts of violence and intimidation by their supporters, and abuse of incumbency at federal and state levels. Inconsistent numbers during collation, lack of clear checks and explanations, and insufficient public information undermined the integrity of the elections. Citizens did not have sufficient means to scrutinise results. INEC did not provide centralised information on the declared results for the different locations and has not posted complete results data on its website. Similarly, there is a lack of disaggregated results by local government, ward or polling unit, which would allow for thorough checking of results.[30]

The EU report concludes:

> Nigeria's 2019 general elections were marked by severe operational and transparency shortcomings, electoral security problems, and low turnout. Positively, the elections were competitive, parties were overall able to campaign and civil society enhanced accountability. However, the last-minute postponement of the elections put an undue burden on voters, results' collation procedures were not sufficiently robust, and inadequate information was provided to the public. Fatalities escalated and the role of security agencies became increasingly contentious. The leading parties were at fault in not reining in acts of violence and intimidation by supporters, and in abusing incumbency at federal and state levels. Except for federal radio, state media primarily served the interests of the president or the governor at state level. Journalists were subject to harassment, and scrutiny of the electoral process was at times compromised with some independent observers obstructed in their work, including by security agencies. The suspension of the Chief Justice of Nigeria by the president a few weeks before the elections was seen to lack due process and reportedly undermined judicial independence. The number of women elected fell again. These systemic failings show the need for fundamental reform so elections better serve the interests of the Nigerian people.[31]

Several reactions attended the EU final report. First, Festus Keyamo, spokesman of the APC Campaign Council, declared what the ruling party expected as follows:

---

30 EU, "European Union Election Observation Mission in Nigeria 2019 Final Report: General Elections, 23 February 2019 and 9 and 23 March 2019," page 3, https://www.ecoi.net/en/file/local/2020744/nigeria_2019_eu_eom_final_report-web.pdf (accessed 10 October 2020).
31 EU, "European Union Election Observation Mission."

The results of the election reflected the overall wishes of Nigerians. That was the report of many observers. If you are an observer, you should come to a definite conclusion. We have 120,000 polling units across the country. In all, I don't think they discussed more than 500 polling units in the report. If you observe anomalies in those units, how does that substantially affect results coming from 120,000 polling units? It is not enough for the EU to discuss the anomalies, they must discuss overall results of the country, whether it reflects the wishes of the people. After all, there were problems in the U.S. elections. There were problems in Europe, and even in U.K. recently.[32]

Keyamo also accused the U.S. Ambassador to Nigeria, W. Stuart Symington, of tactically supporting the PDP presidential candidate, Atiku Abubakar. This accusation resembles that made by the PDP and President Goodluck Jonathan in 2015 against the U.S. Ambassador James F. Entwistle and President Barack Obama.

Yekini Nabena, the APC Deputy National Publicity Secretary, added thus:

In all elections conducted in the country, we have always welcomed local and foreign monitors and observers. In our view, this is a best practice and geared to ensure the transparency of our elections. But comments on our election processes coming from some Western diplomats and accredited foreign observer missions have been downright meddlesome and tantamount to interference. Nigeria is a sovereign nation and such actions by these Western countries negate the principles of international law which outlaw interference in the domestic affairs of a sovereign nation by another country. While the electioneering process might not be perfect as seen with the last-minute postponement of the general elections, we must all work together to make it better. Statements and actions by these Western diplomats and accredited foreign observer missions that erode confidence in the elections are inexcusable and strongly condemned. As a country, we will always find local solutions to our local challenges whenever they arise. The US, UK and EU have enough already on their hands. Their time and energy should be spent on the probe of alleged Russian interference in the immediate-past US elections, the breakdown of the Brexit deal between the UK and EU and many other serious challenges they face.[33]

Once more Nasir el-Rufai, incumbent governor of Kaduna State and a strong APC member, was quoted on national television to have said:

We know the history of those countries that are trying to teach us these things; we have read their history. We also know that in their stages of development they went through these challenges. So, please, let's work together; let's advise one another but don't lecture

---

[32] "EU report on elections: Presidency insists elections fair, PDP alleges fraud, killings," 10 June 2019, https://www.EU+report+on+elections%3A+Presidency+insists+elections+fair%2C+PDP+alleges+fraud%2C+killings (accessed 10 October 2020).

[33] John Owen Nwachukwu, "Leave Nigeria alone, face your many troubles–APC tells US, UK, EU," https://www.Leave+Nigeria+alone%2C+face+your+many+troubles%E2%80%93APC+tells+US%2C+UK%2C+EU (accessed 8 May 2019).

us. We have confidence that INEC will conduct credible elections and we challenge everyone, the opposition parties, to point out what part of the logistical arrangements or electoral preparations gives room for any manipulation, otherwise, they should shut up.³⁴

These reactions show ruling parties to be allergic to final election observer reports; and opposition parties to both welcome and accept election reports from foreign observer missions as reflecting the true position of the concluded election.

Political Developments Prior to the 2019 Presidential Election

Some interesting political developments took place in Nigeria shortly before the 2019 presidential election. These included the suspension of the Chief Justice of Nigeria (CJN), Justice Walter Onnoghen, and the refusal by President Buhari to assent to the Electoral Amendment Bill. For these political developments, various reactions were observed. The international community expected these political developments to cast shadows on the outcome of the 2019 elections. On the occasion of the suspension of the Chief Justice and its possible implications on the 2019 presidential election, the U.S. and U.K. threatened to place visa and travel bans on any politician and family members culpable in committing irregularities before, during and after the elections.³⁵ The U.S. Embassy further stated that the decision to suspend the Chief Justice was unconstitutional, unpopular, undermines the independence of the judiciary, and possibly undercuts the determination of government, aspirants and political parties to proceed with afree, fair and transparent elections that would lead to a credible result.³⁶

The PDP and APC also reacted on the Chief Justice's suspension saga. The PDP presidential candidate, Atiku Abubakar, condemned the suspension and for three days stopped his campaigns to register his displeasure. He noted: "it is our hope that President Buhari will listen to the voice of all lovers of democracy the world over and restore democracy in Nigeria immediately and without

---

34 Adepegba, Ramon and Nwogu, "2019 polls: PDP slams el-Rufai."
35 Mojeed Alabi, "2019: US, UK threaten visa ban on Nigerian election riggers," https://www.2019%3A+US%2C+UK+threaten+visa+ban+on+Nigerian+election+riggers (accessed 20 May 2019).
36 Mojeed Alabi, "2019 elections: Nigeria warns U.S., U.K. against meddling in country's internal affairs," https://www.2019+elections%3A+Nigeria+warns+U.S.%2C+U.K.+against+meddling+in+country%E2%80%99s+internal+affairs (accessed 20 May 2019).

qualifications."³⁷ Cheta Nwanze, a Lagos-based analyst, remarked: "the timing, and all the effort being put, indicates that the president's party is really scared of losing the elections and will stop at nothing to ensure that they have all the arsenal of state at their beck and call."³⁸ Expectedly, these reactions from the PDP and other observers of Nigeria's democratic landscape attracted stern responses from the APC-led government as well as Islamic religious bodies such as Muslim Rights Concern (MURIC). The Minister of Foreign Affairs, Geoffrey Onyeama, during a meeting on 11 February 2019 with representatives of the U.S. National Security Council stated:

> *I met a representative for Africa on the US National Security Council and we discussed elections in Nigeria and I pointed out that the government was absolutely determined to have free, fair, credible and transparent elections; that Mr. President has invested in that.* And also, that I had summoned the US Ambassador to discuss some of the utterances that have been made and some of which we felt were not helpful and that while we welcome very much the role they had played in 2015, and the role that they are continuing to play, that they should be careful not to cross the line between observing and supporting the process and appearing to be partisan and interfering in the process.³⁹

Elsewhere, at a joint briefing of heads of diplomatic missions and international organisations accredited for the elections, Onyeama alongside the Chairman of INEC and the Inspector-General of Police said:

> We welcome very much your engagement. We appreciate very much the support of all other countries in this process. [...] We welcome international observers to the country and all other friends and media to be fully engaged, but what we are concerned about, has sometimes been just the way the engagement has been communicated. We have expected, and hope, that you will also be impartial and just help and observe to see if the elections will be free, fair and credible and not to give any sense of indication that there might be preference.⁴⁰

While the Minister was diplomatic in his utterances, the Senior Special Assistant on Media and Publicity to President Buhari, Garba Shehu, was not economical with his words. He unequivocally stated:

---

37 Neil Munshi, "Nigeria warns over 'foreign interference' ahead of election," *Financial Times*, 27 January 2019. https://www.Nigeria+warns+over+%E2%80%98foreign+interference%E2%80%99+ahead+of+election (accessed 12 July 2019).
38 Munshi, "Nigeria warns over 'foreign interference'."
39 "2019 Elections: FG warns US again not to interfere," https://www.2019+Elections%3A+FG+warns+US+again+not+to+interfere (accessed 12 July 2019).
40 "Nigeria Will Not Allow Foreign Interference."

Nigeria reserves the right to be insulated from suggestions and or interference with respect to wholly internal affairs and commends international laws, customs and norms that mandate and require nations and the comity to respect this prerogative to all. Nigeria is confident of its electoral processes and her preparation for the imminent elections and the Federal Government has supported the independent electoral umpire in both its independence and resources needed to accomplish our desire and insistence on free and fair elections. Although, the question of foreign interference, whether state-sponsored, promoted or otherwise has dominated recent elections and outcomes globally, the Federal Government assures citizens and the global community that it will fiercely and assiduously promote the will and the right of Nigerians to choose and elect their leaders without pressure or assistance from persons or entities that are not constitutionally empowered to participate in the process.[41]

The Muslim Rights Concern (MURIC), an Islamic socio-political group, condemned the U.S. and the U.K. over their hurried positions on the suspension of the Chief Justice without due consideration of the issues surrounding it. MURIC's director, Ishaq Akintola, presented the group's position as follows:

Western countries should not just jump to conclusions. They should not just make it look as if the [Chief Justice] is being suspended to clear the way for some undemocratic practices. Neither the U.S. nor Britain will allow a judge to accumulate wealth illegally because it is dangerous for the judicial system. While we appreciate the interest of U.S. and U.K. in evolving healthy democracies around the world, particularly in Nigeria, we will appreciate it more if these countries show equal concern for Nigeria's war against corruption, particularly in the judiciary and in the repatriation of Nigeria's looted funds in those two countries. Advanced democracies are not under any special obligation to listen only to the opposition and echo its propaganda. They also owe it a moral duty to hear the government's side before making policy statements. To this end, we expect that both the U.S. and U.K. will equally show interest in the allegation bordering on corruption made against the former CJN as they have expressed concern over his suspension.[42]

Besides Justice Walter Onnoghen's suspension, the international community was also interested in the government's anticorruption crusade and the role of the security agencies on the conduct of elections in the country. For example, on the deployment of security agencies on electoral roles, France, Germany, United Kingdom, Australia, Austria, Bulgaria, Canada, the Czech Republic, Denmark, Finland, Greece, Hungary, Ireland, Italy, Japan, Netherlands, Norway, Portugal, Republic of Korea, Romania, Slovakia, Spain and Sweden in a joint communiqué

---

[41] "Again, Nigerian Govt Warns Against Foreign Interference in Elections," https://www.Again%2C+Nigerian+Govt+Warns+Against+Foreign+Interference+in+Elections (accessed 12 May 2019).
[42] Alabi, "2019 elections."

cautioned that security agencies have key roles to play in providing a safe environment for voters to perform their franchise. More so, they maintained:

> We wish to draw particular attention to the fundamental role of the security agencies in providing a safe and secure environment for the Nigerian people to exercise their democratic rights. It is vital that security agencies act, and are seen to act, in an impartial manner that maintains the high standards of professional conduct...The Delegation and the United States said they were gravely concerned over widespread incidents of intimidation, interference and vote buying during the recent gubernatorial elections. We were also perturbed by irregularities and violence during party primaries. They also expressed desire for greater participation of women, youth and people living with disabilities.[43]

Worried by such foreign interests in the 2019 general elections, the APC leadership raised alarm by accusing the international community of intending to impose a particular presidential candidate on Nigeria by any means possible. The party concluded that the international community was determined to commit this unwholesome act because the Buhari administration's anticorruption crusade since 2015 had adversely impacted on the economies of the West. According to Steven Chukwu, the Director of Publicity for the Nigerian Democratic Forum (NDF), there is:

> anecdotal evidence that the High Street shops in the UK suffered a slump in December of that year simply because looters in Nigeria were unable to patronise the stores as they were unable to steal money to spend in that country, many of the shops have since folded up. Almost four years later, other sectors of all the meddling countries have taken hits from not having cash injection bankrolled with stolen funds from Nigeria. Their situation became desperate because other African countries are beginning to follow in the examples of President Buhari, which means another four years of his leadership style will leave the US, UK and EU in dire economic situations while Africa would have made progress in truly being liberated.[44]

Conclusion

External interventions in electoral processes are disliked throughout the globe. While nations in the Global North appear to react moderately to it, many nations of the Global South express extreme disdain for it. This chapter considered how Nigeria's major political parties – the PDP and APC – responded to external in-

---

[43] Niyi Bello, et al., "EU, U.S. Warn Police, DSS, Others on 2019 Elections," https://www.EU%2C+U.S.+Warn+Police%2C+DSS%2C+Others+on+2019+Elections (accessed 10 June 2019).
[44] Godwin, "2019: US, EU, UK others warned."

terventions in the 2015 and 2019 presidential elections. The authors identified those domains that were of interest to Western nations, which the PDP and APC strongly contested. Without a doubt, the two parties responded in a similar fashion to foreign interests. In 2019, the APC accused the West of supporting the PDP during the presidential election. This was the same way that the PDP accused President Obama and his government of helping President Buhari and the APC to win the 2015 presidential election. One major implication of the above is the ensuing lack of public trust in the operations of political parties in Nigeria. No political system survives for long without the support of its citizens where enormous discontents from the citizenry are preponderant. Public trust in the APC is waning rapidly, which of course suggests that the public momentum or electoral pendulum that swept the PDP away in 2015 would likely be the fate of the APC in the coming elections in 2023. Another implication of Western democracy promotion and the two parties' reactions to it is the proof that none of the two parties is the messiah of Nigeria's democratisation effort especially as they respectively helped to stagnate the consolidation of democracy in Nigeria.[45] No wonder Oyediran and Agbaje warned Nigerians in 1991 not to be uncritically optimistic about the country's transition to democracy.[46]

---

[45] Aduku A. Akubo and Adejo U. Yakubu, "Political Parties and Democratic Consolidation in Nigeria Fourth Republic," *Global Journal of Political Science and Administration* 2, no. 3 (2014): 79–108; Robert O. Dode, "Political Parties and the Prospects of Democratic Consolidation in Nigeria: 1999–2006," *African Journal of Political Science and International Relations* 4, no. 5 (2010): 188–194.

[46] Oyeleye Oyediran and Adigun Agbaje, "Two-Partyism and Democratic Transition in Nigeria," *The Journal of Modern African Studies* 29, no. 2 (1991), 234.

Patrick Agbedejobi
A Tale of Defective Democracy: De-Democratisation in Nigeria

Abstract: In the field of democratic studies, scholarly attention has shifted away from democratisation and democratic consolidation studies to conceptualising and operationalising democratic backsliding. The notion of democratic backsliding is putatively regarded as a useful and well-understood concept in the annals of democratic research. Democratic backsliding, as a notion, is familiar in Western democratic research with the likes of consolidated democracies under investigation in the United States of America and the central and eastern European countries, especially in the United Kingdom and Italy. Nevertheless, despite this significant shift in research scope, most African countries' experience of democratic backsliding remains under-researched. The starting point of this article is a reference to Nigeria's democratic turmoil and challenges during the Fourth Republic. In other words, this article will investigate the declining nature of Nigeria's fourth attempt at democratic governance. This will be undertaken via adaptation of Merkel et al.'s concept of democracy, composed of three dimensions – vertical legitimacy, horizontal accountability alongside the rule of law, and effective government. The chapter will specifically examine Nigeria's current democratic status under President Muhammadu Buhari in terms of de-democratisation.

Keywords: democratic defects, democracy, Frankenstate, democratic decay, de-democratisation, democratic consolidation and democratic deconsolidation

Introduction

Until relatively recently, scholars focused on the impact of the third wave of democratisation on developing economies, especially African countries making the transition from military dictatorship to democracy.[1] In Nigeria, democracy

---

[1] D. S. Gberevbie, "Democracy, democratic institutions and good governance in Nigeria," *Eastern Africa Social Science Research Review* 30 (2014): 133–152; B. J. Dudley, *Instability and political order: Politics and crisis in Nigeria* (Ibadan: University of Ibadan Press, 1973), 55–58; P. O. Mbah, C. Nwangu, and S. C. Ugwu, "Contentious elections, political exclusion, and challenges of national integration in Nigeria," *Cogent Social Sciences* 5 (2019): 1–21.

Patrick Agbedejobi, Independent Researcher, Germany

https://doi.org/10.1515/9783110766561-009

seemed to be the perfect currency for enabling competition for public office and for laying claim to legitimacy since its introduction post-independence. This presupposition, fostered by democratisation waves that occurred elsewhere in Central Eastern European countries (CEEC) alongside the attractive lure of democratisation as constituted by the European Union (EU), generated a viral impact. In addition, there were sustainable merits of adopting democracy. This includes an open market as well as international recognition and cooperation in a commonwealth of democratic allies, which foster greater levels of foreign direct investment (FDI), aid, security, and pooling of resources to fight a common enemy, among other appeals.[2]

However, Nigeria's tale of democratisation and its gradual transition is a distorted history of civil war, military coups, political assassinations, ethnic riots, despotic rule, repression, human rights infringements, betrayals, conflicts, and general chaos. A succinct historical review is crucial in demonstrating the trials and challenges of democratisation experienced by the Nigerian state. Nigeria went through a disjointed form of transition – witnessing the installation of democratic rule, usurpation of power by military rule, and a merry-go-round of transitions, both regressive and progressive. One initial experiment at democratisation, in making the transition from colonial to post-colonial rule, was disrupted by the Nigerian Civil War (also known as the Nigeria-Biafra War), which spanned from 1966 to 1970.[3] At the end of the war, military rule followed from 1970 to 1979. The assassination of General Murtala Mohammed in 1976 led to the ascension of General Obasanjo and, consequently, the initiation of a transition process to end military rule in 1979.[4]

The Second Republic, under the leadership of President Shehu Shagari, was succeeded by military rule engineered by Major General Muhammadu Buhari. A decade of military rule followed – a rule of tyranny and dictators. The Second Republic was relatively short-lived, lasting from 1979 until 1983. The Third Republic was constituted in 1993 out of the constitution that had been drafted in 1989 under military rule. The 1990 election that had been promised by the then military head of state, General Ibrahim Babangida, was postponed until 1993 due to political unrest. Eventually, when the election was conducted, Gen-

---

[2] D. Acemoglu, "Oligarchic versus democratic societies," *Journal of European Economic Association*" 6 (2008): 1–44; P. O. Agbese, "Demilitarisation and prospects for democracy in Nigeria," *Bulletin of peace proposals* 22 (1991): 315–327.
[3] L. R. Jackson, "Nigeria: The politics of the First Republic," *Journal of Black Studies* 2 (1972): 277–302.
[4] O. Oyediran and A. Agbaje, "Two partyism and democratic transition in Nigeria," *Journal of Modern African Studies* 29 (1991): 213–235.

eral Babangida annulled it, citing electoral irregularities. This led to the legitimacy of Moshood Kashimawo Abiola, the apparent winner of the election, being contested and interrogated. Successive difficulties in effectively realising the democratic dream ultimately threw Nigeria into political unrest.[5] The impasse, which was not resolved by the Babangida regime's annulment of the election results and the ensuing protests, remains to date unsettled.

What followed, after external pressure, was the installation of an interim national government headed by Ernest Shonekan who was in office from 2 January 1993 to 26 August 1993, who also was the leader of Babaginda's transition team. General Sani Abacha, however, overthrew Shonekan and suspended the constitution and other democratic institutions.[6] This made Abacha the absolute ruler, with powers and decrees that facilitated detention, assassination of citizens, and several acts of repression. Consistent with his absolutist tendencies and repression of democracy, General Abacha planned to run for president as the sole candidate in October 1998, but this scheme was never realised as he died in June 1998. His successor, General Abdulsalami Abubakar, ushered in the next phase of transition to democratic governance.[7] He assured the public of a return to democracy and made good on it by transferring power to the president-elect, General Olusegun Obasanjo (Retired), on 29 May 1999. This paved way for the Fourth Republic – another phase of democratic transition and governance.

Having briefly reviewed the turmoil of democratic transitions and military intervention along this path, this chapter will now concentrate on the Fourth Republic, which started in May 1999 and continues to the present. This democratic dispensation has witnessed several presidents assuming office. The electoral successes, however, are often typically marked with the presence or absence of political violence, either during the elections or afterwards. Endogenous issues related to political violence can be traced to the chaotic nature of electioneering in Nigeria and the profitable venture of holding a public office, as well as political violence, ethnic and religious democracy, weak institutions, the nature of competition among political parties, pseudo-sharing formulas, and federalism, among other factors.[8]

---

[5] K. A. Shettima, "Engendering Nigeria's Third Republic," *African Studies Review* 38 (1995): 61–98.

[6] Oyediran and Agbaje, "Two partyism and democratic transition," 215–217; A. Ajagbe, "Civil Military Relations in Nigeria (M.A/MSc. Thesis, University of Freiburg and University of KwaZulu-Natal, 2008), 23–27.

[7] Ajagbe, "Civil Military Relations," 27–30.

[8] M. Mustapha, "The 2015 general election in Nigeria: new media, party politics and the political economy of voting," *Review of African Political Economy* 44 (2017): 312–321; L. Demarest and A.

In order to render these embedded political constraints amenable to thorough analysis, it is crucial to define democracy and its utilisation in the context of this article. Democracy has no universal definition. Nonetheless, it can be depicted as a system of government that embraces certain values, norms, procedural and constitutional benchmarks. In its simplistic or minimalist form, democracy, according to Schumpeter in *Capitalism Socialism Democracy*,[9] is a means through which the people have the opportunity of accepting or refusing the men who are to rule them through competitive elections. The simplistic form of this definition reduces democracy to mere elections or the competitive chaotic nature of selecting public officeholders. In other words, several other definitions of democracy over the years have been limited within certain norms, procedures, or rules expected of a democratic system.[10] Therefore, the definition proposed in this article stems from a combination of minimalist and maximalist requirements and allows for an effective overstretching of the term democracy. Thus, when I refer to democracy, the term is holistically defined as a system of government governed by four main pillars from which numerous conditions of a democratic government is expected. These pillars are liberalism, constitutionalism and the rule of law, election, and institutional autonomy.

In terms of liberalism, democracy must embrace the freedom of speech, freedom of movement and freedom of the press, among many other liberal normative requirements necessary for democracy to thrive. Constitutionalism, or the rule of law, concerns every citizen and public officeholder who is bound to the rule of law or the constitution of the land. The implication that follows, is that no one can be above the law or can exercise absolutism or decisionism at the expense of the constitution. Elections, as a necessary condition of democracy, must be free and fair in terms of the element of competition amongst political parties. Competition here implies that no political party has an advantage in terms of finance, campaign funds, monopoly of the press, or the use of force in comparison to other

---

Langer, "Reporting on electoral violence in Nigerian news media: "saying it as it is?" *African Studies Review* 62 (2019): 1–27; M. T. Aluaigba, "Democracy deferred: the effects of electoral malpractices on Nigeria's path to Democratic consolidation," *Journal of African Elections* 15 (2016): 136–158.

9 J. A. Schumpeter, *Capitalism, Socialism and Democracy* (Melbourne: George Allen & Unwin Publishers, 1942), 269–275.

10 Minimalist definition of democracy emphasizes or prioritizes certain variables above others. For instance, electioneering and voters' rights might be vastly operationalized as against institutions or human rights, the rule of law, or freedom, whereas a maximalist definition embraces other areas such as liberalism, freedom, quality of governance and equality of citizens. However, a holistic approach might be lacking in such definitions, which makes democracy a barely interpretive or exclusive concept that can be given meaning by political actors and citizens alike.

political parties engaged in the race. Acceptable forms of competition are usually entrenched in the constitution or written acts or convention. Institutional autonomy captivates the need for checks and balances and protects against the usurpation of power or a situation leading to delegative democracy. A probable usurpation of power or abuse of power is endemically corrected by the designated institutions. In a nutshell, democracy encompasses these four pillars and several other aspects, which are outstretched due to the demands of post-modernity, alongside a dynamic and interconnected global society.

Defective Democracy

Before deconstructing what defective democracy entails, it is crucial to examine the typologies of democracies. Contemporary typologies include electoral democracy, constitutional democracy, liberal and illiberal democracy, semi-liberal democracy and defective democracy.[11] In 2019, Freedom House classified Nigeria as a partly free country, with an aggregate freedom score of 50/100.[12] This score shows that certain elements of liberalism, such as constitutional liberalism and rights, are constantly repressed or relegated. Cases of insecurity posed by Boko Haram, the Fulani herdsmen, criminalisation of LGBT rights, electoral violence, lack of free and fair elections in 2019, and unfair competition despite the country's multiparty system, further buttress the received wisdom of Freedom House.

Electoral democracy posits that elections be based on formal and universal suffrage, free and fair elections, and fair competition of political parties and actors. Constitutional democracy prioritises the supremacy of the rule of law in terms of procedural adherence to the constitution in the daily running of the state. Liberal democracy is based on protection and adherence to freedoms and human rights provided by the constitution. It also goes further to consolidate those rights on the political rights of citizens and procedures that govern or shape a liberalised government. Illiberal democracy, on the other hand, represses any form of freedom, rights offered by the constitution, or human rights conventions. It relies on absolutist powers and decisionism to dictate the level of freedoms obtainable in certain institutions of government and relational dealings with the citizenry.[13] Semi-liberal democracy is, however, a middle point be-

---

11 W. Merkel, "Embedded and defective democracies," *Democratization* 11 (2004): 33–58.
12 Freedom House, "Freedom in the world 2019," https://freedomhouse.org/report/freedom-world/2019/nigeria (accessed 24 August 2019).
13 Z.T. Pállinger, "Direct democracy in an increasingly illiberal setting: the case of the Hungarian national referendum," *Contemporary Politics* 25 (2019): 62–77; Merkel, "Embedded and de-

tween liberal and illiberal democracy. It emphasises the adoption of piecemeal patterns or elements of both negative and positive forms of democratic consolidation.[14] In other words, cases of unfair electoral competition, electoral uncertainty, partial repression of rights, and other partial negative deeds might self-enforce a semi-liberal democracy.

Bogaards depicts delegative democracy as a product of the proliferation of adjectives utilised in qualifying democracy.[15] The delegative democratic state is perceived as a minimal democratic country that lacks horizontal accountability, embraces illiberal democracy, and is an electoral democracy where civil liberties are compromised. Such a definition reiterates the Frankenstate condition of illiberal democracies like Hungary. The Frankenstate condition, according to Scheppele, exists when a state adopts piecemeal elements of several types of democracy in order to lay hold of power.[16]

Defective democracy, however, is a disembedded form of democracy in which partial regimes are disjointed and one can no longer point to an intact embedded democracy.[17] Partial regimes in this sense include democratic electoral regimes, political rights of participation, civil rights and horizontal accountability, and they inherently guarantee that power to govern lies in the hands of democratically elected representatives. This highlights Przeworski's assertion that democracy only becomes consolidated when democratic norms are "the only game in town."[18] However, Przeworski's template of democracy, as the only game in town, is simplistic as it fails to account for what happens when institutions of democracy themselves are employed as tools of deconsolidation.

---

fective democracies," 53–55 ; S. P. Huntington, *The Third Wave. Democratization in the Late Twentieth Century* (Norman: University of Oklahoma Press, 1991), 13–19.

14 G. Pridham, "The International Context of Democratic Consolidation in Southern Europe in Comparative Perspective," in *The Politics of Democratic Consolidation. Southern Europe in Comparative Perspective*, eds. Richard Gunther, N Diamandouros and J. H. Puhle (Baltimore: Johns Hopkins University Press, 1995), 166–203.

15 M. Bogaards, "How to classify hybrid regimes? Defective democracy and electoral authoritarianism," *Democratization* 16 (2009): 399–400.

16 K. L. Scheppele, "The Rule of Law and the Frankenstate: Why Governance Checklists Do Not Work," *Governance* 26 (2013): 559–562.

17 W. Merkel, H. Puhle, A. Croissant, C. Eicher and P. Thiery, *Defekte Demokratie, Band 1: Theorie* (Wiesbaden: Budrich Publishers, 2003), 39–64.

18 A. Przeworski, *Democracy and the Market: Political and Economic Reforms in Eastern Europe and Latin America* (Cambridge: Cambridge University Press, 1991).

The crux of the matter here is that a regime can become less democratic or even undemocratic in numerous ways.[19] Consequently, Nigeria's transition to democratic rule is apt for analysis – to determine whether it has deviated from a democratic path to an undemocratic path. Analysing this, Merkel et al's concept of democracy embraces three complementary dimensions: vertical legitimacy, horizontal accountability alongside the rule of law, and effective government. Vertical legitimacy represents the relational value between citizens and government alongside rules through elections and political rights.[20] The horizontal dimension incorporates elements such as liberal constitutionalism, rule of law, and horizontal accountability. Effective governance implies that only duly elected representatives can make authoritative decisions.

These three regimes are further buttressed by five partial regimes such as elections, political participation rights, civil rights, horizontal accountability and effective government. The three regimes, according to Bogaard's submission, translate into 10 criteria that can be depicted as conditions highlighting the existence of a defective democracy.[21] It is argued that democratic elections must provide a platform for active suffrage, passive suffrage, free and fair elections, political participation or political rights, freedom of opinion, a free press, freedom of association, and freedom to engage in deliberative democracy without financial constraints.

Lastly, horizontal accountability and effective government are complementary, as they evaluate governance in terms of how leaders are perceived by the electorate through the ballot box. Effective government also extends beyond the rule of law; it extends to the execution of inclusive policies, institutional independence and the monopolistic use of force.[22] Hence, once certain elements are disjointed within a partial regime, it is no longer mutually embedded. Therefore, the logic of constitutional or liberal democracy alongside rights is disrupted and defective features remain the only visible feature of democracy left intact.

Merkel presented the typologies of defective democracy to include exclusive democracy, domain democracy, illiberal democracy, and delegative democracy.[23]

---

[19] W. Merkel, "The consolidation of post-autocratic democracies: A Multi-level Model," *Democratization* 5 (1998): 33–67.
[20] Merkel, Puhle, Croissant, Eicher and Thiery, *Defekte Demokratie*, 65–95.
[21] M. Boogards, "How to classify hybrid regimes? Defective democracy and electoral authoritarianism, Democratization 16, no.2 (2009): 400–404; and M. Boogards, "De-democratization in Hungary: diffusely defective democracy," *Democratization* 25 (2018): 1481–1499.
[22] Merkel, Puhle, Croissant, Eicher and Thiery, *Defekte Demokratie*, 65–95; Merkel, "The consolidation of post-autocratic democracies," 37–39.
[23] Merkel, "Embedded and defective democracies," 33–58.

From the perspective of exclusive democracy, sovereignty is the basic concept of democracy. It must guarantee universal electoral rights and fair execution. Domain democracy occurs when exclusive powers, such as the use of force within the exclusive reserve of the state, are hijacked from democratically elected representatives and instead wielded by non-state actors.[24] This leads to the creation of political domains, which are extra-constitutional or exogenous to the constitution. Also, it represents a form of defective democracy with cases replete in Latin America and Southeast Asia where military juntas take over political veto roles. In an illiberal democracy, the rule of law is damaged and substituted by illiberal elements or partial adherence to the constitutional provisions. It is also likely that the constitution has been amended to accommodate such illiberal acts or elements. Issues such as freedom of expression, human rights, free and fair elections, and independence of the judiciary are non-existent or partially existent in illiberal democracy.[25] Today, countries such as Turkey, Russia and Hungary are among the most cited cases of illiberal democracies.

Democracy in Nigeria: Descriptive Indicators

In order to operationalise the phenomenon of defective democracy, this chapter adopts indicators that conform with Merkel et al's postulation of defective democracy.[26] Table 1 presents the Bertelsmann Transformation Index (BTI) indicator, as evidenced in political and social integration, the stability of democratic institutions, rule of law, political participation, and stateness. These indicators, with an average aggregate score, show the rationale behind Nigeria's depiction as a highly defective democracy. However, the BTI indicators of democratic health are classified differently, as there exist classes such as highly defective democracies, democracies in consolidation, defective democracies, moderate autocracies, and hard-line autocracies.

The Bertelsmann Transformation Index 2018 ranks Nigeria as a highly defective democracy, alongside countries such as Ecuador, Honduras, Ivory Coast, Lesotho, Guatemala, Madagascar, Mali and Nepal, all of which scored between 4.9 and 6.0 on a 10-point scale (where 1 is classified as worst and 10 as best). Nigeria, for instance, garnered a 5.4 score on democracy and, with a 70-point aggregate score, tied with Madagascar, while Nepal and Guatemala had 76 and 74

---

24 Merkel, "Embedded and defective democracies," 33–58.
25 Merkel, "Embedded and defective democracies," 33–58.
26 Merkel, Puhle, Croissant, Eicher and Thiery, *Defekte Demokratie*, 65–95.

points, respectively. In 2018, Nigeria's democracy score of 5.4 indicates the rationale for the highly defective democracy label.[27] Table 1 makes reference to indicators such as civil rights, prosecution of abuse, monopoly on the use of force, party system and social capital, which were all within the worst point-scale bracket.

Table 1: Quantitative Indicators from BTI Pointing Towards Defective Democracy in Nigeria (2018)[28]

Political and Social Integration (Mean Score = 4.5)	Stability of Democratic Institutions (Mean Score = 5.5)	Rule of Law (Mean Score = 5.3)	Political Participation (Mean Score = 6.5)	Stateness (Mean Score 5.0)
Party System = 4	Performance of Democratic Institutions = 5	Separation of Powers = 6	Free and Fair Elections = 7 Effective Power to Govern = 6	Monopoly on the Use of Force = 4 State Identity = 8
Interest Group = 4 Approval of Democracy = 6 Social Capital = 4	Commitment to Democratic Institutions = 6	Independent Judiciary = 7 Prosecution of Office Abuse = 4 Civil Rights = 4	Association/Assembly Rights = 7 Freedom of Expression = 6	No Interference of Religious Dogmas = 4 Basic Administration = 4

Table 2: Freedom House Indices (Nigeria)[29]

Aggregate Freedom Score Nigeria = 50/100 (partly free)	Score (1 = most free), (7 = least free)
Freedom	4/7
Political Rights	3/7
Civil Liberties	5/7

---

27 Bertelsmann Stiftung Transformation Index BTI, "Nigeria Country Report, 2018," https://www.bti-project.org/en/reports/country-reports/detail/itc/NGA (accessed 26 August 2019).
28 Source: Bertelsmann Stiftung Transformation Index, "Nigeria Country Report, 2018."
29 Source: Freedom House 2019, "Freedom in the world 2019."

In Table 2, Freedom House indicators are a partial reflection of Table 1. Indications from Table 1 show that freedom, civil rights and political rights are partly free. To further supplement the picture captured from both operational systems of defective democracy, the succeeding four sections disclose a descriptive evaluation of the state of Nigeria's democracy by examining the four types of defective democracy – exclusive, illiberal, delegative, and tutelary/domain in different sections.

Nigeria as an Exclusive Democracy

Nigeria as an exclusive democracy is emphasised by the ability of eligible people to vote during an election. Recent and previous elections, however, have excluded eligible voters, both at home and in the diaspora. The former is a function of security concerns and political apathy. These security concerns, in terms of violence on election day, include hardware or software malfunctions, lack of personnel to exploit digitalised forms of voting, logistical deficiencies, safety concerns and cases of intimidation of voters in urban and rural areas. Other concerns, such as eligible voters in the diaspora and a systemic lack of coordination to involve them, further question the administrative and technical competence of the electoral commission (INEC).

In addition, the lack of security in polling stations and adequately functioning electronic devices, as well as other logistical constraints, further elevate political apathy of the electorate, thereby increasing the probability of 'stomach infrastructure', vote buying and gigantic election expenditures.[30] The Nigerian case evinces how the political class exploits the patience and 'longsuffering' of Nigerians. Hence, elections, which should be a tool for validating leaders or rejecting their performance in office through voting them out, are non-existent due to self-enforcing institutional capabilities like election rigging, favouritism, non-accountability, godfatherism and patrimonialism. Persons with disabilities or displaced citizens are often excluded from the voting process or running for elections, since social work services, discriminatory laws, or acts executed to foster the voting process such as the Nigerian Electoral Act of 2011 are either non-existent or partially existent in several states and local councils. Notably, there is an active lobby for the representation and wellbeing of people with dis-

---

30 O. O. Ayeni, "Commodification of Politics: Party Funding and Electoral Contest in Nigeria," *Sage Open* (2019): 1–8.

abilities in Nigeria, although the argument is that this effort is poorly served given institutional deficiencies.

This theoretical treatment of Nigeria as an exclusive democracy draws attention to the perspective of the diaspora's exclusion in local politics. Since Nigerians abroad cannot vote from their host countries, the only remaining option is travelling back to Nigeria to exercise their constitutional rights. Another issue is administrative bottlenecks, such as acquiring a voters' card, which confers voting eligibility on the election day. Furthermore, Nigerians in the diaspora face additional constraints and must make sacrifices, including abandoning jobs or responsibilities abroad and dealing with the logistical complexity of participation in elections in Nigeria. These challenges are a product of a failed system, facilitated by institutional incapability, despite the huge budgets allocated to INEC. In 2018, the sum allocated was 234.5 billion naira (equivalent of US$61.7 billion.[31] Institutional incapability is further evinced by the spiral of inconsistencies, election postponements, lack of electronic voting as previously promised, and election malpractices such as those uncovered in the 2019 elections.

Exclusion is also noticeable in party politics. Nigeria is, in reality, a two-party system. Competition, party affiliation or membership, funding, and campaign structures only favour the two main political parties – All Progressives Congress (APC) and the People's Democratic Party (PDP) – especially when it comes to competing for federal government and state government positions. Youth participation or age discrimination in politics is also a form of exclusion in Nigeria. Although the 'Not Too Young To Run' bill was enacted on 31 May 2018, materially this legislation is a mockery of youth empowerment and mobilisation.[32] This is because it reinforces the institutionalisation of gerontocracy and patrimonialism. As discussed, the institutional or structural capacities to enforce such bills at the party level of dominant political parties are demonstrably lacking. Thus, youthful figures are quite rare in parties such as the APC or PDP, except where they possess political capital or come from a renowned political family. Furthermore, youthful politicians in other parties are similarly bedevilled by the institutionalised and semantic notion of gaining experience in politics before running for public office. The lack of accountability by public servants, coupled

---

[31] Q. E. Iroanusi, "Senate approves N234.5 billion for INEC, to consider security budget later," *Premium Times*, 11 October 2018, https://www.premiumtimesng.com/news/headlines/289734-just-in-2019-senate-approves-n234-5-billion-for-inec-ignores-buharis-security-request.html (accessed 14 August 2019).

[32] Sani Tukur, "Buhari signs 'Not too Young to Run' bill," *Premium Times*, 31 May 2018, https://www.premiumtimesng.com/news/headlines/270538-breaking-buhari-signs-not-too-young-to-run-bill.html (accessed 20 November 2019).

with the "political culture of evergreen longsuffering or suffering and smiling mentality by the electorates,"[33] all but deepens the issue of exclusion and its impact on social learning and democratic consolidation.

Nigeria as an Illiberal Democracy

As evinced in Tables 1 and 2, Nigeria partly represses human and civil rights, creating a struggle between constitutional liberalism and constitutional democracy, in which illiberal acts or actions prevail. There are several areas in which illiberal democracy is thriving in the country. Such areas are evinced in constitutional and procedural adherence, as well as civil rights, freedom of speech infringement, right to liberty and personal security, right to life, assembly or protests.

All of these illiberal acts reflect Nigeria's political history and unstable democratic transitions. This also weighs on the strength of the institutions that should be gatekeepers of the constitution or the rule of law. Hence, a suitable analogy of the situation is this: if a democratically elected president tries to manoeuvre or strategically violate the constitution, the gatekeeper institutions, such as the judiciary and legislative, should protect the constitution at all costs. The lack of adherence to the rule of law by the incumbent government is frankly alarming. First, there were incessant trips abroad by President Muhammadu Buhari, lasting three to six months and without procedural transfer of power to the vice president, Professor Yemi Osinbajo. According to Section 145 (1) and (2) of the 1999 Nigerian Constitution (as amended),[34] the law is only infringed upon when an absence extends to 21 days. Therefore, Section 145 (2) calls for the National Assembly to intervene and pass a resolution empowering the vice president to become acting president when the president is absent for a continuous period of 21 days. Another prominent example was President Buhari's suspension of Chief Justice Walter Onnoghen and the immediate swearing in of Justice Ibrahim Tanko Muhammad as the acting chief justice of Nigeria. This action breaches the doctrines of separation of power; it exemplifies an act of absolute decisionism – unhindered or uncontested illiberal governance where the president or the executive arm of government has absolute powers over other branches of government. This is further demonstrated by the disregard for court orders by the incumbent administration. Serial violation of

---

33 P. Chabal, *Africa: The politics of suffering and smiling (World Political Theories)* (London: Zed Books Ltd., 2009), 127–140.
34 The Constitution of the Federal Republic of Nigeria 1999 (as amended).

court orders is an explicit contravention against the rule of law. This is evinced by various courts granting Colonel Sambo Dasuki, the national security adviser to the former president of Nigeria, Goodluck Jonathan, bail on at least six different occasions; yet the incumbent government incessantly refused to comply with such court orders.

Freedom of the press has also been an issue, excluding several news outlets owned either by the state or federal government. Privately owned news outlets are on the receiving end of abuse and illegal raids. Such raids, like that on 6 January 2019 at the *Daily Trust* or the arrest of journalists by the State Security Service (SSS), prove a wanton disregard for liberalism or constitutionalism. The arrest of Omoyele Sowore and some of his supporters on 3 August 2019, based on Omoyele Sowore's call for a revolution and their attendance at a peaceful demonstration, exemplifies a lack of freedom of expression or right to assemble in Nigeria.

Table 3: Nigeria as a Frankenstate[35]

Dimensions	Five partial regimes	Ten criteria	Nigerian evidence	Type of democratic defect
Vertical legitimacy	Elections	Active suffrage	Voting rights for eligible voters exist. 'Not Too Young To Run' bill makes a mockery of youths. APC/PDP main parties are inaccessible due to godfatherism/patrimonialism.	Exclusive democracy
		Passive suffrage	Nigerians in diaspora cannot vote from their host countries. Handicapped/disabled/displaced citizens are disenfranchised due to logistics and security.	
Vertical legitimacy	Political participation	Free and fair elections	Chaotic and unorganised/institutional mechanism of election rigging. Devoid of transparency.	
		Elected officials	The cost of political participation is high, with incidents of bribery and vote buying. Competition amongst political parties are unequal. Reduced opportunities for direct democracy.	

---

35 The Constitution of the Federal Republic of Nigeria 1999 (as amended).

Table 3: Nigeria as a Frankenstate *(Continued)*

Dimensions	Five partial regimes	Ten criteria	Nigerian evidence	Type of democratic defect
Horizontal accountability and rule of law	Civil rights	Freedom of opinion association	Repression of freedom of opinion and association, especially when it is connected to the incumbent government.	Illiberal democracy
		Freedom of press, information. Individual protection rights against state and private actors	Government control of media, corruption and nepotism, tribalism in governance and discrimination. Tribalistic- and ethnic-focused governance at the expense of meritocracy or technocratic skills.	
	Horizontal accountability	Equal treatment and access to courts	Power sharing, revenue sharing all a bane to federalism as well as democracy. Repression of human rights or lackadaisical stance to such. Non-existent; those with political capital, the rich, and loyalists of the incumbent regime are untouchable or above the law.	Delegative democracy
Effective government	Effective governance	Elected officials with real power	Institutionalised/patron-based control of INEC and other arms of government by the executive arm of government. Monopoly on the use of force limited.	Tertiary/domain democracy.

Nigeria as a Delegative Democracy

Delegative democracies are void of horizontal accountability. This suggests that decisionism and absolutism exist in the executive arm of government. The suspension of the chief justice of Nigeria and his immediate replacement further demonstrates a direct attack on the rule of law alongside the usurpation of powers in the form of hiring and firing of judges. The anomalous strings of events thereafter confirm the non-existence of checks and balances, not to mention little or no protests from civil societies and the electorate alike. This problem is further exacerbated by the utilisation of executive power in persecuting political opponents. The use of the Economic and Financial Crimes Commission (EFCC), with the 'smart targeting' of political opponents of the incumbents, is an example. The high-profile arrests of presidential candidate Abubakar Atiku's son-in-law, accused of money laundering, as well as Senator Dino Melaye and the former senate president, Bukola Saraki, (all PDP members) on criminal charges suggest a campaign aimed at silencing opponents. Of course, it can be argued that such public figures are not saints; however, the specific targeting of political opponents to the benefit of those in the ruling party (APC) denotes abuse of power and disregard for procedural adherence or checks and balances.

In a similar vein, the arrest of presidential candidate of the African Action Congress (AAC), Omoyele Sowore, on grounds of inciting violence or terrorism based on his call for a 'Revolution Now' movement, once more demonstrates the lack of horizontal accountability in Nigeria. The SSS sought permission to keep Sowore and his cohorts in detention for 90 days, supporting its application with Section 27(1) of the Terrorism (Prevention) Amendment Act.[36] Lewis and Ololajulo rightly sum up the above occurrences as an aftermath of Nigeria's weak transition, ambiguous political ideology, the presence of a rentier state, ethnic-motivated loyalties and mobilisation, alongside historical feuds of the legislative and executive arms of government.[37] What is particularly alarming is the rate at which democratic principles are ignored and autocratic principles are embraced in a so called 'democratic polity'. A relevant case is the recent 'End Sars' protest nationwide, particularly in Lagos, which ended in loss of civilian lives due to the reckless use of force by the military to disperse the protesters.[38] The response of the federal government as well as state government to such use of force against peaceful protesters was met by denials and gaslighting strategies.[39]

---

[36] Source: Author's compilation based on Merkel, Puhle, Croissant, Eicher and Thiery, *Defekte Demokratie* (2003).
[37] P. Lewis, "Nigeria: Elections in a fragile regime," *Journal of Democracy* 14 (2003): 131–144; B. O. Ololajulo, "'Eating with One Spoon': Zoning, Power Rotation and Political Corruption in Nigeria," *African Studies* 75 (2016): 153–169.
[38] BBC News, "End Sars protests: People 'shot dead' in Lagos, Nigeria," 21 October 2020, https://bbc.com/news/world-africa-54624611 (accessed 12 December 2020.)
[39] BBC News, "End Sars protests."

The Drivers of De-Democratisation in Nigeria

In terms of operationalising the drivers of de-democratisation, Merkel et al. posited five clusters that facilitate the emergence of democratic defects in a polity. These are: (a) socio-economic development and modernisation, (b) socio-cultural factors, (c) former regime type and mode of transition, (d) stateness and nation-building and (e) the international context. Each cluster comprises at least two factors of which many of these are further broken down, culminating in a total of 23 variables that are thought to be conducive to either the development of democratic defects or the facilitation of a functioning democracy. For instance, 'exclusive and confrontational' regime change is connected to democratic defects; however, 'inclusive-cooperative transition' is said to facilitate an embedded democracy. These cases all fall under historical and structural factors that clearly pose a different set of analytical problems. In the case of African polities, with a different history and structural competence, many theorists grow too quickly enamoured with Merkel et al.'s five clusters, foregoing other endogenous factors which may deeply influence de-democratisation. Hence, in addition to Merkel's stipulated five clusters, one might include other clusters which are specific to the Nigerian case, such as: (i) ethnic path dependency (which brings to the fore the impact of ethnic and tribal mobilisation as well as quota systems or power-sharing; this should allow for cooperation, though often it facilitates favouritism, schism, and nepotism), (ii) pseudo federalism (linked to reliance on central government and lack of creativity or innovativeness in the states, which can be linked to socio-cultural factors or socio-economic development; however, this is a robust source of ailment specifically in the Nigerian state), (iii) modernisation and sustainability stagnation (this part is crucial to explaining democratic de-democratisation, political apathy, and corruption). The industrialisation of Nigeria is yet to take full force, with several structural issues (electricity, alternative sources of power, accountability, and maladministration) impeding its path to self-sufficiency without recourse to oil revenues. The argument raised by the possibility of modernisation and sustainability stagnation suggests that Nigeria is lacking in terms of a traditional value or modern value that should impact its self-sufficiency and sustainability.

With Nigeria's given lack of infrastructure, stable source of electricity and lack of investment in human capital, Rostow's five-stage model of development situates Nigeria in a bubble of stagnation.[40] The first stage of dependence on farming was witnessed in the early pre- and post-1960s post-independence peri-

---

[40] W. W. Rostow, "The stages of economic growth," *The Economic History Review* 12 (1959): 1–16.

od (the cocoa boom era), while the second stage concerning preconditions for rapid industrialisation (science and technology to improve agriculture, infrastructure, roads, transport system and industrial capacity) are absent in Nigeria's case. Investment in science and technology is substituted by hope, faith and religion. A highly networked and efficient transport system remains yet to be actualised as does functional infrastructure, good roads constructed by Nigerians and investment in training employees, along with updating their knowledge whenever appropriate.

While the five partial regimes provided for the sake of operationalisation are quite relevant in certain cases, the underlying variables might differ in other cases – especially in the Nigerian situation, due to diverse endogenous factors. Thus, the additional three clusters proposed herein situate the Nigerian problem within a peculiar case for the drivers of de-democratisation. Nevertheless, Merkel and colleagues suggest five propositions on the emergence of specific types of defective democracies that partly fulfil the drivers for de-democratisation. Exclusive democracy is largely caused by social and economic inequality based on the adoption of majoritarian institutions in an ethnically divided society.[41] In the Nigerian case, this ethnically divided society is subjected to marginalisation and a majoritarian rule of a specific ethnic majority group. This can be evinced in executive appointments and the strategic positioning of a specific ethnic group in influential or key positions. Delegative democracy is a function of presidential systems of government in which the executive usurps power and further expands his or her powers. Such seems to be the case in Nigeria, with the 2019 election and its aftermath, or as the actions of the incumbent government precisely confirmed, the usurpation of power and further expansion. Illiberal democracy is caused by a combination of asymmetry in societal resources, potential issues with stateness, and an undemocratic past. This vividly illustrates the Nigerian situation, and with its history of military incursions and political violence, a likely turn to illiberal democracy cannot be overlooked. In terms of tutelary or domain democracies, the competition of non-state actors in the reserved domain is visible, with multinational corporations, religious institutions, and militant groups influencing policy making or invalidating the powers of the democratically elected government.

Lastly, Samuel Huntington's perspective of democratic consolidation is worth disclosing. He posits that the public must learn that democracy is not an answer to all societal problems, but rather the ability to remove the govern-

---

[41] Merkel, Puhle, Croissant, Eicher and Thiery, *Defekte Demokratie*, 65–95.

ment from power through elections.[42] Specifically, democracies become consolidated when the public learns that democracy is a panacea to tyranny, but not to anything else.[43] The learning process suggested by Huntington further raises the issue of the imperfection of democracy – suggesting a successive reiteration of trial and error phases until such lessons for a full democracy suitably sink in. The idea of the learning process further suggests that consolidation has no endpoint; rather it builds on several experiences as building blocks to a sustainable form of democracy. In other words, effective conceptualisation and operationalisation of democratic consolidation is an inherently difficult task, considering the diversity and historical differences alongside generational attitudinal shifts of the public.

Conclusion

My chapter explored the democratic typology of Nigeria through a mixed-method investigative analysis. Based on both Merkel et al.'s and Scheppele's models, I characterise Nigeria as a highly defective democracy and essentially a 'Frankenstate' by which the Nigerian state possesses several characteristics of autocratic legalism, while as a defective democracy, as opined by Merkel et al., Nigeria borrows piecemeal from each defective democracy typology for the sustenance of government.

The current situation of the Nigerian polity, especially post-2019 election, is evidentially suggestive of Nigeria taking an illiberal democratic turn. This article provides a conceptual exploratory framework on which the quality, health of democracy and emancipative values in a polity can be analysed. Howbeit, this submission is subject to debate, and assessments of its validity should be weighed against specific countries' cases and experiences. Nevertheless, there have been continued human rights violations in the Buhari administration, more so than in any other democratic administration in the history of Nigeria. Since many of the democratic defects reviewed by this article have gone largely unopposed by the democratic institutions charged with the protection of the rule of law, one can ultimately suggest that democracy is in decline, and the quality of democracy, as shown by Tables 1, 2, and 3, is regressing over time.

---

42 S. P. Huntington, *The Third Wave. Democratization in the Late Twentieth Century* (Oklahoma: University of Oklahoma Press, 1991), 123–128.
43 Huntington, *The Third Wave*.

John T. Tsuwa and Faeren M. Agaigbe
INEC, the Electoral Process and the Conduct of Elections in 2019

Abstract: The electoral process in Nigeria as in many developing democracies of the world has been fraught with several challenges ranging from personnel to operations and logistics. These challenges have resulted in irregularities in the Nigerian electoral process thereby undermining the conduct of free, fair and credible elections. The recently concluded 2019 General Election was not spared these challenges or the consequent questionable and contested outcomes of the election in many parts of the country. In lieu of the foregoing, this chapter discusses the challenges the Independent National Electoral Commission (INEC) confronted during the 2019 election such as insufficient personnel, operations and logistics difficulties right from the time of voter registration, collection of Permanent Voters Card (PVC), campaign regulation, and logistics on election day. These challenges made it difficult for INEC to meet its mandate of delivering free, fair and credible elections. The analysis shows that INEC needs to strengthen her departments of procurement and operations to enable the commission to both recruit and train ad-hoc staff early and deliver electoral materials on time. There is also need to integrate field study in the training of ad-hoc staff in order to get them familiar with their soon-to-be work environment.

Keywords: Democracy, INEC, election, electoral process

Introduction

Electoral processes have shaped the nature of elections and by extension the fate of modern nations in their quest to enshrine and consolidate democratic governance. This is because elections are crucial as they provide the avenue by which diverse interest groups within the nation negotiate to peacefully resolve their claims to power.[1] Elections determine the manner and methods by which legitimate changes in the social order occur. However, elections in Nigeria have continued to generate controversies due to the challenges in the electoral process

---

[1] Festus Iyayi, "The Conduct of Elections and Electoral Practice in Nigeria" (paper presented at the Annual Nigerian Bar Association Conference, Abuja, 24 August 2004).

John T. Tsuwa and Faeren M. Agaigbe, Benue State University, Makurdi

https://doi.org/10.1515/9783110766561-010

particularly with regards to the activities of political parties, political elites, security agencies, as well as the level of independence of the Electoral Management Bodies (EMBs), their professionalism and the public acceptability of the elections they conduct.

Since Nigeria's return to democratic governance in 1999, the electoral process has been questioned for lack of transparency, integrity, credibility and inclusivity. The Independent National Electoral Commission (INEC), vested with the constitutional powers to conduct elections since 1999, has not been spared varying degrees of controversies and accusations concerning the nature of elections it has conducted. This is largely an outcome of the various challenges that the Commission faces during election seasons. Nonetheless, INEC has consistently accused political actors and weak institutional and legal frameworks of collaborating institutions in the electoral process for the challenges it faces in the quest to conduct free, fair and credible elections. Against this multi-dimensional problematic, this chapter critically analyses some of the challenges that confronted INEC during the 2019 general election. Structurally, this chapter proceeds in seven parts. The first, which is the introduction, is followed by conceptualization of key terms – election and the electoral process. Thereafter, the establishment and mandate of INEC would be examined. A key sector of the chapter dealing with INEC and the conduct of the 2019 general election follow, before both the conclusion and some recommendations.

Conceptualizing Election and the Electoral Process

Election is fundamental to the process of representation in liberal democratic settings. It is a systematic strategy in selecting, among choices, a preferred actor to lead on behalf of a group of people.[2] Ejumudo sees it as the technical means or instrument of ensuring popular participation in governance with the dictates of modern democracies and hallmark of legitimacy.[3] Even so, elections entail the ability and freedom of members of a particular organization, associa-

---

[2] John T. Tsuwa, "Making the Votes Count: Interrogating the Role of Collation Officers in Benue North-East Senatorial Elections in 2015 Elections," in *The 2015 Elections in Nigeria: Emerging Issues*, John T. Tsuwa and Elijah T. Ikpanor, eds. (Ibadan: Don Afrique. 2010), 7–16.

[3] B. Kelly and O. Ejumudo, "A Critical Analysis of Fiscal Federalism Palaver as Exposition of the Pseudo and Quasi Nature of Nigeria's Federal Arrangement," *International Journal of Political Science and Administration* (2010): 14–20.

tion or society, within the guidelines provided in their constitution, to express their choice by selecting among their members, especially those who indicate interest, who to govern them. Elections are complex set of activities with different variables that act and feed on one another.[4] Election can be conceptualized as a "formal" act of collective decision-making that occurs in a stream of connected antecedents, with subsequent behaviour aimed at selecting among group members an arrowhead that would provide direction for group members to follow towards achieving their coordinated objectives. In another dimension, elections are periodic legitimate instruments that give the choice makers (electorates or voters) the power to confer authority on the choice (leader) who would authoritatively carryout out specified functions on behalf of the choice makers. It also makes provision for the conferred authority to be stripped off when the leadership fails to deliver the collective aspirations of the people into achievable outcomes.

In a strict sense, electoral process has been viewed in many ways by several authors. This diversity stems from the objectives of their studies. However, Jinadu sees the electoral process as the rules, procedures and activities relating to the establishment of electoral bodies, the appointment of their members, selection and training of electoral officials, constituency delimitation, voter education, registration of political parties, registration of voters, nomination of candidates, balloting, counting of ballots, declaration of results and, in some cases, supervision of party nomination congresses.[5] Ajayi opines that the electoral process is the management and organization of all the activities and stages of an electoral cycle (i.e. the pre-election, election and post-election stages) by an electoral body.[6] Jega and Ibeanu observe that there is a widespread misconception of equating the electoral process to the election itself.[7] They argue instead that the electoral process transcends the method of choosing public office holders and includes the entire gamut of all the institutional procedures, arrangements and actions involved in elections. These include suffrage, voters' registration, delimitation of constituencies, electoral competition between rival political parties, the body charged with the conduct and supervision of election, the method of

---

[4] Festus Okoye, Assessing the credibility of elections in Nigeria (Abuja: Human Rights Monitor, 2007).
[5] Adele L. Jinadu, "Matters Arising: African Elections and the Problem off Electoral Administration," *African Journal of Political Science* 2, no.1 (1997): 1–11.
[6] Kunle Ajayi, "Elections Administration in Nigeria and the Challenge of 2007 Elections," *The Social Science Medwell Journal* 2, no.2 (2007): 142–151.
[7] Jega M. Attahiru and Okechukwu Ibeanu, eds., "Elections and the Future of Democracy in Nigeria" (paper presented at the Nigerian Political Science Association Conference, Abuja, 2007).

selection of candidates within political parties, the nomination of candidates, the method of voting, the actual conduct of the election, the determination of election disputes, electoral malpractices and their consequences. Going by the INEC Proceedings, electoral process includes a long and complex range of activities that are aptly represented in the diagram below.

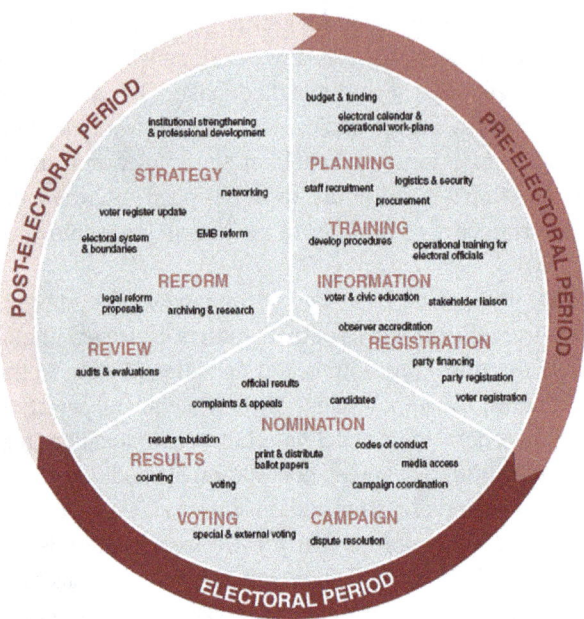

Figure 1: Diagram showing INEC's proceeding of electoral process
Source: The Electoral Institute, Abuja 2015.

Fig. 1 shows that election is a long process that starts not only from the election management bodies (EMBs) but also from the political actors because the actors also begin by indicating intentions to contest, carryout consultations, mobilize and organize campaign teams, carryout publicity, participate in party primaries before coming in direct contact with the EMBs.[8] It is therefore noteworthy that elections are not necessarily about election day activities only as it encompasses a wide-range of activities before, during and after the election day proper. Put differently, election process includes the formation and construction of the legal and constitutional frameworks of elections – the registration of political parties, voter registration, collection of voters' cards, party campaigns, the activ-

---

[8] Tsuwa, "Making the Votes Count," 7–16.

ities of the security agencies, the activities of (international and local) election monitors/observers (missions), and the electorates. The evidence here is that the electoral process is not unidirectional, but involves all the state and non-state actors that play different roles leading to the actual conduct of the election and the post-election activities.

Establishment and Mandate of the Independent National Electoral Commission (INEC)

INEC is Nigeria's electoral body charged with the mandate and responsibility to conduct elections in Nigeria. The Commission was established in accordance with Section 153(f) of the amended 1999 Constitution of the Federal Republic of Nigeria with a Chairman and 12 National Commissioners.[9] The functions of the Commission as stipulated in part 1 of the third schedule of the 1999 Constitution are as follows:

a) Organize, conduct and supervise all elections and matters pertaining to elections into all elective offices provided in the Constitution of the Federal Republic of Nigeria 1999, as amended, or any other enactment of law.
b) Register political parties in accordance with the provision of the relevant enactment or law.
c) Monitor the organization and operation of the political parties, including their finances.
d) Arrange for the annual examination and auditing of the funds and accounts of political parties and publish report of such examination and audit for public information.
e) Conduct registration of persons qualified to vote and the preparation, maintenance and revision of the register of voters for the purpose of any election.
f) Monitor political campaigns and provide rules and regulations, which shall govern the political parties.
g) Delegate power to Resident Electoral Commissioner
h) Carryout such other functions as may be conferred upon it by a Decree or any other enactment of law.
i) Divide the area of the Federation, or as the case may be, into such constituencies as may be presented by law for the purpose of elections to be conducted by the Commission.

---

[9] Babayo Sule, "The 2019 Presidential Elections in Nigeria: An analysis of the Voting Pattern, Issues and Impact," *Malaysian Journal of Society and Space* 15, no. 2 (2019): 129–140.

Situated within the above constitutional powers are the principles guiding INEC in the fulfillment of its mandate. These principles were designed to serve as the code of conduct so as to create confidence in the EMBs and the process adopted towards the conduct of the elections. These include:

a) Transparency – INEC will be open and transparent in all its activities and in its relations with political stakeholders, media organizations, INEC service providers and the people of Nigeria.
b) Truthful and honest in all its dealings with people, its political stakeholders and each other
c) Credibility – INEC will strive to ensure that the people of Nigeria and in particular, the political stakeholders will readily accept all its actors.
d) Impartiality – INEC shall endeavour to create a level playing field for all political actors.
e) Dedication – INEC shall be committed to providing the highest quality election services to the people of Nigeria and will also work to ensure that merit will continue to be the basis for compensation, promotion and recruitment of staff.[10]

Methodological and Theoretical Considerations

A mixture of primary and secondary sources was used for this chapter. For the primary source, two focus group discussions (FGDs) were held each with INEC staff, politicians and INEC ad-hoc staff in Makurdi, Abuja, Lokoja, Obudu and Wukari areas. In addition, 10 key informant interviews (KII) were conducted among INEC staff, ad-hoc staff and politicians. The findings from these primary sources were analyzed in thematic and descriptive formats and collaborated with secondary data, which were derived from relevant books, journals, INEC publications and credibly verified Internet sources.

The theory of structural functionalism was used to analyse the data collected. Structural functionalism has its intellectual roots in the writings of social anthropologists such as Redcliffe Brown and Bronislaw Malinowski, which was adopted into the field of political science by Gabriel Almond. At its basic level, structural functionalism posits that a political system is made up of institutions (structures) such as interest groups, political parties, the executive, legislative and judicial branches of governments and bureaucratic machinery.

---

[10] "Regulations and Guidelines for the Conduct of Elections, 2019," https://inecnigeria.org/elections/regulations-and-guidelines-for-the-conduct-of-elections/ (accessed 28 September 2021).

This theory stipulates that all these institutions function together to make the political system work more effectively. For Almond, a better understanding of the society emerges only when one begins to examine how these institutions act within the sphere of a specific political process.[11] As Almond describes it, interest groups serve to articulate political issues, parties then aggregate and express them in a coherent meaningful way, while government enacts public policies to address them, and bureaucracies finally regulate them.

Almond and Powell, in modifying and expanding this theory, added an important set of system functions to this model by acknowledging the crucial role played by political culture in determining the unique characteristics of a political system.[12] According to Tsuwa, the major assumptions of structural functionalism are: the social system is the prior causal reality and the system parts are functionally interrelated; all social phenomena have functions for the larger social system; the higher the level of integration between these intermediate groups, the more cohesive society will be as a whole.[13]

The functionalism theory, therefore, serves as a means of explaining the roles performed by the structures in a political system. It argues that some of the roles are unintended and unrecognized while others are manifest and intended roles, and therefore recognized as latent. These social patterns that contribute to the maintenance of a political system are regarded as functional, while those that have negative consequences are considered dysfunctional.[14] This if further buttressed by Adejoh who holds that a political system is made up of interrelated parts that are supposed to work harmoniously to ensure the survival of the whole system.[15] However, when related to politics, structural functionalism is the means of explaining basic functions of political structures within the political system.

Since every political system is made up of various parts, this theory has proven vital in helping to explain the relationship between the various existing parts (structures) within any given institution. These structures being many, can take any form, but it is the contribution of each part (structure) that sustains the whole (political system). Thus, building upon the tenets of the functionalism theory, this chapter makes a strong postulation that for the Nigerian political sys-

---

[11] Gabriel A. Almond, "Comparative Political Systems," *Journal of Politics* (1956): 391–409.
[12] Gabriel A. Almond and Bingham G. Powell. *Comparative Politics: A Developmental Approach* (Boston: Little Brown, 1966).
[13] John T. Tsuwa, "Collective Security and Peace in Africa: A study of the AU Collective Security Architecture," *NPSA* 2, no. 3 (2017): 74–88.
[14] Pius Adejoh, "Elections and Democracy in Nigeria," *Journal of Politics* 1, no. 3 (2019): 51–64.
[15] Adejoh, "Elections and Democracy."

tem to consolidate its democracy and ensure collective survival, INEC and all stakeholders need to perform strategic functions in the electoral process as parts (structures) of the whole system, by so doing, INEC would succeed in fulfilling its constitutionally given mandate.

Conduct of Elections in Nigeria: An Overview

The Election Management Bodies (EMBs) mandated to conduct elections in Nigeria, starting from the colonial era, have consistently changed in form, nature and character over the years. These EMBs include: the Electoral Commission of Nigeria (ECN) in 1959, the Federal Electoral Commission (FEC) in 1964, the Federal Electoral Commission (FEDECO) in 1978, the National Electoral Commission (NEC) that conducted the June 12 elections in 1993, and the National Electoral Commission of Nigeria (NECON) in 1994. The General Abubakar Abdulsalami-led administration established the current EMB, INEC, in 1998, which would go on to conduct the 1999 elections when Nigeria reverted to civilian rule. INEC has since then conducted six general elections in Nigeria, making it the longest serving EMB in Nigeria's political history. Over the years, as Adejumobi and Agbaje note, the autonomy and capacity of EMBs in Nigeria became suspect.[16] This appears to reflect in their endless renaming and restructuring, not to mention the varying levels of influence on it by successive governments. This has largely accounted for the twin malady of malpractices and violence that characterized elections in Nigeria, which severally threatened and even successfully truncated democratic rule.[17]

Since Nigeria's return to civilian rule in 1999, the succeeding elections of 2003, 2007 and 2011 were embroiled in controversy, rejection and legitimacy crisis because of the massive fraud and violence that attended them. Although the blame may not be completely laid on the shoulders of INEC alone, nonetheless, there were blames for acts of commission or omission by INEC, which largely contributed to the wide-scale irregularities that characterized the 2003 and 2007 elections, thus, generating a massive lack of confidence in the electorates. Consequently, the 2011 elections started on a pessimistic note as many Nigerians doubted the sincerity of INEC to conduct credible elections going by its past re-

---

[16] Said Adejumobi and Adigun Agbaje, "Do votes count: The Travails of electoral Politics in Nigeria" (CODESRIA Special Working Paper, Dakar, 2006).
[17] E. Obioye and A. Emesibe, "Elections and Governance in Nigeria's Fourth Republic," in *The 2015 Elections in Nigeria: Emerging Issues*, eds. John T. Tsuwa & Elijah T. Ikpanor (Ibadan: Don Afrique, 2015).

cords.[18] INEC, under the leadership of Professor Attahiru Jega, however, rose to the challenge of conducting credible elections beginning with a more transparent and effective registration of voters. As a result, the pessimism that initially greeted the INEC chairman and his commission members gradually gave way to trust and promise as the Commission assured the Nigerian electorates of free, fair and credible elections. Though INEC recorded giant strides in the 2011 elections that attracted applause from both national and international election observers' missions, the election also had certain shortcomings and challenges. Nonetheless, the confidence of several Nigerians in INEC towards conducting credible elections in subsequent election seasons was rejuvenated.

Attahiru Jega's second election in 2015 was historic for two major reasons. Firstly, the introduction of an electronic accreditation process (EAP) remarkably increased the credibility of the entire election process. Secondly, it was the first time in Nigeria's electoral history that an incumbent president and his political party would lose elections and concede defeat to the opposition. Yet, the 2015 general election administration process as Moveh reports was not without controversy.[19] Responses from FGDs conducted indicate that the 2015 elections were unique especially in the manner in which the campaigns were carried out by political parties and their candidates. According to our respondents, Abu Amali and Benson Oogwu, political campaigns in the pre-election period were heated with hate speeches, fake pictorial representations of opposing candidates and debates were non-issue based. In several states across Nigeria, the pre-election period recorded varying degrees of election-related violence more than on the actual day of election. They noted that the election and post-election activities were more peaceful than the pre-election period. Indeed, the 2015 general election was described as the most keenly contested set of elections in the history of Nigeria, but at the same time, regarded as the most free and fair election since 1999. Little wonder that expectations were high that the 2019 general election would be an improvement of the 2015 experience.

---

18 E. Obioye, "Elections and Governance."
19 David O. Moveh, "INEC and the Administration of Elections in Nigeria's Fourth Republic: The 2015 General Elections in Focus" (paper presented at the National Conference Organized by the Electoral Institute, Abuja, 27–28 July 2015).

INEC and the Administration of the 2019 General Election

The elections of 2019, originally scheduled to hold on 16 February and 2 March 2019, respectively, were postponed to 23 February and 9 March 2019 because of logistics challenges. Prior to the postponement, however, there were high expectations from Nigerians that the exercise would be an improved version of the 2015 general election. According to two key informant interviews and aggregation of FGDs, the conduct of the 2019 general election was questionable and the expectations of many Nigerians were shattered as the neutrality of INEC was strongly questioned because of the postponement. Ukiwo identified three further factors that fueled this suspicion.[20] The first factor was that contrary to convention, President Muhammadu Buhari appointed a person from his own geopolitical zone as INEC chairperson. Besides being against the norm, it was construed as having serious implications on the neutrality of the Commission's chairman and, indeed, the conduct of elections for that season.

The second factor was the decision of President Buhari to decline assent to the proposed amendment of the Electoral Act, which was supposed to enhance the independence and capacity of INEC to deliver free, fair and credible elections. And the third factor was the postponement of scheduled elections by INEC six hours to the commencement of accreditation and voting. This called into question INEC's neutrality as the conditions surrounding the shift in date was not satisfactorily explained to Nigerians. Even so, the Peoples' Democratic Party (PDP), the main opposition party to the ruling All Progressives Congress (APC), and other political parties joined millions of Nigerians to condemn the postponement of the elections and INEC was accused of incompetence and biases in its dealing during that election season.[21]

Reports from the FGDs, collaborated by Key informant interviews, indicate that INEC's activities commenced from voter registration, the sourcing and distribution of materials and personnel to the final announcement of results. Based on INEC's election process presented earlier in diagram 1 and Elklit and Reynold's steps in election administration process presented in Table 1, INEC activities in the 2019 general elections are discussed thus:

---

20 Ukoha Ukiwo, "Democracy, Development and Governance: Nigeria's 2019 General Elections: A Postscript" (SSRC on Kujenga Amani, April 2019).
21 Ukiwo, "Democracy, Development and Governance."

Table 1: Elklit and Reynold's steps in Election Administration Process.[22]

	Steps in the EAP	Important element
1.	Legal framework of the EMB's structure	• Constitutional/legal basis • Rules/regulations/guidelines • Set allocation system
2.	Elections management	• Electoral commissions appointment & independence, including terms of tenure • Commission/ administration relationship • Method of allocation of resources
3.	Constituency and polling district demarcation	• Relevant body identified and active • Principles for delimitation identified • Rules about automatic periodical revision • Adequate resources available • Rules for handling complaints in place
4.	Voter education	• Timing • Quality • Outreach • Adequate resources available • Relationship between electoral commissions efforts and efforts by parties and NGOs
5.	Voter Registration	• Automatic or voluntary registration • Appointment and training of registration personnel • Adequate time for registration and access to registration stations. • Rules for public scrutiny of voters register • Complaints procedure
6.	Access to and design of the ballot, nomination and registration of parties and candidates	• Registration of parties/ candidates • Rules about independent candidates • Mechanism for ballot paper access • Ballot paper design
7.	Campaign Regulation	• Spending rules • Public funding of party expenditure/ campaign costs • Access to public media • Rules for meeting and rallies • Codes of conduct

---

22 Source: Jorgen Elklit and Andrew Reynolds, "The Impact of Election Administration on the Legitimacy of Emerging Democracies: A New Research Agenda," in *Commonwealth Comparative Politics* 40, no. 2 (2000): 86–119.

In the light of the above table, the authors integrated these two processes and discussed their findings in four thematic areas in the electoral process namely; legal framework, voter education, voter registration and permanent voter card (PVC) collection, campaign regulation and logistics.

Legal Framework

Elections and the electoral process in Nigeria are governed by laws domiciled in the Constitution and the Electoral Act, which from time to time need amendment for maximum results. For the 2019 general election, a number of alterations were made to the constitution in 2018. Some of these alterations bore on election matters such as: reducing the age limit for running members of House of Representatives (HoRs) and State House of Assembly (SHoA); governorship and presidential candidates; and increasing the time for INEC to conduct re-runs for the office of president and state governors from the initial 7 to 21 days.[23]

Since 1999, it has become an established norm for the Electoral Act to undergo some amendment after every general election. This is usually informed by the lessons taken from preceding elections. The preparation for the 2019 elections were not different; several changes were initiated and put into process by the National Assembly towards the amendment of the Electoral Act. However, the Electoral Act (Amendment) Bill went back and forth between the lawmakers and the president who rejected it on several occasions. The amendment proposals as put together by the National Assembly, contained provisions that were to made significant and positive impacts on the conduct of elections in Nigeria. For instance, the use of biometric technology would have helped in preventing inflation of figures in the registers of voters as multiple registrations would be rendered technically impossible. Unfortunately, the non-approval of the amendment proposals of the Electoral Act Bill (EAB) cast a shadow of uncertainty around the 2019 elections. INEC was constrained to work with the existing Electoral Act of 2015 with its already identified imperfections.

---

23 "Regulations and Guidelines for the Conduct of Elections, 2019."

Voter Registration and Permanent Voters Card (PVC) Collection

A register of voters is an indispensable document for the conduct of election; it should consist of only eligible voters in a constituency.[24] According to Moveh, a reliable voters' register is devoid of names of under aged, deceased, fictitious or fake names. Rather, the register should consist of names of eligible voters' resident in the area where they intend to vote. The process of voter registration is a major test of credibility of an election process as well as for the EMB.[25] In Nigeria, a registration of voters conducted by INEC precedes every general election. The most significant development of the continuous voter registration exercise was the decision to issue permanent voters' cards to the electorate. Agaigbe, describes this decision as a "highpoint" in the attempt to develop a credible voter register as well as conduct credible elections in Nigeria.[26]

For the 2019 elections, the enrollment of new voters in the continuous voters' registration began in April 2017 and was scheduled to last until August 2018. Eventually, the deadline was extended by two weeks to give as many people as possible the opportunity to register. Ugbede notes that during the exercise, apart from enrolling new registrants, INEC replaced 998,993 cards and transferred 640,796 cards to new voting centres. In all, over 84 million voters were registered across the country and a close scrutiny of the state-by-state registration of voters revealed a remarkable successful turnout of voters for registration.[27]

At the level of Permanent Voters Card (PVC) collection, no state was able to achieve 100% collection after the public verification of the register of voters.[28] On a general note, however, there was an increase in voter registration and a rise in PVC collection rates between 2015 and 2019. The percentage was from 82.03% to 86.63%.[29]

---

24 "Regulations and Guidelines for the Conduct of Elections, 2019."
25 "Regulations and Guidelines for the Conduct of Elections, 2019."
26 Faeren M. Agaigbe, "Voter Apathy and Voter Turn Out in the 2015 General Elections: The Benue Experience" (paper presented at the National Conference on Elections organized by the Electoral Institute, Abuja, 27–28 July 2015).
27 Fredrick Ugbede, "Nigeria: 2019–INEC Appoints Controversial Officials as Head key Election Committee," *Premium Times*, 3 January 2019, https://www.premiumtimesng.com/news/top-news/303981-2019 (accessed 15 June 2019).
28 "Regulations and Guidelines for the Conduct of Elections, 2019."
29 "Regulations and Guidelines for the Conduct of Elections, 2019."

Campaign Regulation

One major feature of the electoral process in Nigeria is that electioneering campaigns in the country hardly address the major issues that border on the interests, welfare and security of the people. Instead, campaigns were often characterized by name-callings, mudslinging, thuggery, hooliganisms, maiming and even killing of political opponents.[30] The challenge of campaign regulation in the electoral process in Nigeria arises to a large extent from two inter-related factors, namely; the inability to effectively regulate the finance and funding of political parties and the inability to establish and enforce a code of conduct for political parties and the mainstream media.

Aderemi notes that political party funding is the process whereby parties generate monies and assets that are used in running their day-to-day activities and funding of political campaigns. In addition to private funding, all registered political parties in Nigeria are entitled to receive public funding to support general operations and costs of campaigning. Public funding of political parties began in Nigeria during the Second Republic, prior to which there was no clearly defined regulatory framework on party finance. Funding of political parties was predominantly through private funding as parties and candidates were responsible for election-related expenses.[31] Nonetheless, the 2019 general election saw robust campaigns among parties. Even so, a few of the parties that conducted primary elections failed to conduct transparent primaries and such anomalies led to allegations of the imposition of candidates. The two main political parties that dominated the campaign circle were the incumbent APC and the main opposition PDP. Indeed, there was a flagrant abuse of electoral law by both the APC and PDP. In addition, there were activities such as intimidation, use of hate speech, fake news and eventual vote-buying and selling during the 2019 election.[32] The failure of political parties to abide by the laws guiding campaign regulations during elections as well as the monetization of the entire electoral process and the inability of INEC to enforce a code-of-conduct for political parties contributed in no small measure to their heating up the polity during the elections. And such a scenario affected the ability of INEC to delivering a free, credible and transparent election.

---

30 Moveh, "INEC and the Administration."
31 Adewale Aderemi, "Election Funds and The Conduct of 2015 General Elections in Nigeria" (paper presented at the National Conference on Elections organized by the Electoral Institute, Abuja, 27–28 July 2015).
32 "Regulations and Guidelines for the Conduct of Elections, 2019."

Operations and Logistics

For the 2019 general election, an Electoral Logistics Committee (ECL) was set up to coordinate logistics support as well as the clearance and transportation of election materials to designated locations nationwide. This logistics support included the delivery of sensitive and non-sensitive materials to almost 200,000 locations ranging from polling units to the various wards, local governments, states and national collation centres for the 1,558 constituencies in which elections were to be conducted. The Electoral Logistics Committee included relevant security agencies whose roles were clearly defined in Section 29(3) of the Electoral Act of 2010 (as amended). The ECL was also charged with the recruitment, training and deployment of INEC ad-hoc staff. Even though the INEC National Commissioner of Operations (NCO), Professor Okechukwu Ibeanu, and its chairman, Professor Yakubu Mahmood, had assured Nigerians of INEC's preparedness for the conduct of 2019 elections, there were significantly two components of the operations and logistics that flawed the entire process during the 2019 exercise. These, on one hand, were the recruitment, training and deployment of ad-hoc staff and, on the other, the distribution and transportation of election materials.

The report on Nigeria's 2019 elections indicates that out of all the states where elections were supposed to have taken place on Saturday, 16 February 2019, prior to its postponement, the following 18 states, along with the Federal Capital Territory (Abuja), were yet to receive sensitive election materials: Abia, Akwa-Ibom, Benue, Cross River, Delta, Ebonyi, Enugu, Gombe, Imo, Kaduna, Kano, Kogi, Lagos, Nasarawa, Niger, Ogun, Taraba, and Zamfara States and Abuja.

As mentioned, the recruiting and training of ad-hoc staff was another responsibility that INEC unsatisfactorily executed. All categories of ad-hoc staff had only three days of training. In many cases, they had only two days. Consequently, such a deficiency in training those who would be in the field to conduct the elections ensured INEC was left with improperly trained and unequipped ad-hoc staff. In most of the local government areas like in Benue State, for instance, the Presiding Officers (PO), Assistant Presiding Officers (APO) I, II and III only completed two days of training meaning that they were improperly trained to carry out their assigned roles. Consequently, several ad-hoc APO II staff could not deal with problems that arose from operating the smart card readers (SCR).

In sum, INEC operations fell short of its expected role and obligations as set in the threshold document. Logistic and operational challenges, therefore, marred the credible conduct of elections and the integrity of INEC. The first sign of this flaw manifested itself in the unexpected postponement of election in the early hours of the election start date on 16 February 2019. The second manifestation was the inability to move ad-hoc staff and election materials to the various constituencies where elections were to hold. By the time the postponement of the election was declared by the INEC chairman, all ad-hoc staff were still at their various local government INEC offices. Again, in Benue State, for instance, the ad-hoc staff were yet to know the polling units and registration areas (RAs) they were posted to.

Postponing voting six hours to the start of polls exposed how ill-prepared INEC was for the 2019 general election. It also dampened citizens' enthusiasm that had built up towards the election. It made it almost impossible for many who had travelled out of their states of residence in order to vote in their constituencies to make a second trip back to vote the next weekend. This situation exacerbated voter apathy in the 2019 general election. The inability and failure of the respective INEC organs to perform their functions and work together for the success of the 2019 general election led to low output of the system. This indeed confirms the assumptions of the functionalist perspective that the conduct and outcome of the 2019 elections, which should have greatly improved on performance of the 2015 elections, invariably fell below expectations. Instead, the 2019 general election revealed serious shortcomings that cast doubts on the credibility of the exercise and, indeed, INEC's integrity and independence to conduct credible, free and transparent elections in the future.

Conclusion

This chapter identified some major steps in the electoral process of 2019 and also highlighted some major challenges that characterized the process. The two key flaws that undermined the 2019 election exercise bordered on operations and logistics: the movement of personnel between the time of voter registration up to the election day and the movement or distribution of election materials. These constituted the biggest challenges in the conduct of the 2019 general election. INEC's inability to adequately address these problems in a timely manner resulted in a flawed process that heightened citizen's doubts over its capacity to conduct free, credible and transparent elections in the future. The findings from this study underscore the need for INEC to strengthen her procurements and operations departments in order to enable timely delivery and distribution of election materials to the designated destinations for elections to hold as scheduled. Further, ad-hoc staff should be recruited and trained early as well as getting them adapted to their various constituencies of assignment. Lastly, INEC should carry out its oversight functions on political candidates and their parties and conform them to carry out their electioneering process within the provisions of the laws guiding elections in Nigeria. This, will, in turn, minimize the challenges INEC confronts while trying to deliver on its constitutionally given mandate.

Patrick Chukwudike Okpalaeke and Tony Johnson Ekpo
Murdering Their Consciences, 'Right to Vote' and Ethno-Political Conflict in Lagos during the 2019 General Election

Abstract: The sporadic attacks on the Igbo by political thugs in Lagos State during the 2019 general elections did not only reaffirm the continuous play of politics along ethnic lines, but also exposed the weaknesses in Nigeria's electoral laws. In fact, it is disturbing to consider that an international legal instrument – Right-to-Vote – to which Nigeria remains a signatory has not been domesticated to help curb the challenges confronting Nigeria's electoral system. This chapter provides an understanding of the changing dynamics of ethno-political conflicts as displayed during the 2019 general election in Lagos State. It draws a link between the 2015 'lagoon threat' issued by the Oba of Lagos to the series of attacks recorded in various parts of Lagos State in 2019. Research results show that the Oba's threat in 2015 was calculated to curtail the extent to which the Igbo have permeated the political space of Lagos State in a manner that appears antithetical to Lagos' political ambitions. The chapter further sheds light on how Lagos indigenes perceive Igbo economic activities that propelled the development of Lagos. The study concludes by highlighting key issues that must be addressed to avert future attacks on the Igbo during elections.

Keywords: constitution, elections, ethnic-politics, Igbo, Lagos State and Nigeria

Introduction

Lagos, Nigeria's mega-city,[1] was thrown into disarray after the 23 February 2019 general election when reports of attacks on the Igbo ethnic group by political hoodlums circulated on social media. Such tension was reminiscent of the age-long political fault lines that had existed between the Igbo of southeastern Nigeria and the Yoruba ethnic group of southwestern Nigeria since the colonial

---

[1] Matthew Gandy, "Learning From Lagos," *New Left Review* 33 (2005): 37–52.

Patrick Chukwudike Okpalaeke and Tony Johnson Ekpo, University of Uyo

https://doi.org/10.1515/9783110766561-011

era.[2] Following Nigeria's return to democratic rule in 1999 and the amendment of the constitution, elections were to be held quadrennially. Election periods are when Nigerians are presented with the opportunity to decide, through the ballot box, who leads them for another four years in the various elective positions. It was in the bid to put this constitutional provision into practice that electorates, especially those of Igbo extraction, were attacked by political hoodlums in some polling units, as well as after elections in various market places in Lagos State.[3] Such ethno-political violence, however, has a deep-seated history that dates to the colonial era, after the Clifford Constitution of 1922.[4]

The Clifford Constitution of 1922,[5] and its provision for a Legislative Council,[6] paved the way for party politics. Between 1923 when the first political party, the Nigerian National Democratic Party (NNDP), was formed[7] and 1948, there was "a regionalization of nationalism"[8] and political party leaders began to exhibit what James Coleman describes as "regional thinking."[9] This ethnic ideology led to the formation of political parties along ethnic lines: the Northern People's Congress (NPC) was for the Hausa-Fulani or the North; Action Group (AG) for the Yoruba or the West, and the National Council for Nigeria and Cameroon (NCNC) for the Igbo, the East and northern Cameroon.[10] The formation of political parties along ethnic sentiments created the platform for ethnic nationalism in Nigerian. This development would later compel scholars to attempt crit-

---

[2] Rotimi Fasan, "2019 elections: The Thing about tension between Yoruba and Igbo," *Vanguard Newspaper*, 6 March 2019.

[3] Samuel Awoyinfa, Ifeoluwa Ogunfuwa and Oluwatosin Omojuyigbe, "Two Feared Dead as Thugs Invade Polling Units in Lagos," *The Punch Newspaper*, 24 February 2019.

[4] Richard S. Sklar, *Nigerian Political Parties: Power in an Emergent African Nation* (New York: Nok Publishers, 1963), 18.

[5] John Hatch, *Nigeria: A History* (London: Martin Secker & Warburg Ltd., 1971), 165; Victor B. E. Abia, *Understanding Nigerian Government and Politics* (Lagos: Concept Publications, 2002), 88; Richard Bourne, *Nigeria: A New History of a Turbulent Century* (Ibadan: Bookkraft, 2016), 20–29.

[6] Hatch, *Nigeria*, 164–165; J. D. Fage, *A History of West Africa: An Introductory Survey* (Cambridge: Cambridge University Press, 1969), 181.

[7] Sklar, *Nigerian Political Parties*, 23–46.

[8] James S. Coleman, *Nigeria: Background to Nationalism* (Berkeley: University of California Press, 1958), 320–322; Fred Omu, "Ethnicity, Nationalism and Federalism," in *Foundations of Nigerian Federalism, 1900–1960*, eds. J. Isawa Elaigwu and G. N. Uzoigwe (Abuja: National Council on Intergovernmental Relations, 1996), 177–180

[9] Coleman, *Nigeria*, 323.

[10] Alexander Madiebo, *The Nigeria Revolution and the Biafra War* (Enugu: Fourth Dimension Publishers, 1980), 5.

ical epistemological and pedagogical exploration of the effect of ethnic-politics on every facet of the Nigerian state starting from colonial times.[11]

As a modest contribution to the literature on ethnic politics in Nigeria, this chapter, sitting at the intersection of electoral violence, constitutional gaps, and host-settler relations, explores in a historical sense, the changing dynamics of hostility among ethnic groups during election seasons using the Lagos State situation as a case study. The authors postulate that existing gaps in Nigeria's electoral laws occasioned electoral violence in most parts of Nigeria during the 2019 general election. What is more? A critical engagement with the issue being examined reveals that the 2015 'lagoon threat' issued by the Oba of Lagos to the Igbo community in Lagos did not only provide the needed impetus for the 2019 attacks on the Igbo in places like Ajegunle, Okota and Olodi-Apapa, where they dominate, but underscored the urgency to prove that the need to checkmate non-indigenes' involvement in the political narrative of Lagos, and other southwestern states, is of great significance.

Ethnic Politics: The Genesis of a Reverberating New State Order

Ethnic consciousness, which reared up in Nigerian politics early in her history right after the 1914 amalgamation exercise,[12] has continued owing to factors such as mutual suspicion among the various regions and ethnic groups in the country, lack of visionary leadership and struggle over national resources, among other core issues. Ethnic politics took concrete shape within the "Ikoli-Akinsanya election crisis in 1941" that led to the virtual collapse of the Nigerian Youth Movement (NYM).[13] The ethno-political conflict within the NYM saw political leaders such as H. O. Davies, K. A. Abayomi, Ernest Ikoli and Nnamdi Azi-

---

11 Okwudiba Nnoli, *Ethnic Politics in Nigeria* (Enugu: Fourth Dimension Publishers, 1978), 215–216; Max Siollun, *Oil, Politics and Violence: Nigeria's Military Coup Culture, 1966–1976* (New York: Algora Publishing, 2009), 12; Chinua Achebe, *The Trouble with Nigeria* (Ibadan: Heinemann Educational Books, 1983), 5; Eghosa E. Osaghae, *Crippled Giant: Nigeria Since Independence* (Ibadan: John Archers Publishers, 2015), 58; Richard A. Joseph, *Democracy and Prebendal Politics in Nigeria: Rise and Fall of the Second Republic* (Cambridge: Cambridge University Press, 1987), 5; Larry Diamond, *Class, Ethnicity and Democracy in Nigeria: The Failure of the First Republic* (New York: Syracuse University Press, 1988), 7.
12 Omu, "Ethnicity, Nationalism and Federalism," 172.
13 Sklar, *Nigerian Political Parties*, 52–54.

kiwe at verbal loggerheads with one another, carried out through the well-planned strategic propaganda of their respective media outlets.[14]

While the emergence of ethnic antagonism among the various ethnic groups took root in the 'divide and rule' strategy employed by the British colonial government as far back as 1914,[15] its persistence in Nigeria's post-colonial political milieu certainly has nothing to do with colonialism.[16] Struggling for Nigeria's independence, Dr Nnamdi Azikiwe, Alhaji Tafawa Balewa, Sir Ahmadu Bello and Chief Obafemi Awolowo, among others, expressed regional allegiance as a critical strategy for gaining political power and support.[17] Rather than seek social, economic and political freedom for the post-colonial Nigerian state, which obviously was very much trapped in economic exploitation and political dominance via deceptive structures put in place by the British colonial government, Nigerian political elites were concerned with securing political power based on the support they could draw from their respective ethnic enclaves.[18]

This phenomenon was so glaring that Okwudiba Nnoli remarked: "under conditions of politicization of ethnicity and the use of governmental powers for inter-ethnic socio-economic competition, ethnic rivalry is inevitable."[19] The understanding of this sad reality, by the likes of Sir Ahmadu Bello, Alhaji Balewa, Dr Azikiwe, Chief Obafemi Awolowo and others, created a tense atmosphere of mutual suspicion and the fear of dominance of one ethnic group over the others. These political elites' exhibition of ethnicity was captured in several dailies. The *Daily Trust,* on 17 October 1944, for example, reported the nature and praxis of ethnic politics thus: "We anticipate [...] an era of wholesome rivalry among the principal tribes of Nigeria [...], while they must guide against chauvinism and rabid tribalism, the great Yoruba people must strive to preserve their individuality."[20] Similarly, in 1948, Sir Adeyemo Alakija, the president of the Pan-Yoruba group, *Egbe Omo Oduduwa,*was quoted to have said: "The Big Tomorrow [for

---

14 Sklar, *Nigerian Political Parties*, 53.
15 Diamond, *Class, Ethnicity and Democracy,* 26 – 28; W Alade Fawole, *The Illusion of the Post-Colonial State: Governance and Security Challenges in Africa* (Lanham: Lexington Books, 2018), 23.
16 Hatch, *Nigeria*, 199; James A. Ekah and Patrick C. Okpalaeke, "The Dilemma of Poor Leadership, Ethnicity and Corruption in Nigeria, 1960 – 2015," *Kaduna Journal of Humanities* 2, no. 3 (2018): 222 – 245.
17 Arthur A. Nwankwo, *The Power Dynamics of Nigerian Society: People, Politics and Power* (London: Camelot Press Ltd., 1988), 1.
18 Fawole, *The Illusion of the Post-Colonial State,* 21 – 36.
19 Nnoli, *Ethnic Politics in Nigeria,* 216.
20 Coleman, *Nigeria,* 345; Godwin Onuoha, *Challenging the State in Africa: MASSOB and the Crisis of Self-Determination in Nigeria* (Berlin: Lit Verlag, 2011), 71 – 72.

the Yoruba] is the future of our children [...] how they will hold their own among other tribes [ethnic groups] of Nigeria. How the Yoruba will not be relegated to the background in the future."²¹ Dr Nnamdi Azikiwe also displayed a radical posture towards the *Egbe Omo Odudu* with the response:

> Henceforth the cry must be one of battle against the *Egbe Omo Oduduwa*, its leaders, at home and abroad, uphill and down dale, in the streets of Nigeria and in the residence of its advocators. It is the enemy of Nigeria; it must be crushed to the earth [...] there is no going back until the fascist organization of Sir Adeyemo Alakija has been dismembered.²²

Reacting to Azikiwe's comment, Oluwole Alakija, a prominent figure in the *Egbe Omo Oduduwa*, made the following statement, further depicting ethnic antagonism:

> We are bunched together by the British who named us Nigeria. We never knew the Igbo, but since we came to know them, we have tried to be friendly and neighbourly. Then came the Arch Devil [Azikiwe] to sow the seeds of distrust and hatred... We have tolerated enough from a class of Igbo and addle-brained Yoruba who have mortgaged their thinking caps to Azikiwe and his hirelings.²³

These statements are among the plethora of ethno-political propaganda that presaged Nigeria's independence. The incident of the 7 January 1952 Western Region House of Representatives' crisis that was to determine the premier political leader in Western Nigeria lends further credence to ethnic politicking.²⁴ The outcome of the incident led many political historians to adjudge the event as a critical juncture in the consciousness of ethnic politics in Nigeria; and both Azikiwe and Awolowo, regrettably, the architects of the national crisis, which have reverberated ever since.²⁵ Okudiba Nnoli and Kalu Ezera adequately provided the details of this episode.²⁶ The ripple effect of the January 1952 incident snowballed

---

21 Onuoha, *Challenging the State in Africa*, 346.
22 G. O. Olusanya, *The Second World War and Politics in Nigeria, 1939–1945* (Lagos: Evans Brothers Ltd., 1973), 39.
23 Olusanya, *The Second World War and Politics*, 346.
24 Deji Ogunjobi, "1952 National Assembly: Awo Stopped Zik-Tribal Politics Snowballed," *Historical Flashback: The Historical Memoir Newspaper*, 9 December–5 January 2016.
25 Patrick C. Okpalaeke "Ethnic Politics in Nigeria: Issues and Lessons from the First Republic," (B. A. project, University of Uyo, 2016), 42; Udida A. Undiyaundeye, "The 1951 Elections and the Origins of Electoral Malpractices in Nigeria," *Lapai Journal of Humanities* 4, no. 5 (2014): 242–252.
26 Kalu Ezera, *Constitutional Development in Nigeria* (Cambridge: Cambridge University Press, 1960); Nnoli, *Ethnic Politics in Nigeria*, 104–279.

into the Eastern Regional House, where it was reported that Azikiwe and his associates ensured that Eyo Ita, Head of Government Business in Eastern Nigeria, lost his position.[27] Reacting to this event, Achebe writes: "I was an eye-witness to that momentous occasion when Chief Obafemi Awolowo 'stole' the leadership of Western Nigeria from Dr Nnamdi Azikiwe in broad daylight on the floor of the Western House of Assembly and sent the great Zik scampering back to the Niger whence he came."[28] Balancing his critique, Achebe further remarks:

> A true nationalist who championed the noble cause of 'one Nigeria' to the extent that he contested and won the first general election to the Western House of Assembly. But when Chief Awolowo 'stole' the government from him in broad daylight he abandoned his principles which dictated that he should stay in the Western House as Leader of the opposition and give battle to Awolowo. Instead, he conceded victory to reaction by ethnic politics, fled to the East where he compounded his betrayal of principle by precipitating a major crisis, which was unnecessary, selfish, and severely damaging in its consequences.[29]

Achebe's view suggests that ethnic base became a *conditio-sin-qua-non* for the political class during the period preceding 1960. In fact, the event of 1953 in the Eastern House of Assembly:

> contributed in no small measure to the suspicion of the majority Igbo by their minority neighbours in Eastern Nigeria – a suspicion that far fewer politicians than Eyo Ita fanned to red-hot virulence, and from which the Igbo have continued to reap enmity to this day.[30]

Ethnic consciousness in the political arena found its way into Nigeria's academic circle as two pivotal incidents portray. First, Eni Njoku, an Igbo Professor of Botany, had nurtured the University of Lagos from its embryonic stage as the premier Vice-Chancellor, luring academics from across the globe. However, Njoku's second-term bid as Vice-Chancellor was torpedoed (despite endorsement by the University Senate) by Samuel Ladoke Akintola's Western Region Government, which gave full backing to the candidature of S. O. Biobaku, a Yoruba Professor of History, because in their opinion, "Lagos was a Yoruba city and the University ought to be headed by a son of the soil."[31] The second instance was when Kenneth O. Dike, University of Ibadan's first indigenous Vice-Chancellor, had to en-

---

27 Sklar, *Nigerian Political Parties*, 121–124; Omu, "Ethnicity, Nationalism and Federalism," 180.
28 Achebe, *The Trouble with Nigeria*, 5–8.
29 Achebe, *The Trouble with Nigeria*, 58–59.
30 Achebe, *The Trouble with Nigeria*, 59.
31 Arthur A. Nwankwo, *The Making of a Nation: Biafra* (London: C. Hurst and Company, 1969), 56.

dure the refractory display of insubordination from the institution's Bursar, who was of Yoruba extraction. On his departure from the institution, Dike lamented that the Nigerian intellectual had become "the greatest exploiter of parochial and clannish sentiments."[32]

To understand why the Yoruba began to act in parochial ways would be to first understand Azikiwe's statements in 1947 when he mused: "it would appear that the God of Africa had chosen the Igbo race to lead other African peoples."[33] The Yoruba understood this as a threat to Yoruba leadership and security, which must be checked. From this background, it appears, ethnic politics was designed to protect and promote parochial interests amidst struggles for national relevance. The struggle, however, has snowballed from the first republic, through the second, third and into the fourth, where the praxes of ethnic politicking have become more vitriolic.[34]

A Legal Lacuna?

The Nigerian constitution of 1999, as amended, has often been faulted by constitutional lawyers and, by extension, the generality of the Nigerian populace on many grounds. The general criticism is that it does not reflect the desire and aspirations of the various ethno-religious and cultural groups that make up Nigeria. For others, the constitution is not a true and logical encapsulation of what a secular state like Nigeria needs if the country must function appropriately to actualize the much anticipated economic growth and development. Notwithstanding, in this discourse, the lacuna in the constitution, which is to be examined, is if the document is vocal enough on the right of electorates residing outside their states of origin, and, if the right to vote as enshrined in the context of interna-

---

32 Pierre L. van den Berghe, *Power and Privilege at an African University* (London: Routledge and Kegan Paul, 1973), 224.
33 Anthony I. Nwabughuogu, "Unitarism Versus Federalism: A British Dilemma, 1914–1954," in *Foundations of Nigerian Federalism, 1900–1960*, 52; Hatch, *Nigeria*, 201.
34 Larry R. Jackson, "Nigeria: The Politics of the First Republic," *Journal of Black Studies* 2, no. 3 (1972): 277–303; P. C. Lloyd, "The Ethnic Background to the Nigerian Crisis," in *Nigerian Politics and Military Rule: Prelude to the Civil War*, ed. S. K. Panter-Brick (London: Athlone Press, 1970), 1–13; Diamond, *Class, Ethnicity and Democracy in Nigeria*, 23–25; B. Salawu and A. O. Hassan, "Ethnic Politics and its Implications for the Survival of Democracy in Nigeria," *Journal of Public Administration and Policy Research* 3, no. 2 (2011): 28–33; and Innocent Onyeanuna Ene, "Ethnicity: The Bane of Democracy and Development in Nigeria," in *Culture, Democracy and Development in Nigeria*, ed. Alexius Amtaika (Austin: Pan-African University Press, 2017), 95–105.

tional law, and ratified, is well articulated in the amended 1999 Nigerian constitution.

As already established in existing democracies, the right to vote is strictly hinged on the tenets of democracy, and democracy has been re-echoed across the globe as a fundamental and core value system within the framework of the United Nations. Oludolapo Makinde, a constitutional lawyer, muses: "the principle of holding periodic and genuine elections by universal suffrage are essential elements of democracy. As such, the right to vote is an indispensable right and the fulcrum upon which democracy rests."[35] The question, therefore, is why harass electorates who desire to exercise their constitutional franchise in line with global best practices?

As a member of various international governmental (ING) and non-governmental organizations (NGOs), Nigeria has ratified various instruments that expressly support the right of her people to vote and be voted for. For example, Article 25 of the International Covenant on Civil and Political Rights holds that every citizen has the right "to vote and to be elected at genuine periodic elections, which shall be by universal and equal suffrage and shall be held by secret ballot guaranteeing the free expression of the will of the electors."[36] Incidentally, the myriad of threats and physical attacks on electorates in a bid to coerce them into voting against their will has become a recrudescence in Nigeria, particularly in Lagos State, and the offenders go unpunished.

In view of the extent to which electoral thuggery and violence has continued to dot Nigeria's political landscape in recent election seasons, it is "disconcerting to discover that voting rights in Nigeria are not guaranteed under Chapter IV of the constitution, which [invariably] stipulates the fundamental rights that accrue to every Nigerian citizen."[37] It is possible that Section 77, Registration of Voters Act (Section 1(2), as well as the Electoral Act (Section 12 (1) might be misinterpreted as ensuring the right to vote. However, a thorough examination of the Act shows otherwise since these laws are arguably more concerned with the proper registration and eligibility of voters, as well as the procedure and bases for putting forth challenges in fraudulent elections in the tribunals. Unfortunately, the right to vote as enshrined in many international legal conventions has not been expressly articulated in Nigeria's 1999 constitution. This lacuna has created grounds for voters' abuses, attacks and undue coercion by anti-democratic persons and groups. The attack on non-indigenes by indigenes, witnessed during

---

35 O. Makinde, "1999 Constitution and Right to Vote," *The Punch Newspaper,* 22 February 2018.
36 Makinde, "1999 Constitution and Right to Vote."
37 Makinde, "1999 Constitution and Right to Vote."

the 2019 general elections, would not have occurred if the right-to-vote and other protection clauses were expressly captured in the constitution. These omitted clauses would have prevented any form of attack or bullying during elections. Besides, the level of impunity witnessed during elections in Nigeria could as well be informed by the fact that unscrupulous politicians and their thugs act as being above the law.

Besides contravening the 1999 constitution, attacks on non-indigenes during elections in Lagos State negate the principle of the 'One Nigeria' project. The attacks on the Igbo and attempts to coerce them into voting candidates against their will show that the One Nigeria project is a mirage. For instance, in 2015, during a forum with Igbo leaders in Lagos, ahead of the governorship election, Oba Rilwan Akiolu verbally threatened that Igbo residents in Lagos who refused to vote for the APC-governorship candidate, Akinwumi Ambode, risked being drowned in the Lagos lagoon.[38] This became known as the lagoon threat. Such a statement makes one to ponder whether Lagos is not one of the federating units in Nigeria; and, if the right, as enshrined in the constitution, on freedom for citizens to reside in any part of Nigeria is mere rhetoric.

Politics of the Lagoon and the Trailing Reactions: Building Blocks for 2019 Attacks?

Scholars and political pundits have discerned events characterizing the 2015 general election in Nigeria via the socio-economic,[39] political and ethno-religious[40] conduits. Ebenezer Obadare contextualizes the degree of influence Pentecostalism has had on the politics of Nigeria since 1999.[41] Obadare, however, alludes that the traditional institution, unlike Christianity and Islam, have not had as much impact on political decisions.[42]

---

38 Joe Agbro Jr., "Adaora Ukoh Lightens Up 'Lagoon Threat'," *The Nation*, 11 April 2015.
39 Emmanuel Shebbs and Ray Njoku, "Resource Control in Nigeria – Issues of Politics, Conflict and Legality as Challenge to Development of the Niger Delta," *Journal of Good Governance and Sustainable Development in Africa* 3, no. 3 (2016): 32–45.
40 John Paden, "Religion and Conflict in Nigeria: Countdown to 2015 Elections" (Washington DC: Special Report of the United States Institute of Peace, 2015), 1–13, https://www.usip.org/publications/2015/01/religion-and-conflict-nigeria (accessed 28 May 2019).
41 Ebenezer Obadare, *Pentecostal Republic: Religion and the Struggle for State Power in Nigeria* (London: Zed Books Ltd., 2018), 37–156.
42 Obadare, *Pentecostal Republic*, 73–123.

The 2015 election in Lagos was unique as it reaffirmed the fact that traditional rulers had long established themselves as a major force to be reckoned with during elections. After the 2015 presidential election in which President Goodluck Ebele Jonathan lost to General Muhammadu Buhari, Lagos, which doubled as the base and stronghold of one of APC's national leaders, Asiwaju Bola Ahmed Tinubu, was perceived to be in danger on the basis that many non-indigenes (particularly the Igbo) were set to vote for Jimi Agbaje, the PDP governorship candidate and not his APC rival. Consequently, Igbo leaders across Lagos were summoned to the Oba's palace for an emergency meeting, where Oba Akiolu issued a stern warning to them that jolted the social and print media. In reaffirming his implicit support for the APC candidate, Akinwumi Ambode, Oba Akiolu declared to Igbo leaders: "If anyone of you goes against the Akin Ambode I picked, that is your end! I tell you in the name of God Almighty Allah!"[43] Continuing with his threat, Oba Akiolu stated:

> because this [the throne] is an undivided chair, the palace belongs to the dead, the living and those who would soon come. On Saturday [making reference to the 2015 gubernatorial election day] if anyone of you, I swear in the name of God Almighty Allah, goes against my wish, that Ambode, Inshall Allah, would be the next governor of Lagos State, the person is going to die inside this water [lagoon]. I am not ready to beg or appeal to anybody [...] what you people [Igbo] cannot do in Onitsha, what you cannot do in Aba or anywhere, if you do what I want, Lagos will continue to be prosperous for you, if you go against it, you will perish in the water, finish![44]

Evidently, the Oba's threat epitomized an episode of ethnic politicking in Nigeria's Fourth Republic. As a royal father, Oba Akiolu has a duty to protect the interest and constitutional rights of everyone, irrespective of their ethnic, political or religious affiliation. The Oba's threat attracted serious attention from many quarters.

Reacting to the Oba's speeches, Dr Dozie Ikedife, a former president-general of *Ohaneze Ndigbo*, the Igbo apex socio-political and cultural body, notes "in as much as I do not believe that the Oba, with all his exposure and position made that statement, it should be sounded as a warning that the Igbo had [sic] been threatened enough in Nigeria."[45] Sensing the political damage the Oba's speech

---

43 "Raw Video: Oba of Lagos Threatens Igbos over Governorship Election," *Sahara Reporters*, 6 April 2015, http://saharareporters.com/2015/04/06/raw-video-oba-lagos-threaten-igbos-over-governorship-election (accessed 25 May 2019).
44 "Raw Video: Oba of Lagos Threatens Igbos."
45 Chimaobi Nwaiwu, "Oba's Threat: Ndigbo Cannot be Intimidated – Ikedife," *Vanguard Newspaper*, 7 April 2015.

could cost the party, the APC swiftly issued the statement: "the Oba does not speak for the APC. [...] Bad is bad, irrespective of where it comes from. We highly condemn the comments made by the highly respected Oba of Lagos in strong terms."[46] Moreover, the PDP's director of Media and Publicity, Femi Fani-Kayode, described the Oba's comment as "ominous and unacceptable."[47]

Notwithstanding the above reactions, two major points need exploring to make sense of the politics of the lagoon threat. First, the Oba's vituperation was not spontaneous. It echoes the manner in which non-indigenes had won elections in Lagos State. Pointedly, three non-indigenes on the platform of the PDP defeated at the polls indigenes of Lagos State who contested for the National Assembly (NASS) in 2015 on the APC platform. Barrister Rita Orji of Ajeromi Ifelodun (AJIF) Federal Constituency, for instance, unseated Honourable Taiwo Adenekan of the APC;[48] Honourable Tony Chinedu Nwulu, another Igbo from Mbaise Local Government Area of Imo State, won a seat to represent Oshodi-Isolo II Federal Constituency of Lagos State; and lastly, Chief Oghene Emmanuel Egboh, an Igbo from Delta State won Amuwo Odofin Federal Constituency.[49] The scenario became frustrating for many Lagos indigenes when the newly-elected Honourable Oghene Egboh remarked: "the noise about indigene and non-indigene should not come up. My victory is a testimony to the fact that Lagos belongs to everyone."[50]

Second, Oba Akiolu's threat was a strategy to help avert a repetition of what happened during the 2015 Presidential and National Assembly elections, as the gubernatorial and State House of Assembly elections had many non-indigenes from rival parties contesting against Lagos State indigenes in APC. Some of

---

46 Sani Tukur, "APC disowns Oba of Lagos over Threat to Igbos," *Premium Times*, 7 April 2015, http://www.premiumtimesng.com/news/top-news/180719-apc-disowns-oba-of-lagos-over-threat-to-igbos.html (accessed 20 May 2019).
47 Tukur, "APC disowns Oba of Lagos."
48 "Politics in Ajeromi/Ifelodun Local Government (AJIF) to Abuja," *Salvo Reporters*, 30 March 2018, http://salvonewspaper.com.ng/politics-in-ajeromi-ifelodun-local-government-ajif-to-abuja/ (accessed 12 June 2019); Tolani Abatti, "Lagos APC Loses Seven House of Reps Seats to PDP and Accord Party," *Encomium Magazine*, 8 April 2015, https://encomium.ng/lagos-apc-loses-seven-house-of-reps-seats-to-pdp-and-accord-party/ (accessed 12 June 2019); Sesan Olasupo, "Igbos Clinch 3 Rep Seats in Lagos as APC Loses 6 and Accord Party Wins 1 Seat," *Amazing Stories Around the World*, 31 March 2015, http://www.amazingstoriesaroundtheworld.com/2015/03/igbos-clinch-3-rep-seats-in-lagos-as.html?m=1 (accessed 13 June 2019).
49 "Igbo Candidates Win Lagos Reps Seats," 3 April 2015, https://www.pmnewsnigeria.com/2015/03/31/igbo-candidates-win-lagos-reps-seats/ (accessed 12 June 2019).
50 Charles Kumolu, "I've Opened the Way for Non-indigenes in Lagos – Oghene, Rep-Elect," *Vanguard Newspaper*, 6 May 2015.

these were: Jude Emeka Idimogu (PDP), an Igbo from Umuezeala-Abuke in Ihitte Ubuoma Local Government Area of Imo State and Ifeanyi Udeh of the All Progressive Grand Alliance (APGA), another Igbo, who contested against Olayinka Ajomale (APC), an indigene of Lagos State and son Lagos State APC chairman. The politics of the lagoon threat was therefore a proactive step to curtail what seemed like the use of the Igbo and other non-indigenes by the PDP and other parties, having realized the demographic force of non-indigenes, to grab political power in the state given the fact that population equates to political strength. Conversely, Oba Akiolu used the influence of his position to assist the APC for reasons outlined above. His outburst proved effective as subsequent elections in Lagos State went in favour of his preferred political party, APC.

The Igbo, Lagos, and the 2019 Elections: Some Reflections

Studies have shown that the paucity of arable land and fear of implosion led the Igbo of southeastern Nigeria to migrate to other parts of Nigeria.[51] However, as Roberts July notes "they have found not the relief they have craved for but political resistance and hostility."[52] Indeed, migration is not only peculiar to the Igbo, but a general phenomenon among other ethnic groups in Nigeria.[53] Influenced by colonial labour and economic policies, the movements from one location to the other took a new dimension as people began to seek for economic survivals in cities such as Lagos, Kano, Ibadan, Enugu, Port Harcourt, Onitsha and Aba,

---

51 Robert W. July, *Pre-Colonial Africa: An Economic and Social History* (New York: Charles Scribner's Sons, 1975), 130; Richard Henderson, *The King in Everyman: Evolutionary Trends in Onitsha Ibo Society and Culture* (New Haven, Connecticut: Yale University Press, 1972), 23–25.
52 July, *Pre-Colonial Africa*, 130.
53 A. Adepoju, "South-North Migration: The African Experience," *International Migration Review* 29, no. 2 (1991): 205–222; A. Adepoju, "Structure and Patterns of Rural Society in Relation to Internal Migration in Nigeria," in *Problems of Migration in Nigeria*, eds. I. O. Odumosu, S. A. Aluko and A. Adepoju (Ibadan: National Council of Social Work in Nigeria, 1976); Kevin M. DeJesus," Forced Migration and Displacement in Africa: Contexts, Causes and Consequences," *African Geographical Review* 37, no. 2 (2018): 78–82; Nora McKon, "Getting to the Root Causes of Migration in West Africa-Whose History, Framing and Agency Counts," *Globalization* 15, no.6, 2018: 870–885; G. W. Roberts, "Immigration of Africans into the British Caribbean," *Population Studies: A Journal of Demography* 7, no. 3 (1954): 235–262; Egodi Uchendu, *Islam in the Niger Delta, 1890–2017: A Synthesis of the Accounts of Indigenes and Migrants* (Berlin: Klaus Schwarz Publishers, 2018), 101–152.

among others.⁵⁴ Outside economic gains, the Igbo migrated to Calabar and Lagos due to the remarkable level of political culture that was present at that time, the result of the Clifford Constitution of 1922 that provided these cities with the privilege of having political representatives ahead of others.⁵⁵

The political scorecards of Azikiwe and other Igbo politicians in Southern Nigeria are reminiscent of how Igbo people contributed to the political culture of Nigeria.⁵⁶ Beyond the political milieu, the Igbo were at the forefront of stimulating economic activities in most regions of the country, as witnessed prior to and sequel to the Nigerian Civil War. Kate Meagher observes: "increased Igbo participation in the informal economy has fostered more cohesive social and economic relations with other Nigerian ethnic groups."⁵⁷ The point to note here is that the Igbo especially have been at the fore of the social, political and economic cohesion in Nigeria, with a view to attaining the 'One Nigeria' dream. But their efforts, oftentimes, were met with stiff opposition by their hosts. One important reason for Igbo rejection, which also leads to attacks on them across Nigeria, hinges on the stereotypes framed against them that date to the pre-independence era. These include narratives of untoward behaviour by the Igbo against their host communities. A typical one is the accusation that they always want to dominate their hosts. This became the guise for repeated attacks on them in Northern Nigeria resulting in loss of lives and properties.⁵⁸ It partly also formed the basis for what transpired in Lagos during the 2019 elections as will be discussed below.

---

54 S. O.Ọsọba, "The Phenomenon of Labour Migration in the Era of British Colonial Rule: A Neglected Aspect of Nigeria's Social History," *Journal of the Historical Society of Nigeria* 4, no. 4 (1969): 515–538; A. I. Akinjogbin, "The Economic Foundations of the Oyo Empire in the 18th Century," in *Topics on Nigerian Economic and Social History*, eds. A. I. Akinjogbin and S. O. Osoba (Ife: University of Ife Press, 1980); Carolyn A. Brown, "Locals and Migrants in the Coal-mining Town of Enugu (Nigeria): Worker Protest and Urban Identity, 1915–1929," *International Review of Social History* 60, no. S1 (2015): 63–94; Ihediwa Nkemjika Chimee, "Coal and British Colonialism in Nigeria," *RCC Perspectives* 5 (2014): 19–26.
55 Undiyaundeye, "The 1951 Elections," 242–252; Michael Crowder, *The Story of Nigeria* (London: Faber and Faber Ltd., 1962), 253.
56 Godwin Onuoha, "Contemporary Igbo Nationalism and the Crisis of Self-Determination in the Nigerian Public Sphere," *African Studies* 71, 1 (2012): 29–51.
57 Kate Meagher, "The Informalization of Belonging: Igbo Informal Enterprise and National Cohesion from Below," *Africa Development* 34, no. 1 (2009): 31–46.
58 Sylvester Adakole, "Migration, Animosity and the Impact of the Nigerian Civil War on the Idoma and their Neighbours, 1967–1970," *Kaduna Journal of Historical Studies* 3, no. 10 (2019): 198–212; Meagher, "The Informalization of Belonging," 31–46; and Leonard Plotnicov, "An Early Nigerian Civil Disturbance: The 1945 Hausa-Ibo Riot in Jos," *Journal of Modern African Studies* 9, no. 2 (1971): 297–305.

The elections in Lagos State in 2019 exposed two crucial facts. First, the Igbo residing in Lagos are a demographic force to reckon with given their population. As the then Action Congress of Nigeria (ACN) publicity secretary, Joe Igbokwe, declared in 2013, "Igbos [sic] constitute over 45 per cent of the population of Lagos and they dominate key sectors of the Lagos economy."[59] Second, the Igbo in Nigeria have since 2015 cried against marginalization by the APC-led federal government.[60] Therefore, considering themselves a demographic force in Lagos State, they thought it was better to vote the PDP at all levels in the hope that their lot would improve should the PDP retake power.

Coming to the marginalization of the Igbo in Nigeria, the general mood pointed towards voting for the PDP. This was despite the fact that the PDP had only two Igbo personalities – Dr Alex Ekwueme and Jim Nwobodo – among the founding members of the party.[61] Attempting to justify Igbo support for the PDP, Ayodele Adio observes: "the point is that PDP is not necessarily a party for or of the Igbos, it just appears to be the party that aligns with their [Igbo] interests in Lagos."[62] When the APC in Lagos State perceived that the Igbo would prefer to cast their vote for Alhaji Atiku Abubakar, the PDP presidential candidate from Northern Nigeria, instead of the APC candidate, General Muhammadu Buhari, also from the north, top-ranking members of the APC party made concerted efforts to entreat as well as persuade the Igbo in Lagos to vote for APC at all levels during the 2019 elections. In that vein, one of the national leaders of APC, Bola Ahmed Tinubu, "appealed to Igbo in Lagos State to vote APC candidates in February and March elections."[63] Tinubu reminded the Igbo, during a town hall meeting, of how Lagos State had never discriminated against them and their children and so there might be no better way to reciprocate this 'wonderful' gesture than for them to massively vote for the APC in the forthcoming elections. Ending his appeal, Tinubu warned that the APC "would monitor election results

---

[59] "Lagos is Safe for Igbo, Says CAN" *PM News*, 31 July 2013, https://www.pmnewsnigeria.com/2013/07/31/lagos-is-safe-for-igbo-says-acn/ (accessed 31 October 2020).

[60] Omeiza Ajayi, "Igbo marginalization will end when they join us APC, Nnamani," *Vanguard Newspaper*, 28 September 2017; Ojo Maduekwe, "Ngige, Buhari and marginalisation of the Igbo," *The Cable News*, 26 May 2017, https://www.thecable.ng/ngige-buhari-marginalisation-igbo (accessed 30 May 2020); E. N. Ota, *Igbo Ethnicity in Nigeria: Origin, Evolution, and Contemporary Forms* (Okigwe: Whytem Printing Press, 2017), 119–159.

[61] Ayodele Adio, "Lagos APC: Winning Over Igbo Voters with Carrots and note Sticks," *PM News*, 7 July 2019, https://www.pmnewsnigeria.com/2019/03/08/lagos-apc-winning-over-igbo-voters-with-carrots-not-sticks/ (accessed 7 July 2019).

[62] Adio, "Lagos APC: Winning Over Igbo Voters."

[63] "Tinubu Begs Igbo in Lagos, Osinbajo Appeals to Hausa Community for Votes," *The Punch Newspaper*, 20 February 2019.

in Igbo-dominated areas such as Amuwo-Odofin, Ojo, Ajeromi-Ifelodun and Surulere [Local Government Areas] in anticipation of votes for APC."[64]

In the light of the foregoing, it becomes pertinent to state that the 2019 elections in Lagos State became a convoluted issue between the Igbo and certain indigenes of the state. Aware of the marginalization of the Igbo by the Buhari-led government since 2015,[65] the APC in Lagos knew it would have to persuade the Igbo to vote for APC candidates. Thus, Tinubu and his associates covertly threatened to check Igbo voting patterns as a way of determining the outcomes of the elections. However, even with APC's appeals to the Igbo community in Lagos, results from various polling units after the 23 February 2019 Presidential and National Assembly General Elections showed that the majority of non-indigenes in Lagos, including, and especially, the Igbo, voted for the PDP whose presidential candidate won also the polling units of both the incumbent APC Vice President, Yemi Osinbajo, and the APC gubernatorial candidate, Sanwo-Olu.[66]

Although, ultimately, President Buhari was declared winner of a highly faulted election exercise, his party members in Lagos State were not pleased with the voting result in their state, which showed that Igbo-dominated areas massively voted for PDP. The actions of the Igbo and other non-Yoruba ethnic nationalities in Lagos State during that election sent distressing signals to Ahmed Tinubu and his associates, suggesting that the Igbo whom they entreated would need more than just mere diplomacy to tow their line. Consequently, the Igbo were attacked in places like Okota and Ijesha, among others. This happened when they tried to prevent political thugs who were determined to disrupt the voting after sensing that PDP was leading in most polling units in those vicinities. At the conclusion of voting, sporadic attacks on the Igbo also occurred. Those attacked were accused of not voting President Muhammadu Buhari for a second term.[67] Thugs sympathetic to the APC kept chanting that the "Igbo should go back to their states to do business; that this is Lagos."[68] One of hoodlums espouses thus:

---

64 "Tinubu Begs Igbo in Lagos."
65 Ajayi, "Igbo marginalization will end;" Maduekwe, "Ngige, Buhari and marginalisation of the Igbo."
66 Adejumo Kabir, "Elections: How prominent Nigerian politicians lost in their polling units," *Premium Times*, 27 February 2019, https://www.premiumtimesng.com/news/headlines/316538-elections-how-prominent-nigerian-politicians-lost-in-their-polling-units.html (accessed 08 July 2019); Chux Ohai, et al, "Osinbajo, Sanwo-Olu lose Lagos polling units to Atiku," *The Punch Newspaper*, 24 February 2019.
67 Interview with Onyekachi Okpara, b. 1970, Okota, Lagos, 27 June 2019.
68 "Hoodlums attack Igbo traders on Lagos Island for failure to vote for Buhari," *PM News*, 27 February 2019, https://www.pmnewsnigeria.com/2019/02/27/hoodlums-attack-igbo-traders-on-lagos-island-for-failure-to-vote-for-buhari (accessed 08 July 2019).

> We campaign [sic] for them to vote for Buhari, but they refused and voted for Atiku. They cannot come here to do business again. They must follow us to vote whoever we ask them to vote for. This is just a sample for them, if they ever vote for PDP again, that will be their end.[69]

Reacting to the attacks on the Igbo, Femi Fani Kayode posted on his Facebook page: "I condemn the attack on the Igbo in Lagos. I can confirm that those that attacked them were not members of the OPC but rather APC thugs..."[70] Following Kayode's example, Yoruba indigenes of Lagos State and their kit and kin from other states in southwestern Nigeria, challenged the actions of these hoodlums on the grounds that their acts were totally against the law.[71] Some reasoned that such attacks on the Igbo by the Yoruba would only create more disunity in Southern Nigeria against a more united north. Besides, the attacks were practical contraventions to the constitutional provisions on electoral laws; not to mention that such attacks raise pertinent questions on the essence of constitutionalism with respect to Chapter Four of the 1999 constitution because they grossly negate section 38, dealing with freedom of thought and conscience, and section 39, on freedom of expression, and section 41, on freedom to reside in any part of Nigeria, among others.[72] As a matter of fact, very few condemnations of the attacks came from the APC and the Lagos State government. Nonetheless, various pan-Igbo groups reacted swiftly. The national leader of Biafra Nations Youth League (BNYL), Princewill C. Richard, commented as follows:

> I think it is foolish of southerners to fight and die for two northern brothers; the Western leaders should calm the situation if they don't want war in Lagos... Igbos and other tribes from the east should wage a fight back if the attacks continue... No tribe can push the Igbo away from areas they occupy and develop.[73]

---

69 "Hoodlums attack Igbo traders."
70 Femi Fani-Kayode, 24 February 2019 (07: 09 p.m.), "I Condemn the Attack on the Igbos in Lagos," https://m.facebook.com/story.php?story_fbid=10157137180317210&id+62188827209 (accessed 08 July 2019).
71 Onyekachi Okpara, interview cited. And C. Ezeobi, "Again, Hoodlums attack traders in parts of Lagos," *This Day Newspaper*, 28 February 2019, https://www.thisdaylive.com/index.php/2019/02/28/again-hoodlums-attack-traders-in-parts-of-lagos/ (accessed 30 May 2020).
72 "1999 Constitution of the Federal Republic of Nigeria and Fundamental Rights (Enforcement Procedure) Rules," 2008.
73 F. Olowolagba, "Presidential results: Biafra group warns Yorubas, tells Igbos next action in Lagos," *Daily Post*, 26 February 2019, https://www.dailypost.ng/2019/02/26/presidential-results-biafra-group-warns-yorubas-tells-igbos-next-action-lagos/ (accessed 8 July 2019).

Richard's statement raises a critical question that hovers on Igbo development of Lagos State. This will be discussed in the next section.

Igbo Contribution to the Development of Lagos State: What Relevance to Voting Right?

The 2019 elections for the umpteenth time established the truism that the Nigerian political space is still saturated with unbearable ethnic sentiments. It was so visible that indigenes of a federating state in Nigeria would attack non-indigenes over rights to vote, even when such a right is inalienable. A right that has been expressed in several international conventions to which Nigeria, a federal republic, is signatory. Nigeria's disinclination to domesticate such legal structures has left enormous gaps in her electoral laws. Why consent to an international legal instrument when there is no plan to domesticate such a law? Obviously, this has ensured that the violation of citizens' rights to vote is not given serious legal attention whenever it occurs.

While the domestication of the right-to-vote is yet to be instituted in the constitution, there is need for the Igbo to come to terms with certain realities of contemporary Nigeria. Arguably, economic power has been equated to political power.[74] However, that supposition could be far from the realities in Nigeria. Thus, the Igbo must discern if their economic activities that stimulate development in Lagos and other states in Nigeria are enough to influence political outcomes given the depth of ethnic politics in Nigeria.

As the 2019 elections rolled out in Lagos, the argument that the Igbo contributed significantly towards the development of Lagos was rife on social media. Many argued that since the Igbo have played significant roles towards the economic development of Lagos State through their trading ventures in the state's major markets – Mandilla, Balogun, Computer Village, Alaba International Market, Aspamda and the Lagos Trade Fair; and also infrastructurally, they deserve the freedom to vote according to their consciences. On the contrary, Yoruba indigenes disagreed. Skibanj Gbeleyi, a card-carrying member of the APC and an aspirant for the Lagos State House of Assembly in the 2019 elections, who sought to represent Oshodi-Isolo Local Government Area, but "was asked to step down for

---

74 A. Wood, *The Politics of Social Conflict: The Peak Country, 1520–1770* (Cambridge: Cambridge University Press, 2009), 19.

the incumbent, Akeem Shokunle,"[75] responded to the question of the role of the Igbo towards the development of Lagos State on Facebook as follows:

> The Igbo would say they developed Lagos. If they have such power how come they couldn't develop their own space [Eastern Nigeria]? [...] If Yorubaland is underdeveloped, Igbo will not move their [sic] daily. Igbo didn't develop Lagos; rather, it is Lagos that shaped and made the Igbo what they are today. Without Igbo in Lagos, most Igbo may likely be nothing. They [Igbo] are dirty, stinky, rough, erect illegal shops on the roads, on pipeline and railway lines indiscriminately in these market places that [causes] traffic gridlocks and other dangerous situations. So how have the Igbo shaped and developed Lagos? In fact, most Igbos are causing nuisance in Lagos. [...] The election in Yorubaland is about Yoruba people. If the Igbo people do not like it, they must leave our space. Nigeria is a country of many nations. [...] The Igbo might be citizens of Nigeria, only they are not Yoruba and can never have the same rights and privileges as the Yoruba in Yorubaland. Nigeria is different from Yorubaland. Yorubaland belongs to the Yoruba people, while Igboland belongs to the Igbo people.[76]

The above, which is the personal opinion of the author, again shows how the Igbo are perceived among the Yoruba, at least, with respect to their role in the economic development of the state. Strengthening the foregoing position, Yemi Okon who witnessed the political crises surrounding the 2019 elections in Lagos, posits that it would be foolhardy for the Igbo to continue nursing the mentality of developing Lagos when their home areas are in dire need of development.[77] Okon argues that buying lands and building houses in Lagos State is no wise investment, especially as the southeast is yet to be developed. To him, the argument that since Igbo has contributed towards the economic development of Lagos is not enough ground for them to meddle in the political circle of Lagos State.

The argument as to whether the Igbo have contributed towards the socio-economic development of Lagos State, thus warranting their unsolicited influence in the socio-political circle, has remained an age-long debate among scholars and political analysts. The argument is even made more vitriolic given the fact that many ascribe to Lagos a 'no man's land' status due in part to the multi-

---

[75] Chukwudi Jackson, "Hon. Gbeleyi (SKIBANJ) offers free Jamb forms/tutorial in Oshodi-Isolo Local Government," *Voice for the Voiceless*, 28 January 2020, https://freevoiceforthevoiceless.wordpress.com/2020/01/28/hon-gbeleyi-skibanj-offers-free-jamb-forms-tutorial-oshodi-isolo-local-government/ (accessed 29 October 2020).

[76] Skibanj, 2 March 2019 (03: 40 p.m.), "The Igbo claim over Lagos," Facebook, 3 May 2019, https://m.facebook.com/groups/156215808394854?view=permalink&id=298230820860018.

[77] Interview with Yemi Okon, b. 1965, Uyo, Akwa Ibom State, 28 February 2019.

ple layers and concentric circles surrounding her history.[78] What then needs to be asked is: could the couched claim of Lagos as a 'no man's land' be the reason for the role of the Igbo in the economic development of the state? And, even if this assertion is true, what is the extent of development of the Igbo in Lagos State, which warrants any sort of political influence like the free exercise of the right to vote without intimidation or harassment? Several positions and counter-positions to these questions suffice.

For instance, perturbed by the rate at which Asiwaju Bola Ahmed Tinubu, governor of Lagos State from 1999 to 2007, enlisted many non-Lagos indigenes, including the Igbo, in his cabinet, certain stakeholders of Lagos State under the aegis of Committee of Indigenous Association of Lagos State (CIALS), formed in 2002, queried such incursion.[79] Then, L.O.T. Adams, Secretary of Eko Pioneers, expressed the views of most indigenes of Lagos State in a published article titled "No Vacancy for Igbos in Lagos Politics," which appeared in the *Guardian Newspaper* of 25 March 2002. In reaction, Joe Igbokwe countered with an argument outlining the contributions of the Igbo to the economic development of Lagos:

> You cannot be collecting billions from people and deny them their democratic rights of being involved in how you are spending the money. If Lagos has twelve commissioners and Nigeria is truly a nation-state, there is no reason why six of such commissioners should not come from outside Yoruba stock. If Governor Ahmed Bola Tinubu who is not from Lagos State can be voted in as the governor of Lagos State, there is no reason whatsoever, why somebody from any part of Nigeria cannot be voted as governor of Lagos State.[80]

Igbokwe's submissions compelled another Lagos indigene, R. O. Ojikutu, of the University of Lagos, to ask: "How many indigenes of Lagos are counselors in the South-East? [...] Are Lagosians not living and paying tax in the South-East? [...] Are the Yorubas not paying tax in Anambra?[81] However, beyond such debates, there has been an unprecedented flourishing of studies showing in statistical terms how the Igbo contributed massively towards the economic development of Lagos. For instance, Olarenwaju A. Olutayo provides concrete insights on how since the twentieth century, traversing the colonial period, Igbo entrepreneurial activities helped to enhance the economic growth of Lagos and most

---

78 Ayodeji Olukoju, "Which Lagos, Whose (Hi)Story?" *Lagos Notes and Records*, 2018, https://www.academia.edu/43040512/Which_Lagos_Whose_Hi_Story (accessed 29 October 2020).
79 R. T. Akinyele, "Lagos is our land: Indigeneship associations and the protection of the rights of Lagosians since 1950," *Lagos Historical Review* 15, no. 1 (2015): 89–110. DOI: 10.4314/lhr.v15i1.6.
80 Akinyele, "Lagos is our land."
81 Akinyele, "Lagos is our land."

other states across Nigeria. Specifically, Olutayo argues that by the time of Nigeria's independence, Igbo people, through their communal association, had 68, 220 members in credit associations, the highest of any group, as compared to 5, 776 for the west and 2, 407 for the north.[82] Using more recent data, S. Maliga stated that 74 percent of investments in Lagos State belongs to the Igbo, 5 percent to the Hausa-Fulani, 15 percent by non-Nigerians, and 5 percent to other Nigerians, whereas only 1 percent is owned by the Yoruba people.[83] While making a strong argument for why the Igbo people are the right candidate to take Nigeria to a greater height given their widespread investments across Nigeria, Clement Udegbe, a lawyer, remarks:

> In Lagos, Igbo investment is not less than ₦300 trillion; it is double of that in Abuja at about ₦600 trillion. In Kano and Kaduna, Igbo investments run up to ₦10 trillion respectively; while in Borno, Yobe and Adamawa States, Igbo investment run into ₦5 trillion respectively. In plateau State Igbo investment is hovering over ₦15 trillion! [...] There is no state in Nigeria where Igbo investments in business do not exceed ₦5 billion.[84]

Deducing from the analyses so far, is it any wonder why at the slightest provocation, businesses and properties belonging to the Igbo, whether in Lagos, Kano, Kaduna or any other part of Nigeria, easily come under attacks by their hosts? And there have been countless attacks on the group since 1945 when the earliest civil disturbance occurred in Jos, Plateau State with wanton destruction of businesses and properties of the Igbo in Jos.[85]

The point here definitely transcends the economic contributions of the Igbo people towards the growth and development of Lagos State to include their constitutional privileges of voting and being voted for elsewhere within federal Nigeria. Of course, the issue of who should vote and be voted for can be properly addressed through the instrumentality of the right to vote clearly expressed in international conventions ratified by the Nigerian government. We conclude this section by quoting Professor R. T. Akinyele who noted: "the central issue in the indigene/settler crisis in Lagos centres around the distinction between citizenship and indigeneship in a country that is struggling to achieve the goal of unity and diversity. The possibility of resolving the conflict is remote since the

---

[82] Olarewanju Akinpelu Olutayo, "The Igbo Entrepreneur in the Political Economy of Nigeria," *African Study Monograph* 20, no.3 (1999):147–174.
[83] S. Maliga, "Igbo dominate economically in Lagos because Yoruba's are lazy," 11 October 2013, https://www.Elombah.com (accessed 29 October 2020).
[84] Clement Udegbe, "The Igbos have more at stake in Nigeria," *Vanguard Newspaper*, 26 July 2013.
[85] Plotnicov, "An Early Nigerian Civil Disturbance," 297–305.

politicians can always make it an election issue."⁸⁶ Therefore, the issue of whether Igbo has contributed towards the economic development of Lagos State or not is inconsequential, as politicians would always find a way to stir up issues between the indigenes of Lagos State against non-indigenes especially when their political ambitions are at stake.

Conclusion

One of the concrete observations of this chapter is that the Nigerian political space has remained saturated with ethnic sentiments, which in most cases become virulent during elections. The chapter also established the fact that no ethnic group would condone the unsolicited interference of another ethnic group in their political spaces because doing so could undermine the interests of the aggrieved ethnic group. However, ethnic politics, which took root in the scheme of colonial activities as early as 1941, has undermined the process of democratization in Nigeria's Fourth Republic as evident in both the 2015 and 2019 general elections. Issues like the attacks on the Igbo in Lagos State, which revolve around electoral malpractices, could have been averted, for instance, if the right-to-vote document had been domesticated by Nigeria. The attacks translate into a wake-up call to the Nigerian government to duly domesticate the international instruments it is signatory to.

---

86 Akinyele, "Lagos is our land," 89–110.

Chikaodili Arinze Orakwue
Thuggery and Election Violence in the 2019 Election

Abstract: From the beginning of the Fourth Republic, Nigeria's political experience witnessed increasing intergroup rivalry, thuggery, arson, intimidation, banditry, assaults, harassments, kidnappings and assassinations, among others. Electoral violence has played a significant role in the disintegration of the country's electoral process. Attitudes of politicians and their supporters have also complicated the search for a truly democratic process. This chapter provides an analysis of the political violence witnessed in the 2019 general election. It identifies the trends and phases of electoral violence, and explains their impact on the social and economic wellbeing of Nigerians. A qualitative research methodology was used for this study. The research findings show that the 2019 general election was marred by violence perpetrated by the youth leading to the cancellation of election results in some states and the announcement of inconclusive elections in others. To consolidate Nigeria's democracy, there should be real dialogue between political candidates and voters, and intentional re-education of the electorate. These would make the militarization of the electoral process, as seen in 2019, unnecessary.

Keywords: election, violence, political parties, thuggery and democracy

Introduction

Elections have become the most acceptable means by which eligible citizens of an ever-increasing number of political systems choose their leaders.[1] They are one of the fundamental duties of citizens in a democratic society. In an ideal sense, elections enable people to choose the kind of politicians they want to represent their interest in the government. Unfortunately, elections in Nigeria, and in much of Africa, have gendered much violence that attracted international attention. According to Igbuzor, electoral violence is any act of violence perpetrat-

---

[1] Tony Ogechi Kalu and D. E. Gberevbie, "Election violence and Democracy in Nigeria: A Study of the 2011 and 2015 General Elections in Lagos State," *Kaduna Journal of Humanities* 2, no. 1 (2018): 60–70.

Chikaodili Arinze Orakwue, Erasmus University, Rotterdam, Hague, Netherlands

ed during political activities including during pre-election, election and post-election periods.² These may include any of the following: thuggery, the use of force to disrupt political meetings or voting at polling stations, or the use of dangerous weapons to intimidate voters, interfere with other electoral processes or cause bodily harm or injury to any person connected with the electoral processes. Electoral violence is one of the greatest obstacles to a peaceful democratic process in Nigeria.³ Most election violence occur during intra-party and inter-party activities and, to a greater extent, affects the quality of election results, the rule of law and the entire democratic practice. Violence also affects the degree to which an election is adjudged free and fair, or transparent.

Nigeria can be rightly described as one of the most deeply divided nations in Africa.⁴ From her beginning as a colonial state, Nigeria has faced a perennial crisis of territorial or state legitimacy, which challenged several efforts at national unity, democratization, stability and economic transformation. Her politicians, over the years, have become more desperate and daring in taking and retaining power; more reckless and greedy in their use and abuse of power; and more intolerant of opposition, criticisms and efforts to replace them.⁵ Politicians and their allies have on occasion organized election violence to actualize their ambitions. They achieve their untoward goals by exploiting regional sentiments, ethnic prejudice, religious intolerance, economic greed and sectional desire for political domination.⁶ Often, the youth are mobilized to serve these ends. Armed with weapons, their youth groups organize as political thugs and prosecute elections in their clients' favour by unleashing violence in order to disrupt the political process and the elections.⁷ These youth are hardly arrested and charged for causing havoc because of the protection from their political masters, which they earn as 'compensation' for their services. Undoubtedly, youth are at the heart of most violent conflicts in the country, and responsible for between 90 to 95 per-

---

2 Otive Igbuzor, "Electoral violence in Nigeria" (Asaba, Action Aid Nigeria, 2010).
3 Neville Obakhedo, "Curbing Electoral Violence in Nigeria: The imperative of political education," *African Research Review* 5, no. 5 (2011): 99–110.
4 Louis Cohen, Lawrence Manion and Keith Morrison, "The ethics of educational and social research," in *Research methods in education* (London: Routledge 2013), 99–128.
5 E. E. Alemika and E. O. Etannibi, "Criminal victimization, policing and governance in Nigeria," *CLEEN Foundation Monograph 18* (2013): 1–81.
6 Anthony Egobueze and Callistus Ojirika, "Electoral Violence in Nigeria's Fourth Republic: Implications for Political Stability," *Journal of Scientific Research and Reports* 13 (2017): 1–11.
7 Reuben Sarki and Agatha Orji-Egwu, "Political Thuggery and the Challenge of Electioneering during the 2019 General Elections in Nigeria," *Journal of Mass Communication* 6 (2019): 115–125.

cent of violent political conflicts in Nigeria.[8] They were at the centre of the 2019 electoral violence.[9]

Many of Nigeria's ostensibly elected leaders obtained their positions by demonstrating an ability to use corruption and political violence to prevail in sham elections.[10] Through violent and brazenly rigged polls, government officials have denied millions of Nigerians any real voice in selecting their political leaders. Nigerian youths have been denied political positions for a very long time. Following sustained public dialogue of their exclusion, the age reduction bill was signed into law by President Muhammadu Buhari in May 2018 to make elective positions accessible to youth and thereby encourage their political aspirations. The timing of the bill, incidentally, did not make room for the youth to join the political race and stand for election in 2019. Lack of resources and the expensive nature of elections in Nigeria also undermined youth capacity to participate in the election as candidates for elective positions.

This chapter empirically analyses electoral violence in this Fourth Republic with emphasis on the 2019 elections. It also investigates the dimensions to which political violence has negatively affected democratic process in Nigeria, creating room for the impending destruction of the current republic if not quickly reversed. Violence is a pervasive phenomenon in every society.[11] It cuts across every aspect of human existence, including politics. The tendency to exhibit violence especially in relation to politics is inevitable, but the nature of the display varies from one political system to another. The European Union Election Observation Mission (EU EOM) reported that violence, vote trading and intimidation of voters characterized the 23 February 2019 general election in Nigeria.[12] The mission observed that election across the nation was disturbed and that both the Independent National Electoral Commission (INEC) and security agencies did little

---

8 Francis Oluwaseun Ogbeide, "Youths' Violence and Electoral Process in Nigeria's Fourth Republic: A Case Study of Ota, Ogun State, Nigeria," *International Journal of Education and Research* 1, no. 9 (2013): 1–14.
9 U. G. Ojukwu, C. C. Mbah and V. C. Maduekwe, "Elections and Democratic Consolidation: A Study of 2019 General Elections in Nigeria," *Direct Research Journal of Social Science and Educational Studies* 6, no. 4 (2019): 53–64.
10 Human Rights Watch, *Election or Selection? Human rights abuse and threats to free and fair elections in Nigeria"* (New York; 2007).
11 Kalu and Gberevbie, "Election violence and Democracy," 60.
12 EU EOM Nigeria, " EU election observation mission final report with recommendations for electoral reform (2019)," https://eeas.europa.eu/election-observation-missions/eom-nigeria-2019/64167/press-release-eu-election-observation-mission-nigeria-publishes-final-report (accessed 26 September 2019).

to address the violence and malpractices that occurred in many parts of the country.

Since 1999, Nigeria's elections have historically been fraught with controversy, violence and other abuses.[13] In the 2011 general elections, unprecedented post-election violence was witnessed in the country and about 800 people were killed while more than 65,000 were displaced.[14] The 2015 general election also witnessed large scale violence both before, during, and after the election. In 2019, Human Rights Watch reported that 629 people were killed. There were also reports of voter intimidation and violence within the election cycle both at the federal and state levels. An Africa-focused market intelligence and communications consulting firm, SBM Intel, provided intelligence reports from 14 October 2018 to 19 February 2019 that catalogued 233 incidences of election violence from 67 districts in the six geopolitical zones of Nigeria.[15] States particularly affected by electoral violence during the gubernatorial election were Kogi, Benue, Kaduna, Bauchi, Kano, Sokoto, Plateau and Rivers states. Kano and Rivers were probably the worst hit. They were identified by both local and international analysts ahead of the elections as holding great potential for electoral violence.[16] Both states (Kano and Rivers) were major political strongholds for the two leading political parties, the All Progressives Congress (APC) and the opposition People's Democratic Party (PDP). The Independent National Electoral Commission eventually cancelled elections in places where the elections were disrupted and held supplementary elections later.

Conceptual Clarifications

Ojo regards election as a "formal expression of preferences by the governed, which are then aggregated and transformed into a collective decision about who will govern, who should stay in office, who should be thrown out and

---

[13] Joseph C. Lemchi and Bassey Inyang, "2019 Electoral Violence," *African Journal of Social and Behavioural Sciences* 9 (2019): 374–384.
[14] Human Rights Watch, *Nigeria: Post-Election Violence Killed 800* (New York: Human Rights Watch, 2011).
[15] Birch Sarah and David Muchlinski, "Electoral violence: Patterns and trends," *Electoral Integrity and Political Regimes: Actors, Strategies and Consequences* (2018): 100–112.
[16] Human Rights Watch, "Nigeria: Widespread Violence Ushers in President's New Term," https://www.hrw.org/node/330919/printable/print.

who should replace those who have been thrown out."[17] An election is a procedure that allows members of a given society to choose representatives who will hold positions such as leaders of local, state and national governments.[18] It is an important mechanism for the employment of administrative governance in the democratic social order, a major involvement in a democracy and the way of approving a regime.[19]

Robert traces modern and democratic elections to the seventeenth century as a means through which modern democracies and newly independent colonies can choose those to represent them in governance and effective management of the commonwealth of the country to the benefit of all.[20] The conduct of elections into governmental offices is always preceded by some preparatory events and political schemes such as the internal selection of party contestants ahead of the contest against candidates from competing parties. Other strategies range from campaigns, political movements, lobbying, promotions and private connections.[21] Vote-casting is not as easy as it may initially look, with several experts and researchers classifying it as the turning points for violent acts. This is supported by the Nigerian experience where vote casting during elections has become the climax for violence and uncertainty in many states.[22]

Democracy has no universally accepted definition as various scholars have different interpretations for it. What is important is that people are central to any democratic process; and without giving people the power to elect their leaders and hold them accountable, democracy would be a mirage. In his classic definition, Abraham Lincoln defined democracy as the government of the people, by the people and for the people. To Diamond, Linz and Lipset, democracy as a system of government entails healthy competition between parties for an all effective position of governance, devoid of violence for an all-encompassing

---

17 O. M. Ojo, "Electoral security and democratic consolidation in Nigeria," in *Nigeria's Internal Security Challenges: Strategies for Sustainable Development*, eds. G. Ikuejube and D. Z. Olupayimo (Ibadan: John Archers, 2014), 1–28.
18 Ayo Awopeju, "Election Rigging and the Problems of Electoral Act in Nigeria," *Afro Asian Journal of Social Sciences* 2, no. 2 (2011): 1–17.
19 Neville O. Obakhedo, "Curbing Electoral Violence in Nigeria: The imperative of political education," *African Research Review* 5, no. 5 (2011): 99–110.
20 Henry M. Robert, Daniel H. Honemann and Thomas J. Balch, *Robert's Rules of Order Newly Revised 11th edition* (Hachette, UK: Capo Press, 2011), 438–446.
21 J. O. Adeyemi and R. A. Gbadeyan, "Nigerian Electorates' Perception of Political Advertising and Election Campaign," *Research Journal of Social Sciences* 1, no. 5 (2010): 52–60.
22 Tersoo Johnkennedy Ikyase and Anthony Ejue Egberi, "Political Violence and Democratic Stability in Nigeria: Reflecting on the past and Chatting the Way Forward," *Review of Public Administration and Management* 400, no. 3617 (2015): 1–9.

level of political involvement in the selection of leaders through the conduct of periodic free and fair elections, fundamental human rights and political participation.[23] This system of governance offers participatory opportunities for citizens to choose reliable representatives from a pool of political aspirants through periodic elections.[24] It also assures the electorate's fulfilment and promotes the rule of law when elected leaders act responsibly towards the electorate. Any democracy that fails to consider the citizen's vote and voice is not a practicing democracy. A democracy promotes citizens' participation in the entire electoral process.

The concept of electoral violence is made up of two distinct concepts: electoral and violence. The word electoral in the opinion of Bamgbose is the process involved in the conduct of elections either at the public or private level.[25] The electoral process at the public level involves planning and conducting elections to choose representatives of the people in public offices of governance, such as the executive, legislative and judicial arms of government, at state and national levels.[26] Similarly, at the private level, it includes all the processes involved in the successful conduct of elections into other types of groups, other than those of government, such as associations and clubs.[27] On the other hand, scholars have examined the concept of violence from diverse perspectives and these relate to either positive or negative views towards achieving a given goal. Johan Galtung refers to violence as the cause of the difference between the potential and the actual.[28] He categorized violence into three: physical violence, structural violence and psychological violence. Zizek, on the other hand, affirms that violence also takes three forms: subjective, objective and systemic.[29] Subjective violence is with a clear perpetrator such as crime or terror, objective violence is always invisible and widespread that comes through racism, discrimination and hate speech, while systemic is embedded in the disastrous effect of an economic

---

[23] Larry Diamond, Juan Linz and Seymour Martin Lipset, *Democracy in Developing Countries: Latin America* (London: Rienner, 1989).
[24] K. Ajayi, "Problems of Democracy and Electoral Politics in Nigeria," in *Issues in Nigerian Government and Politics,* ed. D. Kolawole (Ibadan: Dekaal Publishers 1998), 37–42.
[25] A. J. Bamgbose, "Electoral Violence and Nigeria's 2011 General Elections," *International Review of Social Sciences and Humanities* 4 (2011): 205–219.
[26] Bamgbose, "Electoral Violence and Nigeria's 2011 General Elections."
[27] Robert, Honemann and Balch, *Robert's Rules of Order,* 438–446.
[28] Johan Galtung, "Violence, peace, and peace research," *Journal of Peace Research* 6, no. 3 (1969): 167–191.
[29] Slavoj Žižek, *Violence: Six Sideways Reflections* (London: Picador, 2008).

or political system, making it inherent in the system.[30] In the opinion of Bamgbose, violence is a choice, an art and a force that negates agency.[31]

Electoral violence is one of the major problems that have affected Nigeria's democratic sustainability, undermining her achievement of good governance.[32] It manifests as thuggery, brutality, hooliganism, gangsterism, assassination, intimidation, ballot box snatching, destruction of election materials, injuring voters or opponents and disruption of political process with dangerous weapons.[33] The act of thuggery often perpetrated by the youth, under the watchful eyes of politicians, is an interference with huge consequences on democratic stability and national security. Across Nigeria, different youth groups serve politicians during elections. In the South-West geopolitical zone, they go by the name 'area boys.' Coming to the north, they go by the name *Karare* in Kano State; *yan daba*, *kwaye* or *yan mage* in Kaduna State; *sara suka* in Bauchi State; and *ecomog* in Borno State.[34] These youth bands are composed of unemployed and unskilled self-employed persons.

Trends, Dynamics and Phases of Political Violence in the Fourth Republic

Under the current Fourth Republic, Nigerians went to the polls in 1999, 2003, 2007, 2011, 2015 and 2019. These elections recorded series of violent events before, during and after the process. The 1999 elections had a minimal record of violence largely because the military supervised the exercise.[35] The 2003 elections, conducted by President Olusegun Obasanjo's administration who also was seeking his second tenure in office, were characterized by manipulations, rigging, thuggery and the assassination of perceived political opponents. The ruling PDP swept the polls and consolidated its hold on the country's political landscape. After completing two terms as president, Obasanjo's administration con-

---

30 Žižek, *Violence: Six Sideways Reflections*.
31 Bamgbose, "Electoral Violence."
32 Daniel Eseme Gberevbie, "Democracy, democratic institutions and good governance in Nigeria," *Eastern Africa Social Science Research Review* 30, no. 1 (2014): 133–152.
33 Reuben Sarki and Agatha Orji-Egwu, "Political Thuggery and the Challenge of Electioneering during the 2019 General Elections in Nigeria," *Journal of Mass Communication* 6 (2019), 115–125.
34 Shankyula Tersoo Samuel, "Political thuggery and elections in Nigeria and the law," *Law and security in Nigeria* 2 (2011): 24–53.
35 Olakunle Olowojolu, et al., "Trends in Electoral Violence in Nigeria," *Journal of Social Sciences and Public Policy* 11, no. 1 (2019): 37–52.

ducted perhaps the worst election in Nigeria's history. The 2007 election was preceded by his assertion that it would be a "do-or-die" event for the ruling PDP. Animashaun identified massive irregularities in that election, characterized by inflation of votes, declaration of results where elections were never held or not conclusive, intimidation of voters as well as manipulation of security personnel.[36] Also, scores of political killings, bombings and armed clashes between rival political groups were reported.[37] The outcome of the 2007 elections generated much controversies and widespread condemnation from both local and international observers. President Obasanjo admitted shortcomings in the election with the comment: "Our elections could not have been said to have been perfect, cases of electoral fraud were reported from parts of the country."[38]

Shortly after assuming office as the next president, Musa Yar'adua instituted an Electoral Reform Committee headed by Justice Uwais intending to correct the ills in Nigeria's electoral system. Some of the recommendations of the Committee, which were included in the amended Electoral Act, are: appointment of the chairman of the Independent National Electoral Commission (INEC) by the National Judicial Council rather than the president; funding INEC through the consolidated revenue of the federation; having a time limit for electoral petition; and setting up special Electoral Offences Commission to prosecute electoral offenders. Yar'adua's administration also promoted non-interference in the judiciary as manifested in the various judgments over electoral disputes dispensed at both the election tribunal and the appeal courts. Gubernatorial elections in states such as Ekiti, Osun, Edo and Ondo that were initially declared to have been won by the PDP were upturned in favor of the Action Congress of Nigeria (ACN) and the Labour Party (LP) respectively.[39]

The 2011 elections were adjudged by many observers as the most credible election organized by INEC since 1999. Terence McCulley, the United States' Ambassador to Nigeria, praised the National Assembly election as the first-ever "credible, transparent, free and fair general election" in Nigeria, and declared that it provided a "historic opportunity for Nigeria to consolidate its democracy

---

[36] M. A. Animashaun, "The 2007 elections and the imperative of electoral reform in Nigeria," *Covenant Journal of Business and Social Sciences* 1 (2008): 123–141.

[37] Human Rights Watch, *Election or Selection?*

[38] C. McGrel, "Ruling party candidate wins 'flawed' Nigerian election," *The Guardian*, 23 April 2007, https://www.theguardian.com/world/2007/apr/23/chrismcgreal. (accessed 25 November 2020).

[39] C. C. Aniekwe and J. Kushie, "Electoral violence situational analysis: Identifying hotspots in the 2011 general elections in Nigeria" (Report submitted to National Association for Peaceful Elections in Nigeria, Abuja, 2011).

and further expand its voice on the world stage."⁴⁰ In the same vein, EU Election Observation Mission to Nigeria confirmed that "the 2011 general elections marked an important step towards strengthening democratic elections in Nigeria, but challenges remain."⁴¹

However, before the 2011 presidential polls, some northern politicians including Adamu Ciroma, Iyorchia Ayu, Lawal Kaita, Bello Kirfi, Yahaya Kwande and Bashir Yusuf Ibrahim wrote a letter to the PDP National Chairman on 17 September 2010 requesting the party leadership to restrain Vice President Goodluck Jonathan from contesting the 2011 presidential election under the party's platform. The group argued that the eight-year, two-term presidency mandate the late president Umaru Yar'Adua could not complete should be given to a candidate from that geopolitical zone rather than his deputy taking over the leadership. The group warned that the failure of the ruling PDP to apply the principle of zoning would threaten the stability of Nigeria, saying; "we are extremely worried that our party's failure to deliver justice in this matter (power shift to the North) may ignite a series of events, the scope of the magnitude of which we can neither proximate nor contain."⁴² Inflammatory messages sent through social media worsened the tensions created by religious and ethnic mobilisation by supporters of the two major presidential candidates: Goodluck Jonathan and Muhammadu Buhari.

The northern states of Adamawa, Bauchi, Borno, Gombe, Jigawa, Kaduna, Kano, Katsina, Niger, Sokoto, Yobe and Zamfara were thrown into chaos and anarchy after Dr Goodluck Jonathan was declared the winner of the 2011 presidential election. According to Human Rights Watch, about 800 lives were lost in post-election violence in those states.⁴³ Similarly, they noted that more than 65,000 people were displaced after the post-election violence.⁴⁴ The Nigerian Red Cross Society released a slightly lower figure indicating that the violence displaced 48,000 persons in 12 states.⁴⁵

In the run-up to the 2015 elections, Nigeria's security challenges had become worrisome, especially in some states in the north where the Islamist insurgency group, Boko Haram, became active in 2009. The CLEEN Foundation Secur-

---

40 C. Agbambu and A. Ajay, "US Rates Nigeria's Elections High, Says Country Made History with April Polls...," *Nigerian Tribune*, 29 April 2011.
41 EU EOM, *EU Observation Mission to Nigeria: Final Report on the 2011 General Elections* (Abuja: European Union, 2011).
42 N. Abdallah, "Zoning: Nwodo Snubs Ciroma, Ayu, Others," *Sunday Trust*, 10 October 2010.
43 Human Rights Watch, *Nigeria: Post-Election*.
44 Human Rights Watch, *Nigeria: Post-Election*.
45 Human Rights Watch, *Nigeria: Post-Election*.

ity Threat Assessment published in March 2015 found that 15 states were at high risk of electoral violence. The National Human Rights Commission (NHRC) in its pre-election report stated that at least 58 persons had been killed even before the conduct of the 2015 general election.[46] There were also changes in the political configuration of the country as could be seen in the formation of a mega opposition party, the All Progressives Congress (APC). Formed in 2013, APC was the amalgamation of the following political parties: the Congress for Progressive Change (CPC), the Action Congress of Nigeria (ACN), the All Nigeria People's Party (ANPP), and a faction of the All Progressive Grand Alliance (APGA). A former military ruler, Major General Muhammadu Buhari was picked as the presidential flag bearer for the APC. Meanwhile, the PDP that had dominated Nigeria's political space since 1999 chose the incumbent president, Dr Goodluck Jonathan, an Ijaw from the South-South geopolitical zone, as its presidential candidate. Both the South-East and South-South geopolitical zones adopted Dr Jonathan as their candidate of choice for 2015.

INEC, under the leadership of Professor Attahiru Jega, introduced the use of Smart Card Readers (SCR) and Permanent Voters Card (PVC) for the 2015 elections. Card readers were effectively used, and ensured credible elections, in Ghana, Kenya and Sierra Leone.[47] Introducing same technology in Nigeria was to reduce electoral fraud and irregularities, which in the past impaired Nigeria's electoral process. No doubt, both the Smart Card Readers and Permanent Voters Card improved the quality of elections. The Smart Card Readers ensured the authentication, verification and accreditation of voters to prevented electoral fraud and irregularities during the election.[48] However, there were some drawbacks attributed to their performance such as the malfunctioning of some of the card readers and inability to authenticate some permanent voters card.[49] Generally, the introduction of the SCR improved the efficiency of the voting process and increased the electorate's confidence in the electoral process, but other issues such as management of the elections, weak democratic institutions and widespread insecurity defined the overall election outcome.[50] Notwithstanding all the checks

---

[46] CLEEN Foundation, "Nigeria 2015 elections: Electoral Risk and Hot Spot Mapping" (2015), https://cleen.org/security-briefs/ (accessed 22 September 2019).
[47] Pamela Ukwueze, "48 Smart card readers and Nigeria's 2015 election: To be or not be. (2015). https://www.democracyspeaks.org/blog/smart-card-reader-and-nigeria%E2%80%99s-2015-election-be-or-not-be (accessed 24 September 2019).
[48] "The Card Reader as Hero of 2015 Election," *Daily Trust Nigeria*, 6 April 2015.
[49] A. Fatai, "Smart card readers and the quality of the 2019 general elections in Nigeria: successes and challenges," *The Round Table* 109, no. 4 (2020): 396–405.
[50] Fatai, "Smart card readers."

put in place for a successful electoral experience in 2015, INEC reported 66 cases of violent incidents across the country. This is broken down by the state in Table 1 below.

Table 1: Reported incidents of election violence in the 2015 election

Reported incidents by State	Number
River State	16
Ondo	8
Cross Rivers	6
Ebonyi	6
Akwa Ibom	5
Bayelsa	4
Lagos	3
Kaduna	3
Jigawa	2
Enugu	2
Ekiti	2
Kastina, Kogi, Plateau, Abia, Imo, Kano, Ogun	1 each

Source: *Vanguard*, 12 April 2015.

The European Union Election Observation Mission also reported that about 30 people were killed on 11 April 2015, the election day, as a result of inter-party clashes and attacks at election sites.[51] The roles of certain personalities and the international community in ensuring a peaceful election cannot be overemphasized. A former Minister of Foreign Affairs, Professor Bolaji Akinyemi, appealed to the major presidential contestants to sign a Memorandum of Understanding (MOU) that would commit them to control their supporters against

---

[51] Olowojolu Olakunle, Rasak Bamidele, Ake Modupe, Ogundele Oluwaseun and Afolayan Magdalene, "Trends in Electoral Violence in Nigeria," *Journal of Social Sciences and Public Policy* 11, no. 1 (2019): 37–52.

violence after the 2015 general elections.[52] Similarly, the National Peace Committee for the 2015 general election, led by the former Head of State, General Abdulsalami Abubakar (Retd.), facilitated peace accord between Major General Buhari and President Jonathan.[53] Concerned that Nigeria would degenerate into anarchy, the United States' Secretary of State, John Kerry, visited Nigeria and held separate discussions with President Jonathan and Major General Buhari on the 2015 elections.[54]

Overall, the 2015 election exercise was declared quite successful and more credible than every other election since the commencement of the Fourth Republic. Thus, Muhammadu Buhari who previously contested for the presidency in 2003, 2007 and 2011 won the contest against President Goodluck Ebele Jonathan. The finest hour during the general polls was the noble character displayed by President Jonathan when he accepted his defeat and ensured a smooth transition that ushered in Buhari's administration on 29 May 2015.

The 2019 General Election

Professor Mahmood Yakubu, who replaced Attahiru Jega as the chairman of INEC, conducted the sixth general election in Nigeria's Fourth Republic. Between his assumption of office in November 2015 and the 2019 general election, his team had conducted 196 off-season governorship and other by-elections. The announcement of the date for the 2019 elections was made two years earlier, precisely on 9 March 2017. INEC created a strategic plan from 2017 to 2021.[55] The objectives of the strategic plan include:
a) Provide electoral operations, systems and infrastructure to support delivery of free, fair and credible elections;
b) To improve voter education, training and research;
c) To register political parties and monitor their operations;
d) To interact nationally and internationally with relevant stakeholders;
e) To strengthen INEC for sustained conduct of free, fair and credible elections

---

[52] U. G. Ojukwu, C. C. Mazi Mbah and V. C. Maduekwe, "Elections and Democratic Consolidation: A Study of 2019 General Elections in Nigeria," *Direct Research Journal of Social Science and Educational Studies* 6, no. 4 (2019): 53–64.
[53] Ojukwu, Mbah and Maduekwe, "Elections and Democratic Consolidation," 53–64.
[54] M. Gordon, "Kerry Meets with Nigerian Leaders to Encourage Peaceful Election," *The New York Times*, 25 January 2011.
[55] "INEC Strategic plan 2017–2021," https://www.inecnigeria.org/downloads-all/inec-strategic-plan-2017-2021 (accessed 8 December 2020).

INEC's programme booklet for the 2019 General Election showed that Nigeria had 84 million registered voters out of which 72 million voters obtained Permanent Voter Cards (PVC). It provided information on the 91 registered political parties contesting in the 2019 election; 119,973 polling units; 120 accredited domestic observers, 36 accredited foreign observers and the 23,000 candidates competing for 1,558 positions.[56] Seven elections were also conducted over two Saturdays namely: the Presidential, Senate and House of Representatives elections on 23 February 2019; and the Governorship, State Houses of Assembly, Chairmanship and Councillorship elections of the six Area Councils of the Federal Capital Territory which were held on 9 March 2019.

The election of the president, vice-president, members of the Senate and House of Representatives, which initially was scheduled for 16 February 2019, was eventually postponed by one week. INEC announced the postponement at (03:00 am) on the original polling day, citing logistical challenges in getting electoral materials to polling stations on time.[57] The Institute for Peace and Conflict Resolution, Abuja, had deployed its staff for election observation and, this author, a member of the organisation, was posted to Nasarawa State as a domestic observer. Waking up to the news of the postponement of the general election, we still went out to observe people's reactions. The electorate in Nasarawa were peaceful but many were disappointed by the postponement after they had travelled out of their states of residence to their states of origin where their voting centres were located in order to participate in the election. In states like Rivers, Lagos and Anambra, elections were delayed further by two additional days due to electoral violence, while polling in some areas such as Akoko Tulo and Boni Local Government Areas of Rivers State was deferred until 9 March 2019.[58] In these areas, voting for the federal officials – the president and vice president, senators and representatives – went alongside voting for gubernatorial and state assembly officials.

The results of the presidential election were announced in the early hours of 27 February 2019 and the incumbent President Muhammadu Buhari won his re-election bid, by defeating his closest rival Atiku Abubakar with over 3 million alleged votes. Buhari was declared winner by INEC. He was issued a certificate of return and sworn in on 12 June 2019.[59] Immediately after the elections, there were

---

56 "INEC Strategic plan 2017–2021."
57 "INEC Strategic plan 2017–2021"
58 Msugh Ityokura, "2019: INEC postpones elections in Lagos, Rivers and Anambra State, *The Guardian*, 24 February 2019.
59 Ojukwu, Mbah and Maduekwe, "Elections and Democratic Consolidation."

claims of widespread fraud by the unsatisfied parties in the election and the claims included accusations of ballot box snatching, vote-trading and impersonation. Several reports were released from different observer groups on the 2019 general election. The African Union observer team observed that the elections were largely peaceful. The coalition of NGOs reported that the election failed to meet the threshold of credibility and doubts the future of elections and the quality of Nigerian democracy.[60] The electoral commission also described the elections as the most peaceful. Yet, the 2019 election fell short of expectations. A lot of votes were cancelled by INEC in places where the main opposition candidate were leading on claims that the election was marred by violence, over-voting and non-adherence to the use of Smart Card Readers.[61] Yet, it was observed that while non-adherence to use of Smart Card Readers was applied in opposition enclaves, it was waived in the incumbent's strongholds. Other issues that played out during the 2019 elections were vote buying or financial inducements by APC and PDP party agents at polling stations.[62] The deployment of military officers to the poling units undermined the integrity of the 2019 election because it heightened voter apathy, human rights violations and also strained civil–military relations in the country.[63]

The scenario at the national level was also observed during the state-level election. Millions of cancelled votes resulted in five inconclusive governorship elections in Kano, Sokoto, Plateau, Adamawa and Benue States. Supplementary elections were held in polling units where votes were cancelled. Another unprecedented event in the annals of Nigeria's electoral democracy was INEC's review of the decisions of its Returning Officers in Imo West Senatorial election and Bauchi State governorship election. In the former, the Returning Officer for that election, Professor Innocent Ibeawuchi, alleged that he was forced to announce that the former governor of Imo State, Rochas Okorocha, won the senatorial seat for Imo West district. Ibeawuchi was reportedly held hostage from 19:00 hours (7:00 pm) on Sunday 24 February 2019, till 11:00 hours (11:00 am) on Monday 25 February 2019. Out of fear of being killed, he announced the result of the election, which he claimed was inconclusive because of alleged electoral

---

[60] The Nigerian Civil Society Situation room, "Coalition of NGOs report on 2019 presidential election," *Vanguard*, 1 August 2019).
[61] Ojukwu, Mbah and Madukwe, "Elections and Democratic Consolidation."
[62] Ruth Maclen and Elomo Egbejule, "Nigeria's Election Marred by Vote buying, Technical failure and Violence," *The Guardian*, 23 February 2019.
[63] Freedom Chukwudi Onuoha, Joachim Chukwuma Okafor, Oluwole Ojewale and Chigozirim Okoro, "Militarisation of the 2019 general elections and electoral integrity in Nigeria," *The Round Table* 109, no. 4 (2020): 406–418.

fraud in eight Local Government Areas. For supposedly being made to declare result under duress, INEC withheld the Certificate of Return for Okorocha.[64] This decision of INEC's is what a democratic institution should do for a credible electoral process. The court judgement of the federal high court in Abuja later ordered INEC to release the certificate.

In Bauchi State, INEC similarly reviewed the declaration of its Returning Officer concerning the nullification of the result in the Tafawa Balewa Local Government Area. According to the commission, its investigative panel found out that halfway into collation, armed gangs attacked the collation centre and destroyed the Local Government Result Sheet (EC8C) and some collated results from the Registration Areas. The results of seven out of eleven registration areas for governorship, and six out of the eleven areas for the state assembly, elections were affected. The collation officer, also under pressure from party agents who could not wait for the arrival of a replacement result sheet, decided to collate results on an available Registration Area (RA) result sheet instead of the replacement Local Government Result Sheet. These incidents portray the level of interference recorded across the country during the collation of results in the 2019 general election, showing another major weakness in the Nigerian democratic process.

The European Union observation team stated in their report that the 2019 general election was violated and rigged with over 40 percent of returned results by INEC Returning Officers voided and nullified by courts of competent jurisdiction and election tribunals.[65] Reports and feedbacks, from Centre for Democracy and Development (CDD) and Policy and Legal Advocacy Centre (PLAC) that monitored the election in 8,809 polling units spread across the 36 states and the Federal Capital Territory, indicated that a lot of challenges were faced at some of the collation centres monitored. They reported logistics challenges from INEC offices, misconduct, inefficiency and poor technical knowledge of INEC ad-hoc staff; security lapses and intimidation of collation staff by security agencies; inappropriate activities of political thugs and party agents; and the denial of access to media and observer groups.[66]

After dealing with arson in Anambra, Abia and Plateau States, and the postponement of 2019 general election, more challenges lurked around for INEC as apathy threatened the next round of voting slated for federal officials. The citi-

---

64 Ojukwu, Mbah and Madukwe, "Elections and Democratic Consolidation."
65 Sodiq Omolaoye, Shegun Olaniyi and Lawrence Njoku, "Controversy Intensifies over EU Election Report," *Vanguard*, 17 June 2019.
66 Christian Chidi Okeke, "Critical Evaluation of Nigeria's 2019 Presidential Election," *Afro Asian Journal of Social Sciences* 10, no. 9 (2019): 1–36.

zens appeared to have lost confidence in the election. Someone remarked after the postponement of the original dates of election: "I don't trust the system to conduct the elections and I couldn't have risked my life as a result of today's exercise, I stayed home with my family monitoring on TV."[67] After voting, another citizen lamented the lack of confidence in the election due to violence and irregularities.[68] Other challenges INEC confronted concerned questionable figures, which influenced electoral victories against the wishes of the people, especially as results were reportedly declared at gun points.

Social and Economic Implications of Election Violence in Nigeria

The weaponising of election by arming youth with small arms and light weapons to perpetrate election related violence destroys the fabric of any democratic process.[69] The deadly act of thuggery and violence during election eventually became a problem for those youth who after being used for electoral violence were abandoned to their fate afterwards. Since no political contract was signed with their clients, they return to their jobless status after the exercise. Some resort to drug addiction, armed robbery and kidnapping, aided by their possession of arms.

Election violence also negatively impacts on economic activities in the society. When large-scale violence breaks out, economic activities are disrupted leading to losses for individuals directly affected and the government. This was demonstrated during the 2019 election when three INEC offices were gutted by fire in Plateau, Anambra and Akwa Ibom States. In addition to the infrastructures destroyed, PVCs, Smart Card Readers and other sensitive materials were lost. The economic loss on the Nigerian government was huge. The overall electoral violence in 2019 forced the government into making extra budgetary spending to finance the reconstruction of destroyed facilities at the expense of other developmental programmes.

Another implication of electoral violence is communal disruption. About 65,000 persons were displaced during the 2019 election.[70] This exacerbated

---

[67] Mercy Abang, "Voter apathy apparent in Nigeria's local elections" (2019), https://www.aljazeera.com/news/africa/2019/03/voter-apathy-apparent-nigeria-local-elections-190309141520691.html (accessed 25 July 2020).

[68] Abang, "Voter apathy apparent in Nigeria's local elections."

[69] Imran AbdulRahman and Sesan A. Peter, "Political and Economic Effects of Post-Election Violence on National Development," *Journal of Social Science* 6 (2018): 18–26.

[70] Human Rights Watch, *Nigeria: Post-election violence killed 800.*

the vulnerability of people already displaced by the Boko Haram insurgency in Nigeria's North East geopolitical zone. Many ended up in Internally Displaced Persons (IDP) camps while those that ran across the border became refugees. The refugee problems that accompany these disturbances also have implications for social development such as education and reduction in health standards leading to maternal mortality and childhood deaths.[71] Cumulatively, election violence occasions a humanitarian emergency.

Concluding Remarks

The main findings from the study show that political violence has become a key strategy employed by Nigerian politicians during elections in order to secure political positions at state and federal levels. In this process, the youth population is exploited as unemployed and self-employed ones are recruited to dispense violence during elections. And when the season is over, the youth thugs become social miscreants. The situation calls for thorough electoral reforms that would ensure free, fair and credible elections in Nigeria. Recommendations for improved democratic experience in Nigeria include:

a) *The reform and activation of national electoral laws:* Nigeria does not need a national conference to deliberate on a new Electoral Act. The already existing and workable electoral laws, which hitherto spoke only on paper, should be implemented. In addition to this, the Electoral Reform Bill presented to the president ahead of the 2019 election season should be passed and signed into law. If all prohibited electoral misdemeanour received their due legal punishment, political violence will decline considerably in Nigeria.

b) *Enlisting citizens in the fight against electoral violence:* Unless the citizenry determinedly resist the temptation of being used by politicians to perpetrate violence, the fight against political violence will remain an exercise in futility. The electorate should be intentionally educated along this line in order to achieve this goal.

c) *Incumbent political office holders should resign before contesting elections:* Incumbent political office holders should not be allowed to re-contest for political positions without first resigning from their positions some two or three months to election. The power of incumbency, which has introduced phrases

---

[71] Tyavwase Theophilus Aver, Kingsley C. Nnorom and Aondowase Targba, "Political Violence and its Effects on Social Development in Nigeria," *International Journal of Humanities and Social Science* 3, no. 17 (2013): 261–266.

like "carry go," "do-or-die" and "mandatory second term" into the body-politick of the nation, should be stripped.

d) *Youth empowerment is key to the reduction of electoral violence:* Empowering unemployed youth through gainful employment will make this category self-sufficient and therefore not easily coaxed into violence, especially electoral violence. Legal action taken against defaulting youth would strengthen the resolve of others in resisting illegal electoral work as political thugs.

Further, the absence of proper democratic institutions militates against the sustainability of democracy in Nigeria. Democracy is a system of government that promotes citizens' participation in the entire electoral process; and without an election, democracy cannot be achieved. In the words of Gberevbie, "democratic institutions are mechanisms for the facilitation of the democratic process for the election of public officeholders in any democratic society."[72] On this basis, therefore, a democratic institution like the Independent National Electoral Commission (INEC) should put in place structures and election ethos to enable the conduct of smooth and credible elections built on the notion of "one man, one vote."[73]

---

72 Gberevbie, "Democracy, democratic institutions and good governance."
73 Gberevbie, "Democracy, democratic institutions and good governance."

Nsemba Edward Lenshie, Isa Mohammed and
Patience Jacob Kondu

Electoral Politics and Violence in Taraba State

Abstract: The character of electoral politics in Nigeria, since the restoration of democracy on 29 May 1999, has left so much to be desired. No matter how free, fair and credible past elections were, electoral violence trailed them, making it impossible to separate electoral politics from electoral violence especially at the sub-national level. Using data from surveys and documented evidence to interrogate the 2019 general election in Taraba State, North East Nigeria, the authors argue that the nature of the political competition, patron-clientele politics, supporters' polarization and ethnic or religious manipulations were responsible for the electoral violence in the state in 2019. Consequently, reducing the high stakes in the election by decentralising political and economic power to local governments will make electoral politics competitive, attractive and viable, and also minimize the susceptibility for electoral violence in Taraba State.

Keywords: democracy, Taraba State, electoral politics, electoral process, electoral violence, political competition and voting

Introduction

The restoration of democratic rule in Nigeria in 1999 has generated a highly contentious and violent political atmosphere in the country.[1] The uncommon nature of the electoral process – being free from contentions and violence – is factored from the contested patterns of the election, whether it is at the national or state level.[2] Nigeria's electoral process and its hotly contested nature had, over the

---

[1] E. Onwudiwe and Chloe Berwind-Dart, "Breaking the Cycle of Electoral Violence in Nigeria" (Washington DC: United States Institute of Peace Special Report 263, 2010), https://www.usip.org/sites/default/files/SR263Breaking_the_Cycle_of_Electoral_Violence_in_Nigeria.pdf.
[2] O. Peter Mbah, Chikodiri Nwangwu and Sam C. Ugwu, "Contentious Elections, Political Exclusion and Challenges of National Integration in Nigeria," *Cogent Social Sciences* 5, no. 1 (2019): 1–21.

Nsemba Edward Lenshie, Isa Mohammed and Patience Jacob Kondu, Taraba State University, Jalingo, Nigeria

https://doi.org/10.1515/9783110766561-013

years, produced electoral violence with varying casualty rates. Casualties from the 2003 and 2007 elections numbered 57 and 226 respectively. The number appreciated to 800 in 2011 but reduced to 49 in 2015.[3] In the 2019 general election in which the People's Democratic Party (PDP) and All Progressives Congress (APC) were dominant forces, 58 persons died from election related incidents.[4]

In Nigeria, election violence occurs anytime during the electoral process. However, most occur after the elections. The 2011 general election provides a notable example.[5] Nigeria's elections are commonly characterised by violence because the control of political office confers both the opportunity to exert power and to amass wealth. Because election is a means to an end in Nigeria, it is highly characterized by patron-client politics, monetisation of the electorate and tense manipulations of regional, ethnic and religious identities.[6] The national character of electoral politics is also evident at the subnational level. In Taraba State, North-East geopolitical zone, since 1999, electoral politics have leaned towards political zoning as well as ethnic and religious identities. The characterisation of electoral politics along these considerations commonly results in electoral crises in the state. Inter-party and intra-party politics, political competition, recruitments and mobilizations broadly reflect these dynamics. The roles of the traditional and religious leaders and institutions equally contribute significantly in shaping the character of electoral politics in the state. For instance, in 2019, their roles in the electoral process were remarkably felt in two key areas: determining preferred candidates and negotiating electoral choices for the electorates.

The intricacies of electoral politics in Taraba State during the 2019 general election was interposed by two intense bouts: first, the political rivalry and manipulative tendency among politicians struggling to capture state power; and, second, the divisiveness of the electorate tied to the increasing concentration of electoral politics along with ethnic and religious identities. These factors significantly triggered violence. As a corollary, this chapter investigates the dynamics and dialectics of electoral politics and violence in the 2019 general election in

---

[3] N. Orji, "Preventive Action and Conflict Mitigation in Nigeria's 2015 Elections," *Democratization* 24, no. 4 (2016): 707–723.
[4] Friday Olokor, "58 Nigerians Killed in 2019 Elections – Situation Room," *Punch*, 10 March 2019.
[5] Dorina Bekoe, "Nigeria's 2011 Elections: Best Run, but Most Violent" (Washington DC: United States Institute of Peace Peace Brief 103, 2011), https://www.usip.org/sites/default/files/PB 103.pdf.
[6] E. Ikechi Onah and Uche Nwali, "Monetisation of Electoral Politics and the Challenge of Political Exclusion in Nigeria," *Commonwealth and Comparative Politics* 56, no. 3 (2018): 1–22.

Taraba State in order to understand how competition among politicians and their manipulation of the electorate along ethnic, and importantly religious, identities contributed to electoral violence in the state that year. The chapter is organised into five sections. Following the introduction, section two sets out the background to electoral politics in Nigeria and how it manifests in Taraba State. It includes the study methodology, and provides some conceptual clarifications. Section three examines the electoral scenario in Taraba State in 2019, and four interrogates electoral politics, political violence and casualties in the general election. Lastly, the conclusion and recommendations form the content of section five.

The Background

Taraba State is situated in the North-East geopolitical zone in Nigeria. The former military Head of State, General Ibrahim Babangida, created it from the defunct Gongola State on 27 August 1991. The state covers a land area of about 54,473 Km^2. It is situated within latitude 7° 59' N, 10° 00' N and longitude 10° 58' E, 13° 00' E. The population of the state was estimated at 2,294,800 in 2006.[7] In 2019, the Nigerian Investment Promotion Commission gave the state's population as approximately 3,249,970.[8] Taraba State is bounded by Nasarawa and Benue States to the west; Plateau State, Bauchi and Gombe States to the north; Adamawa State and the Republic of Cameroon to the east and south. Taraba State is ethnically diverse across its 16 Local Government Areas (LGA) and two Special Development Areas. The state has three senatorial districts, with each consisting of five local government areas except the Northern Senatorial District that has six. The entire state has 168 wards and 1,912 polling units from which the political competitors' votes are determined through the electoral process. Each ethnic group in the state is distinct in terms of language, culture and tradition. Christianity and Islam have very strong presence in the state, with Christianity being dominant.

This study follows a qualitative research methodology. It is based on the triangulation techniques such as the focus group discussion (FGD), in-depth interview and documented evidence approach. The triangulation is motivated by the fact that they complement each other in generating useful data. In conducting

---

[7] Nigeria Data Portal, "Nigeria Census," http://nigeria.opendataforafrica.org/xspplpb/nigeria-census# (accessed 23 August 2019).
[8] Nigerian Investment Promotion Commission, "Nigerian States – Taraba State," https://nipc.gov.ng/nigeria-states/taraba-state/ (accessed 10 July 2019).

FGDs, Jalingo, Zing, Wukari, Takum, Sardauna and Bali Local Government Areas were selected purposively because of their ethnic and religious heterogeneity, political diversity and susceptibility in almost every election to contention and violence. In each of these areas, the researchers, assisted by field research assistants, conducted one FGD each between May and June 2019 with the focus on the 2019 general election in the state. The composition of each FGD group ranged from 7 to 10 persons who have attained the age of suffrage. What mattered in the selection were participants' level of political awareness, knowledge and involvement in electoral politics and not necessarily their level of education.

Politicians from different political parties, voters and electoral observers featured in the in-depth interviews. Among them were active political stakeholders from both the Christian and Islamic faiths and election observers who had participated in the electoral process in the three senatorial districts. Participation in the in-depth interviews was entirely voluntary. The approach was conversational and flexible. This was meant to generate the required viewpoints while looking for "patterns, themes, relationships, sequences and differences"[9] presented by the participants for understanding and interpreting their individual and collective opinions on the issues under investigation.[10] Documented sources on the 2019 general election were also integrated in the study. These were either state-owned or independently produced records available in the public or private domains. They included visual media, personal diaries and periodicals on the 2019 electoral process in Taraba State.[11] The purpose went beyond understanding the manifest contents to grasping the latent contents of these documented materials to uncover the regular patterns of data related to this study.[12]

Electoral politics and electoral violence, like other concepts in the social sciences, are without universal conceptualisation. At the core of participatory democracy is electoral politics, which is the whole gamut of the electoral process and the election itself. Election starts with politics and ends with politics. Electoral politics, therefore, is a catalogue of activities involving political competi-

---

9 M. de Hoyos and Sally-Anne Barnes, *Analysing Interview Data* (Warwick: Warwick Institute for Employment Research, 2012), https://warwick.ac.uk/fac/cross_fac/esrcdtc/coretrainingmodules/quals/analysing_interview_data_1_-_w6.pdf.
10 S. Kvale, *Interviews: An Introduction to Qualitative Research Interviewing* (Thousand Oaks, CA: SAGE Publications Inc, 1996).
11 M. Helm, "The spectrum of qualitative research – the use of documentary evidence" (paper presented at the Qualitative Evidence-based Practice Conference, Coventry University, 15–17 May 2000), http://www.leeds.ac.uk/educol/documents/00001391.htm (accessed 10 July 2019).
12 Buttolph J. Johnson and Richard A. Joslyn, *Political Science Research Methods* (Delaware: CQ Press, 1995); M. Biereenu-Nnabugwu, *The Methodology of Political Inquiry: Issues and Techniques of Research Methods in Political Science* (Enugu: Quintagon Publishers, 2006).

tion, political recruitment, consciousness building, group mobilisation, interest articulation, communication, and participation.[13] It is a game involving the electorate and the political competitors struggling for state power. In democracies, electoral politics provide the bases for, and the guide that enables, the electorate to make rational decisions during elections. However, the choices the electorates make by voting a particular candidate or party depends on certain tradable incentives. Scholars attribute three reasons for different patterns of electoral choices. The first consists of the psychosomatic choices or attractions (including primordial identities as in the case of Nigeria).[14] The second consists of goals and policies which political parties or candidates present to the electorates that incentivise them.[15] The third consists of the incentive which the electorates gain or would gain as individuals, groups or community in return for their support and votes.[16]

The patterns for supporting or voting certain political parties or candidates depend largely on the deployment and dexterity of electoral politics; for example, using strategies of campaigning along party affiliation, accounting for presidential performance during the campaign process, and the use of the incumbency factor.[17] In developing countries, electoral politics presents a lot of paradoxes. Political parties use influential candidates and stakeholders to influence how the electorates vote and ultimately win election. When political parties fail to engage an effective campaign strategy to win an election, they make violence an alternative. In a broader sense, electoral violence is an aspect of political violence. It encompasses election-related violence, which usually occurs as a result of po-

---

[13] R. Ekaterina Rashkova and Sam van der Staak, "The Party Abroad and its Role for National Party Politics" (International IDEA Discussion Paper 1/2019, Ultrecht University, Strömsborg, Sweden), https://www.idea.int/sites/default/files/publications/the-party-abroad-and-its-role-for-national-party-politics.pdf (accessed 27 July 2020).

[14] M. Larry Bartels, "Partisanship and Voting Behavior, 1952–1996," *American Journal of Political Science* 44, no. 1 (2000): 35–50.

[15] P. Morris Fiorina, *Retrospective Voting in American National Elections* (New Haven: Yale University Press, 1981); B. Roger Myerson, "Theoretical Comparisons of Electoral Systems," *European Economic Review* 43 (1999): 671–697.

[16] A. John Ferejohn and Morris P. Fiorina, "The Paradox of Not Voting: A Decision Theoretic Analysis," *American Political Science Review* 68, no. 2 (1974): 525–536; H. Shalom Schwartz and Wolfgang Bilsky, "Toward A Universal Psychological Structure of Human Values," *Journal of Personality and Social Psychology* 53, no. 3 (1987): 550–562; C. Susan Stokes, "Perverse Accountability: A Formal Model of Machine Politics with Evidence from Argentina," *American Political Science Review* 99 (2005): 315–325.

[17] A. John Ferejohn, "On the Decline of Competition in Congressional Elections," *American Political Science Review* 71, no. 1 (1971): 166–176,

litical activities during the electoral process.[18] This mutually and exclusively includes using force to disrupt campaigns, political meetings and voting during an election.

Electoral violence involves the use of threat to harm persons and destroy properties during the electoral process.[19] It could also mean to intimidate electorates to vote in a particular direction, or using dangerous weapons to affect the electoral process in a way that alters the electoral outcome.[20] Electoral violence occurs among competitors from different electoral camps as an expression of grievances in the struggle to acquire political power. Also, anti-democratic forces can use violence to attack electoral competitors or to defer the electoral process. Some other forms of electoral violence are as a result of individual and group grievances, which may occur during the electoral process, and, sometimes, may not have any connection to the election.[21]

Power Struggle and the Manipulation of the Electorate Ahead of the 2019 Elections

Power struggle to capture political power in Taraba State has repeatedly been characterised by rising political tension and manipulations of the sentiments of the electorate. Ethnicity and religion were the most manipulated identities both in the state and also across the country. Because of the heightened ethnic and religious consciousness in the electorates, political recruitment and mobilisation always followed that pattern. During the 2011 general election, the pair of the former Secretary of Taraba State government, Danbaba Suntai (Christian) and the former Chairman of Karim-Lamido Local Government Area, Alhaji Abubakar Sani Danladi (Muslim) emerged as governor and deputy governor of Tar-

---

[18] K. Ashindorbe, "Electoral Violence and the Challenge of Democratic Consolidation in Nigeria," *India Quarterly* 71, no. 1 (2018): 92–105.
[19] K. Höglund, "Electoral Violence in Conflict-Ridden Societies: Concepts, Causes, and Consequences," *Terrorism and Political Violence* 21, no. 3 (2009): 412–427, https://doi.org/DOI: 10.1080/09546550902950290; Kuro P. Inokoba and Agnes Ebi Maliki, "Youths, Electoral Violence and Democratic Consolidation in Nigeria: The Bayelsa State Experience," *Anthropologist* 13, no. 3 (2011): 217–225, https://doi.org/doi.org/10.1080/09720073.2011.11891200.
[20] Tawfiq M. Ladan and Isyaku Aisha Kiru, eds., *Election Violence in Nigeria* (Lagos: AFSTRAG-Nigeria, 2005), 33.
[21] I. Salehyan and Christopher Linebarger, "Elections and Social Conflict in Africa, 1990–2009," *Studies in Comparative International Development*, Research Brief, 50, no. 1 (2014): 23–49, https://doi.org/doi:10.1007/s12116–014–9163–1.

aba State respectively. The Deputy Governor, Danladi, was later impeached and replaced with a fellow Muslim from his constituency, Alhaji Garba Umar.

Incidentally, Governor Suntai could not govern beyond two-and-half years, after his first tenure, because of a plane crash that incapacitated him. He was flown to Germany, and subsequently the United States of America, for treatment.[22] The political intrigues and manipulations, along ethnic and religious lines, gendered unprecedented negative political consciousness against the process that made his deputy, Alhaji Garba Umar, the acting governor of Taraba State. While dividing the electorates along these identities, the interests of the politicians were to acquire state power, political positions and other forms of economic rewards. The former deputy, now acting governor, Alhaji Garba Umar, mobilized 16 out of 24 legislators to impeach the Speaker, Barrister Istifanus Gbana (Christian) who was replaced with Barrister Sam Haruna Tsokwa (Christian). The latter had agreed to use his powers as the Speaker of the State House of Assembly to actualise Alhaji Garba Umar's quest of becoming the substantive governor of Taraba State.

As it turned out, Alhaji Garba Umar could not also complete his tenure as acting governor before the 2015 general election because the Supreme Court sacked him when it ruled that the removal by impeachment of the elected Deputy Governor, Abubakar Sani Danlad, was illegal and lacking fair hearing. Danladi, who commenced legal battle to challenge his impeachment, first lost at the Appeal Court, but continued to the Supreme Court where he got justice and was restored to his position. With Governor Suntai's lingering illness, Danladi resumed as the acting governor. He therefore became a critical actor in the electoral process of the 2015 governorship election in Taraba State. During this period Darius Dickson Ishaku, who many believed was influenced by the retired General Theophilus Yakubu Danjuma, was brought to contest for the 2015 governorship election. Political intrigues and violence greeted the electoral process, particularly in Wukari, Jalingo and Sardauna Local Government Areas.

Senator Aisha Jummai Alhassan defected from PDP to the APC to contest the 2015 governorship election. When she did not win the election, she petitioned the outcome at the State Election Tribunal. In response, the INEC Returning Officer for the state election ordered for a re-run in some local government areas. Although Senator Alhassan was again defeated in the re-run elections, she continued to contend the ruling and filed suits up to the Supreme Court, which also

---

[22] Fanen Ihyongo, "2015: Suntai, Umar and Succession Drama in Taraba," *The Nation*, 3 March 2015.

upheld Ishaku's victory.[23] The manipulation of religious affiliation and sentiments was instrumental to Darius Dickson Ishaku's second victory in the 2019 governorship election. The roles of religious leaders were highly visible in the electoral process. Christian and Muslim leaders mobilised followers to vote based on religious identities. In fact, the leaders of the Christian Association of Nigeria (CAN) assiduously worked round the clock to ensure the re-election of Governor Ishaku in the 2019 governorship election. CAN leaders knew that the population of Christians alone would not make Governor Ishaku win the election. This was because the governor's failure to deliver the much-anticipated democratic dividends made many Christians to not want to return him as the governor of the state. For majority of the citizens in the state, Governor Ishaku, ethnically a native of Takum Local Government Area in the southern part of Taraba State, lacked the credentials for re-election in the 2019 governorship election.

Besides using religious identity politics, other factors played out in the electoral process to have Governor Ishaku re-elected in the 2019 governorship election. There were:

a) First, the PDP, the preferred party in the state, then operated a zoning system in Taraba State. The position of the governor was zoned to the Southern Zone of Taraba State from where Governor Ishaku came. He also enjoyed the backing of Major General Theophilus Yakubu Danjuma in 2015 and again in 2019.

b) Second, the Chairman of the Traditional Council in Taraba State, Aku Uka of Wukari, Dr Shekarau Angyu Masa-Ibi, also influenced the Jukun political elites to support Governor Ishaku's re-election. The Jukun ethnic group was mobilised to cast their votes in favour of Governor Ishaku, even though other Jukun politicians such as Chief David Sabo Kente and Senator Joel Danlami Ikenya contested in the 2019 governorship election of Taraba State on the platforms of the Social Democratic Party (SDP) and All Progressives Grand Alliance (APGA) respectively. The political argument tendered was that dividing their votes across the three Jukun governorship candidates could lead to Governor Ishaku losing the governorship position. This will mean that the Jukun nation has lost control of state power, a situation that may take about eight years to reverse as it was unlikely that the position will be zoned to southern Taraba before that time.

---

[23] Ade Adesomoju, "Breaking: Supreme Court Upholds Ishaku's Election as Taraba Governor," *Punch*, 11 February.

c) Thirdly, Governor Ishaku had appointed several traditional rulers across the state who were asked to make good on their chiefdoms by ensuring his re-election in 2019.

These factors reinforced ethnic and religious manipulations in the 2019 electoral process in favour of the PDP and their respective candidates in Taraba State.

Electoral Violence in Taraba State During the 2019 Elections

Political competitors and their political parties hotly contested the 2019 general election. Respective party supporters were mobilized along these hotly contested fault lines – ethnicity and religion. Like in previous elections, the 2019 general election was characterised by enormous political intrigues and debacles. As noted, the PDP presented the sitting governor, Darius Dickson Ishaku, as its 2019 governorship candidate following the unanimous decision during the party's primary election in Jalingo to adopt Governor Ishaku as their candidate.[24] Their decision aligned with the PDP zoning principle in the state.

The contrary happened with the APC where several aspirants contested for the governorship candidature; namely Senator Aisha Alhassan, Senator Abubakar Sani Danladi, Senator Joel Danlami Ikenya, Chief David Sabo Kente, Professor Sani Yahaya, Alhaji Alhaji Garba Umar, Comrade Bobboi Kaigama, Alhaji Ibrahim Tumba and Alhaji Aliyu Omar.[25] The APC primary election in Jalingo, which produced Senator Abubakar Sani Danladi as the party governorship candidate, was reportedly marred by fraud. Following the party's primary election, six candidates, including Senator Ikenya, Chief Kente, Professor Yahaya, Alhaji Omar, Alhaji Umar and Alhaji Tumba condemned the process at a press conference and called for the intervention of their party's national headquarters, under the chairmanship of Adams Oshiomhole, chairmanship of Comrade Adams Oshiomhole a former governor of Edo State. As it turned out, Oshiomhole upheld the result of the APC primary election that favoured Senator Abubakar Sani Danladi.

Speculations among party members differed on why the governorship candidature of Senator Danladi was upheld by the APC headquarters. Some believed

---

[24] Interview with Irash John, b. 1967, PDP member, Takum, 25 July 2019.
[25] The names of the aspirants seeking to be governorship candidate in the APC primary election were provided by Abdullahi Mohammed Alabura, an APC defector to PDP on claims of injustice within the APC party.

that the party chairman was bribed; while others believed that Senator Danladi was the only political candidate that could defeat Governor Ishaku in the 2019 governorship election. Senator Alhassan who played a significant role in launching the APC in Taraba State and mobilising supporters for the party was disqualified from the primary election for reasons which she could not decipher. The party chairman, however, claimed that her disqualification was due to anti-party politics:

> As for the Honourable Minister of Women Affairs, she has issues that have to do with party loyalty. Our constitution is clear and it dictates that to contest elections or even hold office in the APC, you must be loyal to the party in every material concern. From all she had said in the past and even her comments and general attitude during the screening, the NWC [National Working Committee] reviewed everything taken together and we arrived at the conclusion that she does not possess the level of loyalty that the APC requires for her to contest elections on our platform.[26]

In the process, Alhassan resigned her ministerial position in President Muhammadu Buhari's APC-led government and defected to a fledging party, the United Democratic Party (UDP), and became its governorship candidate.[27] Her defection with about 5000 supporters to UDP, including APC stalwarts, weakened APC numerical strength in Taraba State.[28] Alhassan's presence in UDP unsettled older members of the party causing a candidate for the State Constituency, Abba Yusuf, to accuse her of hijacking the UDP:

> As I speak with you, the UDP that Tarabans used to know is no longer the party that was working hard to capture power from the PDP. Ever since Senator Aisha defected from APC to UDP, she divided the party members into two; we have the old members and Senator Aisha's group who recently dumped APC for UDP because of selfish interest. Immediately she joined the party, they quickly dissolved the old executives of the party and replaced them with those she felt would work for her interest.[29]

---

26 John Alechenu, "Why APC Disqualified Shittu, Al-Hassan – Oshiomhole," *Punch*, 29 September 2018.
27 News Agency of Nigeria, "2019: Aisha Alhassan Picks UDP Guber Nomination Form," *Today Ng*, 29 September 2018, https://www.today.ng/news/politics/2019-aisha-alhassan-picks-udp-guber-nomination-form-158185.
28 News Agency of Nigeria, "Taraba APC Receives 5,000 UDP Defectors," *Punch*, 10 November 2018, https://punchng.com/taraba-apc-receives-5000-udp-defectors/.
29 Andrew Ojih, "Senator Alhassan Accused of Hijacking UDP Structure," *Leadership*, 5 December 2018, https://leadership.ng/2018/12/05/senator-alhassan-accused-of-hijacking-udp-structure/.

Those supporters of Senator Alhassan who were not comfortable with the APC and her newfound political party, UDP, joined the PDP for better political prospects.[30] The APC candidate Senator Danladi was accused of corruption but was later cleared by a High Court in Jalingo to prevent the Economic and Financial Crimes Commission (EFCC) from arresting him. However, he was faced with another suit at the Federal High Court in Jalingo over falsification of age and other documents.[31] Finally, the High Court seating in Jalingo disqualified him from contesting as an APC candidate in the 2019 governorship election.[32]

While PDP supporters were celebrating these turn of events, Senator Danladi and his party rushed to the Appeal Court in Yola, Adamawa State. The court issued an order of 'stay on execution' thereby barring the Independent National Electoral Commission (INEC) and other agencies from implementing the Federal High Court's judgement.[33] A restraining order by the Appeal Court enabled him to re-join the governorship race. On the election day, the PDP candidate, Darius Dickson Ishaku, received 520,433 votes while the APC candidate, Senator Danladi, received 362,735 votes. The INEC Returning Officer for Taraba State, Professor Shehu Adamu Iya, declared Governor Ishaku of the PDP winner of the election.[34] Senator Danladi's defeat was a big surprise to him because of the alleged "machineries"[35] provided by the federal government to aid his victory as an APC governorship candidate.

---

30 Interview with Abdullahi Alabura, b. 1969, Karim-Lamido LGA, 18 June 2019. Alabura was a staunch supporter of the APC because of Senator Alhassan. With the defection of Senator Alhassan to the UDP, he decided to join the PDP. The probable reason for his decision to join PDP was that it is only PDP and APC that have made strong in-roads in the political landscape of Taraba State. Therefore, it was unlikely for the UDP to win the governorship election.
31 Samson Toromade, "Court Disqualifies APC's Taraba Governorship Candidate, Danladi, for Falsifying Age," *Pulse. Ng*, 6 March 2019, https://www.pulse.ng/news/politics/court-disqualifies-apc-governorship-candidate-in-taraba/wkwb3lm.
32 Idowu Bankole, "Updated: Court Disqualifies Taraba APC Governorship Candidate, Danladi over Age Discrepancy," *Vanguard*, 6 March 2019.
33 Abubakar Ahmadu Maishanu, "Appeal Court Clears Taraba APC Governorship Candidate,", *Premium Times*, 7 March 2019, https://www.premiumtimesng.com/news/headlines/318304-appeal-court-clears-taraba-apc-governorship-candidate.html.
34 Magaji Isa Hunkuyi, "Ishaku Declared the Winner of Taraba Governorship Election," *Daily Trust*, 12 March 2019, https://www.dailytrust.com.ng/ishaku-declared-winner-of-taraba-governorship-election.html.
35 Few days before the governorship election, the Federal Government of Nigeria deployed senior officers of the Nigeria Police Force and the Nigerian Army to Taraba State. Most Tarabans construed the action as aimed at intimidating and scaring electorates in PDP strongholds, while permitting election malpractices in APC strongholds in favour of Senator Danladi, the governorship candidate of the APC. Others argued that the deployment of security officers was to

The manner in which the election was conducted can be sieved from observer reports. The Coalition for Clean Polls (CCP) claimed that the governorship election in the Southern Senatorial District of Taraba State was massively rigged.[36] Also, that they noticed the intimidation of voters and other related electoral irregularities during the electoral process. The group further asserted that in Takum Local Government Area, electoral officers were seen moving from one polling station to another to ensure that certain candidates won the election. On the other hand, in Wukari Local Government Area, electoral officers were maltreated and beaten up by PDP thugs. The officers were also forced to relinquish sensitive and non-sensitive election materials, which were used to commit electoral fraud. In Donga Local Government Area, Douglas Ndatse Yahaya, representing the area at the House of Assembly, was accused of using thugs to disrupt the election and to seize ballot boxes in order to thumbprint the ballot papers for the PDP. In Dampar Ward in Ibi Local Government Area, the PDP was accused of capsizing a boat carrying election results.[37]

Then, in the central and northern senatorial districts of the state, the APC was accused of using security agencies to arrest members of the PDP with the intention of provoking violence to a magnitude that will undermine the credibility and outcome of the election. The APC was also accused of rigging election in Karim-Lamido and Lau Local Government Areas. This informed the reason why the State Security Services (SSS) arrested Danladi Baido Tijos, representing Ardo-Kola, Lau and Karim-Lamido Federal Constituency, and Idi Mali, then Chairman of Karim Lamido Local Government Area. Victor Bala Kona, the PDP Chairman in Taraba State, disclosed that "the introduction of the SSS into the election equation created doubt about the prospect of free and fair polls in Taraba."[38] Moreover, the security agents were accused of arresting, detaining and preventing PDP members from voting in Bali, Kurmi and Sardauna Local Government Areas, all in order to reduce PDP votes and/or rig election in favour of the APC governorship candidate.[39]

---

secure the electoral process from violence because the state was identified as one of the security flashpoints in the 2019 electoral process in Nigeria.
36 Emmanuel Okogba, "Governorship Poll: Group Demands Cancellation of Southern Taraba Results," *Vanguard*, 10 March 2019.
37 Okogba, "Governorship Poll."
38 Ayodamola Owoseye, "Flared Tempers Trail Arrest of Top PDP Officials in Taraba," *Premium Times*, 8 March 2019, https://www.premiumtimesng.com/news/headlines/318548-flared-tempers-trail-arrest-of-top-pdp-officials-in-taraba.html.
39 Interview with Abdullahi Alabura, b. 1969, Karim-Lamido LGA, 18 June 2019.

As noted, Senator Danladi had challenged his disqualification from the governorship race at the Supreme Court, after the Appeal Court in Yola had passed its judgement upholding the verdict of the Federal High Court in Jalingo. However, the Supreme Court dismissed Senator Danladi's appeal upholding the earlier verdict of the High Court in Jalingo.[40] After the election from which Ishaku emerged winner for the second time running, Senator Alhassan congratulated Governor Ishaku on his victory, showing acceptance of the outcome of the 19 March 2019 governorship election. Senator Danladi, however, filed a petition at the tribunal in Abuja challenging Governor Ishaku's victory on the grounds that Ishaku did not garner the majority votes in compliance with the Electoral Act of 2010.[41]

The Election Petition Tribunal sitting in Abuja dismissed Danladi's suit because of the irregularities of false age declaration and other documents that earlier led to his disqualification from the polls. The APC then filed a separate petition to the tribunal against Governor Ishaku, calling for the nullification of the governorship election. For this bid, the APC replaced Senator Danladi with Professor Sani Yahaya as their governorship candidate. The party claimed that on the strength of the evidence at their disposal, Ishaku did not win the 2019 governorship election; and therefore aimed to regain what they assumed was a stolen mandate.

Electoral Politics, Violence and Casualties in 2019 Election in Taraba State

Taraba State is not particularly known for electoral violence, but rather for violence tailored towards ethnic group identities. However, prior to and after the 2019 general election, the state witnessed unprecedented electoral violence.[42] The manifestations followed the nature and pattern of political competition and mobilisation of the electorate. It was clear that the political dominance of

---

40 Channels Television, "Supreme Court Dismisses Appeal By Taraba APC Gov Candidate," *Channel Television*, 5 July 2019, https://www.channelstv.com/2019/07/05/supreme-court-dismisses-appeal-by-taraba-apc-gov-candidate/.
41 Nsikak Nseyen, "Tribunal Rules in APC's Petition Challenging Gov. Ishiaku's Re-Election," *Daily Post*, 10 July 2019, https://dailypost.ng/2019/07/10/tribunal-rules-apcs-petition-challenging-gov-ishiakus-re-election/.
42 Nwangoro Nnaemeka, "Horrendous Aftermath of Taraba Governorship Election," *Channel Television*, 14 March 2019, https://www.channelstv.com/2019/03/14/the-horrendous-aftermath-of-taraba-governorship-election/.

the PDP in the state, as the ruling party, rattled opposition parties, which sought to change the status quo, a political aspiration that was difficult to achieve. As earlier stated, since 1999 the electoral politics in Taraba State was tailored along the fault lines of zoning between the three senatorial districts – the northern, central and southern senatorial districts. Ethnicity and religion played prominent roles in negotiating the pattern of electoral mobilisation and voting among the electorates. Meanwhile, the PDP and APC were the major political parties in Taraba State. Since the PDP governorship candidate, Darius Ishaku, is a Christian and ethnically a Jukun from southern Taraba; and the APC governorship candidate, Senator Danladi, a Muslim and ethnically a Wurkum from northern Taraba, the electorates were mobilised to vote on ethnic and religious lines. The political campaigns of that season were infused with hate speeches that undermined the peace of the state. Rival groups often attacked the governorship candidates of the PDP and APC and their supporters resulting in heightened violence during the campaigns across the state.[43]

The campaigns and attendant political violence during the electioneering process in Taraba State in 2019 can be divided into three phases: (i) electoral violence that occurred during the campaign period; (ii) electoral violence that occurred on the day of election, and (iii) electoral violence that occurred after the declaration of the winner of the governorship election. The reason why violence occurred during the 2019 electoral process could be attributed to: (i) election violence motivated by members of the strong opposition party, the APC, which had strong political patron support; (ii) unequal competitive competency, efficiency, acceptability and followership between political candidates or political parties competing for the same political position leading to violence during the campaign period, (iii) the speculations by some political parties that their candidates were likely to lose the election propelled electoral violence, and (iv) the ill-feelings within some political parties that the election outcome did not favour their candidates also gave rise to election violence. Incidentally, electoral violence before, during and after elections merely reinforces the nature and pattern of political and intergroup relations in the state.[44]

The pre-election period in Taraba State manifested internal democracy deficits and other challenges including the problem of internal party democracy, conflicting role of political representatives, non-adherence to party rules and regulations, and the lack of accountability and inclusiveness. All these exposed the

---

[43] Interview with Gamboro Adi, b. 1976, Jalingo, 12 May 2019.
[44] Shola Omotola, "Explaining Electoral Violence in Africa's 'New' Democracies," *African Journal on Conflict Resolution* 10, no. 3 (2010): 51–73.

inefficiency of state political institutions and the structure of major contending political parties – PDP, APC and UDP. These parties were unable to generate the required cohesiveness and stability needed for effective campaign. These problems occasioned defections by aggrieved members in the PDP, but mainly those in APC. Nigerian political parties lack inter-party tolerance. This is the basis, during this Fourth Republic, for which they entered into agreements to ensure that the electoral process was peaceful and candidates readily accepted election results, but the latter is not often the case. In 2019, however, the governorship candidates of the PDP and APC refused to participate in the peace accord to promote violent-free election. This refusal generated scepticism in the electorates that the electoral process of that season will be peaceful.

As feared, the political atmosphere was tense as political competitors and their supporters showed incivility during the campaigns. Anticipating the possibility for violence during the governorship election in Taraba State, the Commissioner of Police, David Akinremi, invited the major candidates – Governor Ishaku (PDP), Senator Alhassan (UDP) and Senator Danladi (APC) to a peace accord, but none attended.[45] Table 1 presents incidents of violence during the 2019 electoral process in Taraba State.

Table 1: Incidents of violence during the electoral process in Taraba State

Date	Location	Incident and nature of violence
17 January 2019	Ibi roundabout, Wukari	A mob attacked the APC governorship candidate, Senator Danladi, during a campaign trip to Wukari and Ibi Local Government Areas. The same day, Alhaji Hassan Ardo, Nigeria's Ambassador to Trinidad and Tobago (APC) was also attacked by a mob while on the campaign trail in Wukari in the Southern Senatorial District.[46]
7 February 2019	Jalingo Metropolis	APC pre-presidential campaign rally took place at the Jolly Nyame Stadium, Taraba State Capital. The vio-

---

[45] PM News, "PDP, UDP, APC Governorship Candidates Absent at Taraba Peace Accord," *PM News*, 10 January 2019, https://www.pmnewsnigeria.com/2019/01/10/pdp-udp-apc-governorship-candidates-absent-at-taraba-peace-accord/.
[46] Idowu Bankole, "Hoodlums Attack APC Governorship Candidate's Convoy," *Vanguard*, 17 January 2019.
[47] Emmanuel Okogba, "Thugs Allegedly Destroy Buhari's Campaign Posters in Taraba," *Vanguard*, 7 February 2019.

Table 1: Incidents of violence during the electoral process in Taraba State *(Continued)*

Date	Location	Incident and nature of violence
		lence that erupted led to destruction of billboards, bashing of private cars, campaign vehicles and tearing of posters, among others.[47] The APC members generated the fracas by assaulting the PDP members and attacking their billboards.
7 February 2019	Jolly Nyame Stadium, Jalingo	At the APC presidential campaign rally at the Jolly Nyame Stadium in Jalingo, five people died from a stampede caused by overcrowding leading to violence among members.[48]
9 February 2019	Jalingo LGA	PDP Governor Ishaku's convoy was attacked by hoodlums perceived to belong to the opposition after he saw off the President Muhammadu Buhari to Jalingo Airport following the latter's presidential campaign tour. Several vehicles were destroyed, including those belonging to the deputy governor; a special adviser to the governor and the Taraba State Commissioner of Police.[49]
21 February 2019	Government Day Secondary School Baissa, Kurmi Local Government	PDP gubernatorial candidate, Governor Ishaku, was harassed and booed by the APC members during campaigns in Kurmi for failing to fulfil his promise of constructing the road from Mararaba-Baisa to Abong which his predecessor, Governor Suntai, started.[50]
24 February 2019	Amar/Kambari, Karim Lamido Local Government	During the presidential election in Taraba State, gunmen attacked and killed five people returning from Amar and Kambari in Karim Lamido LGA to Gassol LGA.[51]

---

48 Queen Esther Iroanusi, "Presidency Confirms Deaths at Buhari's Campaign Rally in Taraba," *Premium Times*, 7 February 2019, https://www.premiumtimesng.com/news/headlines/311108-just-in-presidency-confirms-deaths-at-buharis-campaign-rally-in-taraba.html.
49 Bolaji Femi, "Hoodlums Attack Gov Ishaku's Convoy, Destroys Vehicles," *Vanguard*, 9 February 2019.
50 Abubakar Ahmadu Maishanu, "Election: Drama as Residents Boo Governor over 'unfulfilled' Campaign Promises," *Premium Times*, 2019, https://www.premiumtimesng.com/regional/nnorth-east/314377-election-drama-as-residents-boo-governor-over-unfulfilled-campaign-promises.html.
51 News Agency of Nigeria, "Five Persons Killed by Gunmen in Taraba – Police," *Punch*, 24 February 2019.

Table 1: Incidents of violence during the electoral process in Taraba State *(Continued)*

Date	Location	Incident and nature of violence
8 March 2019	Nyamusala, Jalingo Local Government	PDP supporters celebrating Governor Ishaku's re-election victory clashed with APC supporters over claims of destruction of properties and attacks on bystanders by the PDP supporters around Nasarawo and Mallam Joda areas in Jalingo. The feeling that APC is a Muslim Party and PDP a Christian Party further aggravated the violence.[52] APC members, mostly Muslims, attacked PDP members celebrating the victory of their candidate, Governor Ishaku. Several people were killed and injured in the clash between the two groups.
8 March 2019	Karim Lamido	Political assassinations and abductions of party candidates and family members occurred. In Karim-Lamido, strong PDP members, Danladi Baido Tijos, a member of the Federal House of Assembly, and Idi Mali, the Council Chairman of Karim-Lamido were arrested ahead of the 2019 governorship election. They alleged that the APC leadership orchestrated their arrest to ensure landslide victory for the APC in the Mambilla Plateau.
14 March 2019	Jalingo LGA	The celebration of Darius Ishaku's election victory led to violence in which eight people were killed and 56 others, wounded. Those wounded were taken to the Federal Medical Centre (FMC) in Jalingo. 36 of the 56 persons hospitalized at FMC sustained life-threatening injuries ranging from gunshots, stabbing and arrow wounds.[53] APC members were alleged to have first attacked PDP members. Disappointment that their candidate lost the election and the feeling that the election was rigged led to the violence.

---

52 Jerry Wright Ukwu, "Group Blames Taraba Government, PDP over Jalingo Post-Election Violence," *Legit.ng*, 17 March 2019, https://www.legit.ng/1228012-group-blames-taraba-government-pdp-jalingo-post-election-violence.html.
53 John Mkom, "Post-Election Violence: 8 Killed, 56 Others Receiving Treatment in Taraba," *Leadership*, 14 March 2019, https://leadership.ng/2019/03/14/post-election-violence-8-killed-56-others-receiving-treatment-in-taraba/.

Table 1: Incidents of violence during the electoral process in Taraba State *(Continued)*

Date	Location	Incident and nature of violence
21 March 2019	Lissam II, Ussa LGA	Post-election period: PDP and APC supporters clashed in Ussa Local Government Area. One person was killed, several others were injured and houses were burnt.[54]

Source: Authors' compilation from national dailies.[55]

These instances of electoral violence in Taraba State, captured above, resulted from different factors and had different magnitudes of manifestations even though the electoral process was relatively peaceful when compared with other states in the country during the 2019 general election. Focused group discussions in the state's three senatorial districts uncovered the factors that necessitated violence during the 2019 governorship election. These factors are presented below in Table 2. Their impacts are shown in percentages.

Table 2: Summary of major FGD themes conducted in three Senatorial Districts of Taraba State

SN	Identified factors of electoral violence (IFEV) in Taraba State	Percentage of IFEV
1	Hate speeches by religious leaders who mobilises members of their churches and mosques to vote for their religious group.	79
2	Internal conflicts within political parties; those of the APC and PDP occasioned disenchantment and violence.	68
3	Disaffection with the existing political order in the PDP, APC and UDP led to members cross-carpeting to rival political parties.	78
4	The pattern of messages/rhetoric during party campaigns among political candidates of different political parties enhances conflict transformation to violence during the electoral process.	80
5	Ethnic and religious polarization within intra-party and inter-party among party supporters and members. Such polarisation has produced the divide that often turns into violence.	82

---

54 Oluwatoyin Bayagbon, "Supplementary Election: 'One Killed, Scores Injured' in Taraba," *The Cable*, 23 March 2019, https://www.thecable.ng/supplementary-election-one-killed-scores-injured-in-taraba.

55 The data presented is not exhaustive, but a representation of the major manifestations of violence during the 2019 general electoral process across Taraba State.

Table 2: Summary of major FGD themes conducted in three Senatorial Districts of Taraba State *(Continued)*

SN	Identified factors of electoral violence (IFEV) in Taraba State	Percentage of IFEV
6	Elite manipulation of group identities such as ethnicity, religion and other related concerns to limit or eliminate other group's share.	69
7	Political thuggery, voter intimidation, hoarding and hijacking of materials carried out by PDP and APC?	70
8	Activities of security agencies during the elections generated volatile security situation for the electorates.	76
9	Youth unemployment and underemployment made the youth to be vulnerable to violence. Politicians exploited youth idleness for their interest. For example, PDP and APC candidates mobilised the youth commit electoral malpractices.	54
10	The interests of the ruling PDP in retaining power in the state, while the APC, ruling at the centre, struggled to remove the PDP from power.	77
11	The pattern of social media uses among party supporters. Social commentators used social media handles to campaign against political candidates to discredit them in the public spaces.	89
12	Destruction of posters of candidates and party emblems carried out by alleged APC supporters. However, this does not exonerate the PDP supporters across the state's 16 Local Government Areas.	73
13	Disruption and clashes during party campaign rallies among the APC and PDP.	86
14	The use of campaign songs to insult political opponents. Politicians in PDP and APC engaged in sponsoring music that insulted their political opponents.	78

Source: FGDs Field Survey, 2019.

Figure 1, in bar chart, graphically summarises the data in Table 2 showing the intensity of the factors responsible for electoral violence during the 2019 general election in Taraba State.

Prior to the 2019 general election, Taraba State had several incubated groups associated with various forms of violence. This was particularly the situation in Jalingo Local Government Area. The membership of these groups consisted of youth within the ages of 18 and 25 years who, using machetes, shillelaghs and other small arms, attack victims and rival groups with the intent to cause damage or harm, whether partially or totally. These restive youth groups were already

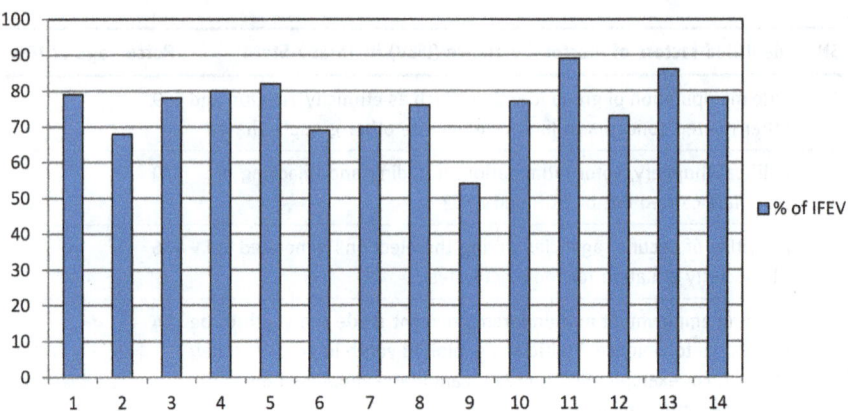

Figure 1: Graphic presentation of the percentage of identified factors of electoral violence in the 2019 general election.
Source: Curled from FGD field survey data, 2019.

clashing violently among themselves over trivial issues; and were found going from one area to another fomenting trouble, raping and killing victims. High-level unemployment among the youth contributed to election violence in Taraba State. The Nigerian Police Force did not do enough to curb the menace until after the killing of an alleged rival member at the Jalingo Central Market early in 2019, before the governorship election that year.[56] In the process of diffusing these groups, the Commissioner of Police was attacked and injured. Isa Mohammed argued that the emergence of a youth gang called the *Base Boys* in 2019 as a result of unfavourable social and economic conditions in the state as well as the country had impacted negatively on the electoral process in the state, particularly in terms of political recruitment and mobilization of supporters.[57]

Political competitors took advantage of the situation to recruit the restive youth in their campaign trails during the pre-election period. It was commonly noticed that the youth were paid to destroy campaign posters and billboards of political opponents, attack vehicles of opponents on electioneering campaigns, and, in some instances, attempt assassinations of opponents and instigate clashes between rival groups. This exploitation of the youth by political

---

[56] Justin Tyopuusu, "One Killed in Jalingo Market Violence," *Punch*, 3 December 2019.
[57] Isa Mohammed, "Youth Restiveness and Insecurity in Jalingo Metropolis," *Jalingo Journal Social and Management Sciences Maiden Edition* 1, no. 1 (2018): 92–106.

competitors during the electoral process marked a return to the political character of the state between 1999 and 2007, during the era of the first democratically-elected governor, Reverend Jolly T. Nyame. Then, the youth were used to disrupt the election, intimidate the electorate to ensure that election did not hold and cancel polling units where political opponents held sway. As politicians exploited restive youths for their political advantage, in the same manner, they were accused of coercing traditional rulers to deliver their domains for certain parties and candidates.

The role of security agencies, particularly the police and military, in the 2019 electoral process in Taraba State raised concerns whether the election would be free, fair and credible. The blame went to the APC for inviting the police and military into the 2019 general election. Sarah Birch and David Muchlinski assert that applying force to win election risk the process of lasting peace with deleterious consequences for the electorate who may be affected by violence.[58] The heavy presence of security agencies before and during the governorship election generated serious tension rather than reducing the existing tension among the electorate across Taraba State. Security agencies were not professionally capable of responding to violence during the election. Many people attributed their massive deployment across the nation to the orders of President Muhammadu Buhari who also ordered them to act ruthlessly.[59] This order generated fear in the electorate, including the sitting governor who responded by calling for the neutrality of the security agencies in the electoral process.

Similarly, retired General Theophilus Yakubu Danjuma, from Takum Local Government Area and former Minister of Defence in the President Olusegun Obasanjo's administration (1999–2007) had reasons to question the neutrality of INEC in the general election and advised the electorate to ensure that their votes counted because there was an unconcealed plan by the APC to rig the election for their governorship candidate, Senator Danladi.[60] This fear was strengthened when Danladi Baido Tijos, the member representing Lau, Karim-Lamido and Ardo-Kola Federal Constituency at the House of Representatives, and other PDP patrons were arrested by the Department of State Security Services

---

[58] Sarah Birch and David Muchlinski, "Electoral Violence Prevention: What Works?" *Democratization* 25, no. 3 (2018): 385–403,
[59] Adamu Abuh, Chijioke Nelson, and Emeka Nwachukwu, "Outrage as Buhari Orders Ruthless Action over Polls," *The Guardian*, 19 February 2019.
[60] "There Are Plans to Rig 2019 Elections, Says TY Danjuma," *Sahara Reporters*, 23 January 2019, http://saharareporters.com/2019/01/23/there-are-plans-rig-2019-elections-says-ty-danjuma.

for undisclosed reasons.[61] The action by the security agency compounded the lingering religious tension in Taraba State. The youth took to social media to react to the activities of security agencies. They also debated the political incivility in the electoral process.

Religious elites and institutions also played significant roles in the electoral process. Christian and Muslim religious leaders and preachers, as well as their youth wings, influenced the pattern of voting with their newsletters, messages and counter hate speeches. What was happening in Taraba State manifested in differing degrees beyond the borders of the state as Christian and Muslim preachers mobilized followers to vote politicians from their religious groups. Those found preaching otherwise were criticised by fellow preachers within their religious groups and preacher were considered by their members as bought over or bribed preachers, and therefore, did not represent the faith which they profess. As religious elites and institutions conflicted at the level of inter-faith relations over electoral politics; in public they enjoined the electorate to be peaceful during the election which is a contradiction.

Conclusion

Generally, electoral politics around the world shows forth various dynamics and dialectics. In Africa, particularly in multi-ethnic democracies like Nigeria, the electoral process had often produced varying levels of violence. Drawing from the exemplary nature of the 2015 general election in Nigeria, many academics, commentators, observers and publicists envisaged credible electoral democracy subsequently. Incidentally, the 2019 general election did not support their assumptions as local and global reports from the electorates, civil society organisations and election observers indicate. Electoral politics at the state level clearly reflects what obtains at the national level – squabbling among political parties, shortcomings of the election management body and connivance of security agencies with political actors, all in the effort to influence or alter electoral outcomes. The use of state machineries to win election threatens the fragile peace and disrupts intergroup relations both in the state and the nation. It is one thing to triumph in an election; it is another to secure peaceful co-existence in Nigeria.

---

61 Fanen Ihyongo, "DSS Arrests Taraba's Federal Lawmaker Danladi Baido," *The Nation*, 8 March 2019, https://thenationonlineng.net/dss-arrests-tarabas-federal-lawmaker-danladi-baido/.

This chapter revealed the dynamics, contradictions and violence in the electoral process in Taraba State in particular during the 2019 general election. The findings established that the nature and pattern of electoral politics in the 2019 general election marketed intense and unhealthy political rivalries among political competitors and political parties in their efforts to win the 2019 general election. It also showed how electoral politics was overtaken by intense power struggles that triggered the manipulative propensity of the three senatorial districts, which fed off ethnic and religious identities that, in turn, weakened the already fragile peace-building process in the state.

Muslims have argued that since Christians were in control of Taraba State power since the state was created in 1991, there was need to change the narrative and have a Muslim elected governor in 2019. Those with this view belonged to the opposition party, the APC. They perceived that state power could simply be handed over to a Muslim candidate without a struggle. The character of power struggle in the state required that serious efforts should be directed at building strong and vibrant political institutions, and not individuals and groups supported by the state institutions because they control state power. The political institutions must play a decisive role in the electoral process, for example, by engaging with communities and community leaders during the electoral process through political education and mobilisation against political incivility and violence.

Since electoral choices in the state are gleaned from the pattern of elite politics, the ruling government and its political party at the national and state levels must prioritise unity, taking it above the individual, group and party interests, as well as other related concerns. When this is achieved, the nature and pattern of politicking at the subnational level would, with some level of certainty, reflect similar character in the electoral process. In this context, political recruitment, campaigns and election in Taraba State, and elsewhere in Nigeria, will manifest commendable civility. Above all, there is the need to reduce the high stakes associated with electoral politics and election in the country by decentralising political and economic power to the local governments. It will in turn reduce the pressure of political competitors at the state level and the susceptibility of electoral politics to violence. The Taraba State government must revive the local government system and make election to the Local Government Council attractive to reduce electoral pressure concentrated on the governorship election in Taraba State.

Obinna Ukaeje
The Security Implications of Election-related Violence in Nigeria and the Way Forward

Abstract: Election-related violence in Nigeria has become a serious security challenge, which the country needs to overcome to achieve its true potential. This is because of the fear, tension, deaths and other humanitarian catastrophes that characterized it. Although election-related violence has been a recurring feature since Nigeria's First Republic, the frequency and intensity of the violence displayed and the ethno-religious and regional dimensions it has assumed in the current Fourth Republic (1999 till date) have become alarming making it a big threat to national security. Not only do citizens bear the brunt of the violence, the knock-on effects to the credibility of Nigeria's political process cannot be ignored. It is in this light that this chapter critically evaluates election-related violence in Nigeria with the aim of articulating strategic measures for containing it so that future elections in the country are conducted in the most peaceful atmosphere.

Keywords: Fourth Republic, election-related violence, future elections and security

1 Introduction

The end of the cold war after the demise of the Union of Soviet Socialist Republics (USSR) and the Eastern bloc, culminating in the installation of democratic systems of government in most parts of the world, marked the triumph of liberal democracy in global politics. One of the critical elements of liberal democracy is election. Contemporary representative democracy is organized through regular elections that determine who will occupy political offices in the state.[1] Every election involves competition among political parties that invokes a winner-

---

[1] A. A. Ujo, "Election Observation and Consolidation of Democracy," *Journal of Political Studies*, Special Edition on Democracy (2006): 170–186.

Obinna Ukaeje, National Defence College, Abuja

takes-all syndrome. With the high stakes that attend these competitions, they are very often accompanied by violence.

Violence has been a major feature of elections in Nigeria, dating back to 1964 during her First Republic. Electoral violence had since remained a recurring social, political and security challenge in the annals of her political system. It creates political tension, leads to destruction of lives and properties, increases insecurity and encourages breakdown of law and order. It also creates fear, simmers division among groups and stokes political instability, which in the end undermine the integrity of the election. In many instances, election-related violence had led to the subversion of the country's political system. Glaring examples were provided by the 1964, 1965 and 1983 elections. The 1983 general election was reminiscent of the 1965 Western Regional elections in the pattern and widespread nature of the violent manifestations, as well as the political instability that followed afterwards.[2] In both 1964 and 1983 general elections, the instabilities that resulted respectively culminated in the subversion, through military coups, of the existing administrations and by inference the First and Second Republics.

However, despite the various transformations the electoral system had undergone in the decades after independence to make national elections credible and reduce incidences of violence, election-related violence in Nigeria seems to be on the increase both in frequency and intensity. The six elections so far conducted in the current Fourth Republic – in 1999, 2003, 2007, 2011, 2015 and 2019 – are all symptomatic of this malaise. Apart from clashes between party supporters, Nigeria's political elites also fuel ethnic and religious sentiments to gain political advantage. This creates ethno-religious tension during election time and expands the already fragile inter-group relationship that exists among Nigeria's various ethnic groupings. Such an atmosphere of insecurity is ominous for the country and should be checked to mitigate the widening strained relationship among her ethnic and religious communities, which, in most instances, are the drivers of conflicts in Nigeria. This chapter discusses election-related violence in Nigeria with particular emphasis on the last three elections held in 2011, 2015 and 2019. It sieves out the security implications violence portends for the survival of democracy in Nigeria and also the survival of the country as one indivisible entity.

---

[2] O. Awofeso and T. I. Odeyemi, "Violence, Security Challenges and Electoral Process in Nigeria: A Futuristic Projection and Management Strategy," *Unilag Sociological Review* 7 (2016): 95–96.

Election, Election-Related Violence and Security: A Conceptual Clarification

The idea of an election suggests a decision making process through which people select who governs them or who holds public office.[3] Elections are premised on the assumption that legitimacy comes from the people from whom the power to govern is derived. Elections also create room for a larger number of people, categorized as eligible electorate, to select a fewer number of people through voting to occupy and exercise powers inherent in such positions.[4] This, however, implies that citizens exercising the power of choice under elections do so in furtherance of their constitutionally imputed sovereignty over those likely to exercise the powers of the state. Elections have been the usual mechanism by which modern representative democracy had operated since the seventeenth century.[5] Elections may fill offices in the legislature, sometimes in the executive and judiciary, and for regional and local governments. This process is also used in many other private and business organizations, from clubs to voluntary associations and corporations.[6] Elections may not in themselves be a sufficient condition for poll representation, but there is little doubt that they are necessary for democratic governance.[7]

Elections, as described above in the realm of electoral context, refer to impartiality and the ability of citizens to participate without coercion or restriction, having equal access to opportunities, thereby ensuring a free and fair election exercise. Gilbert Nduru highlighted the criteria for measuring free and fair elections, which he referred to as the guarantee of political freedom and human rights, the provision of good legislative framework, access to media, good political environment where political campaigns could be carried out and well cleaned up voter register.[8] It therefore means that the presence or absence of these elements highlighted by Nduru determines the validity of elections.

---

3 *Encyclopedia Britannica*, 8th ed. (Chicago, IL: Encyclopedia Britannica, 2015).
4 O.B.C. Nwankwo, "Elections & Democratic Governability in Nigeria," *Journal of International Politics and Department of Studies* 2, No. 3 (2006): 180–201.
5 Henry M. Robert, Daniel H. Bach and J. Thomas, *Roberts Rules of Order*, 11th ed. (Philadelphia: Da Copo Press, 2011), 438–446.
6 Robert, Bach and Thomas, *Roberts Rules of Order*.
7 A. Heywood, *Politics* (New York: Palgrave Macmillan, 1997), 211.
8 G. Nduru, "The Challenges of Conducting Free and Fair Elections and Referenda" (paper presented at the Workshop for District Registrars and Assistant District Registrars in Kampala, Uganda, October 2008).

Electoral violence derives its meaning from the general notion of violence which entails an act of force exerted to impart physical, psychological and structural violence[9] in order to influence the electoral process in favour of the perpetrators and organizers of the violence. It is, therefore, a special type of political violence characterized by election related destructive tendencies, which may be physical, psychological or structural. Otivo Igbuzor refers to electoral violence as:

> Any act of violence perpetuated in the course of political activities, including pre, during and post-election periods, and may include any of the following acts; thuggery, use of force to disrupt political meetings or voting at polling stations, or the use of dangerous weapons to intimidate voters and other electoral process or to cause bodily harm or injury to any person connected with electoral process.[10]

Corroborating the above, Megan Reif sees electoral violence as:

> Any spontaneous or organized act by candidates, party supporters, election authorities, voters or any other actor that occurs during an electoral process, from the date of voters registration to the date of inauguration of a new government, that uses physical harm, intimidation, blackmail, verbal abuse, violent demonstrations, psychological manipulation, or other coercive tactics aimed at exploiting, disrupting, determining, hastening, delaying, reversing or otherwise influencing an electoral process and its outcome.[11]

From the foregoing, electoral violence is similar to any other form of violence, but occurs during elections and are perpetrated for political advantage.

In conceptualizing security, Otivo Igbuzor,[12] Ogaba Oche,[13] Chukwuemeka Nwanegbo and Jude Odigbo[14] placed emphasis on the absence of threats to peace, stability, national cohesion as well as political and socio-economic objec-

---

9 J. Galtung, "Violence, Peace and Peace Research," *Journal of Peace Research* 6, no. 3 (1969): 167–192.
10 O. Igbuzor, "Electoral Violence in Nigeria," 2009, http://www.centrelsed.org/paper (accessed 19 June 2019).
11 R. Majekodunmi and K. D. Adejuwon, "Electoral Administration and the Consolidation of Democracy: An Overview of 2011 General Elections in Nigeria," *International Journal of Physical and Social Sciences* 2, no. 5 (2012): 1–26.
12 O. Igbuzor, "Peace and Security Education: A Critical Factor for Security and Sustainable Peace and National Development," *International Journal of Peace and Development Studies* 2, no.1, (2011): 1–7.
13 O. Oche, "Democratization and the Management of African Security," in R. Akindele and B. Ate, *Nigeria Journal of International Affairs* 13, no.1 (2001): 76–77.
14 C. J. Nwanegbo and J. Odigbo, "Security and National Development in Nigeria: The Threat of Boko Haram." *International Journal Humanities and Social Sciences* 3 (2013): 285–291.

tives of a country. Apparently, there is a general notion that security is vital for national cohesion, peace and sustainable development. Adebayo Akinade reiterates the importance of security to national development when he said that security is inextricably tied to national development.[15] He gave instances of violence to include ethnic crisis, vandalisation of oil pipelines, armed robbery, electoral violence and other forms of violence that have hindered the developmental progress in Nigeria.

Without doubt, the security and welfare of citizens should be the primary objective of every sovereign nation. The 1999 Constitution of the Federal Republic of Nigeria (as amended) categorically states:

> The Federal Republic of Nigeria shall be a state based on the principle of democracy and social justice (2) is hereby accordingly declared that: security and welfare of the people shall be the primary purpose of government; and the participation by the people in their government shall be in accordance with the provision of the constitution.[16]

This allusion by the constitution as regards security is an indication of its importance to national cohesion, peace and development.

The political violence theory undergirds the discussion in this chapter. It describes politically motivated violence by non-state actors against a state or against other non-state actors. It also explains the non-action on the part of a government, also characterized as a form of political violence. Examples of such non-action include the government's refusal to address security concerns or to deny resources to politically identifiable groups within their territory. Among the major proponents of political violence theory are Karl Max,[17] Carl von Clausewitz,[18] James Fearon[19] and John Dollard.[20] These scholars do not share the same views over the causes and dimensions that violence may assume in a society. They, however, contend that each incident of political violence is unique and best understood in its historical specificity. Thus, based on its origin, duration, spread and impact, violence can be multidimensional.

---

15 A. Akinade, "National Security, Social Cohesion and Sustainable Development: Panacea to Conflict, Violence and Xenophobia," *Sociology International Journal* 2, no. 6 (2018): 593–601.
16 Constitution of the Federal Republic of Nigeria as Amended, Chapter II, Section 14 (1), 1999.
17 R. Singh, "Status of Violence in Marx's and Engel's Theory of Revolution," *Review of Political Economy* 24, no. 4 (1989): 9–20.
18 C. von Clausewitz, *On War* (New York: E.P. Dutton & Co, Ltd, 1940).
19 J. Fearon, "Rationalist Explanation for War," *International Organization* 49, no. 3 (1995): 279–414.
20 John Dollard, Doob W. Leonard, Miller E. Neal, Mowrer H. Orval, and Sears R. Roberts, *Frustration and Aggression* (New Haven, CT: Yale University Press, 1939).

Three main theoretical explanations are embedded in political violence theory. These can be used collectively or separately to explain election related violence in Nigeria. They are:
a) relative deprivation, rising expectations and frustration-aggression hypothesis,
b) the systematic hypothesis, and,
c) group conflict hypothesis.[21]

These hypotheses explain election-related violence from different perspectives. The relative deprivation, rising expectations and frustration-aggression hypothesis aptly clarifies why the electorates react negatively and spontaneously through demonstrations, riots and arson when their expectations are disappointed following a manipulated election. Such reactions were witnessed in Nigeria's 2011, 2015 and 2019 elections. Election-related crisis can be avoided by deliberately securing the confidence of the electorate through impartiality and transparency in the conduct of elections. The other two hypotheses throw light on political violence holistically both in their social and group contexts. This author, therefore, limits the analysis in this chapter within the ambit of the relative deprivation hypothesis.

Historical Overview of Election Related Violence in Nigeria

Elections started in Nigeria in 1922 after the introduction of the Clifford's Constitution, but the first national general election was conducted in 1959 by the British colonial administration. Irrespective of the flaws recorded during that election, it remains one of the few relatively peaceful and violent-free elections in Nigeria.[22] The second general election held in 1964 was not anything close to the 1959 parliamentary elections in terms of being peaceful, free and fair. High incidence of violence characterized it. The 1964 general election, which is among the worst elections in Nigeria, also marked the beginning of electoral violence in the country. Although, the violence that attended the 1964 elections was especially intense in the then Western Region, it still extended to other regions of the country. The Western Region electoral violence was tagged '*operation wet e'* meaning 'wet with petrol and burn'. The upheavals that followed

---
21 Dollard, Leonard, Neal, Orval and Roberts, *Frustration and Aggression*.
22 Awofeso, "Violence, Security Challenges and Electoral Process," 85.

that election precipitated Nigeria's first military coup d'état on 15 January 1966, which ended the first republic. Subsequent elections in the second, third and fourth republics were also marred by violence, the intensity of which varied from election to election.

The first post-1964 election, held in 1979, heralded the beginning of the Second Republic. Coincidentally, it was relatively more peaceful than the 1983 general election that followed it. Scholars believe that the military government that organized it adeptly managed all anticipated crises during the military-to-civilian transition period of 1978 to 1979.[23] Amadu Kurfi who studied the 1979 and 1983 general elections notes:

> the calm atmosphere prevalent during the 1979 elections was not brought about by the existence of [a] fine political culture in the Nigerian people but was due to the veiled threat of immediate military retribution should law and order breakdown and the possibility of postponement of date of handover to civilians. Despite the calm atmosphere that pervaded the 1979 elections, there were accusations and counter accusations of ballot stuffing, corruption and other irregularities in the elections.[24]

Dudley,[25] Adamu and Ogunsanwo[26] also noted:

> Surplus ballot papers had been sold to the highest bidder, that polling agents had to thumb-printed ballots for those who paid them, that ballot boxes stuffed with pre-marked ballots were substituted for real ones on the way to counting centres, and that the deliberate invalidation of ballots by polling and counting officials had occurred, also, members of the huge temporary bureaucracy recruited by FEDECO to conduct the elections, as well as the police and other security officials assigned to guard against electoral malpractices, and finally the officers, candidates and supporters of the contesting parties, engaged in extensive act of collusion to manipulate various aspects of the electoral process.[27]

Unlike the 1979 general election, the 1983 exercise was a replica of 1964 both in character and level of violence. There were several electoral irregularities and vices that include manipulation of election result through multiple voting, monetization of the electoral process through bribing of electoral officials, vote buy-

---

23 Awofeso, "Violence, Security Challenges and Electoral Process," 85.
24 A. Kurfi, *The Nigerian General Elections of 1959 and 1979 and the Aftermath* (Lagos: McMillan Publishers Nigeria, 1983), 243.
25 B. Dudley, *Instability and Political Order: Parties and Crisis in Nigeria* (Ibadan: Ibadan University Press, 1973), 43–46.
26 Haroun Al-Rashid Adamu and Alaba Ogunsanwo, *The Making of the Presidential System: 1979 General Elections* (Kano: Triumph Publishing Co, 1983), 125.
27 Richard A. Joseph, *Democracy and Prebendal Politics in Nigeria: The Rise and Fall of the Second Republic* (Ibadan: Spectrum Books Ltd, 1991), 154.

ing, widespread violence courtesy of political thugs, extreme lawlessness, hooliganism and vandalism. Richard A. Joseph succinctly documented the extent to which violence degenerated during the 1983 general election in the following words:

> According to the Nigerian News Agency, more than 60 people died during the electoral campaign. Most of the dead over the last two weeks [died] following a fairly common practice in Nigeria of pouring petrol over and setting alight the victim. In the last few days, several members of the NPN and at least two policemen accused of having 'stolen' votes have been lynched by this method, which is generally reserved for thieves caught red-handed.[28]

Dudley,[29] Post and Vickers,[30] and Madiebo[31] identified electoral irregularities, misconducts and violence among the major excuses used by the January 1966 and December 1983 coup plotters, which correspondingly brought an end to the first and the second republic democratic governments. What seemed like the third republic democratic system was neither here nor there because the military government in place between 1985 until 1993 operated a diarchy – a double government[32] that had both military and civilian personnel in power, headed by a serving General as president. However, the military government of General Ibrahim Babangida could not ensure a full transition to democracy, rather it took the country through an endless transition programme to democratic rule. In 1992, after seven years, it was able to deliver one of the elections acknowledged by both national and international actors as the freest and fairest ever conducted in Nigeria; but this was annulled by the same military government. The annulment was greeted with stiff opposition, expressed in the form of massive political unrest, across the country. The political upheavals combined with international pressure for a democratic government forced General Babangida to relinquish power to an Interim National Government (ING) led by Chief Ernest Shonekan. The ING was ousted within a year in what looked like a palace coup by the then Chief of Defence Staff (CDS), General Sani Abacha.[33]

---

28 Joseph, *Democracy and Prebendal Politics in Nigeria*, 33.
29 Dudley, *Instability and Political Order*, 43–46.
30 K. W. J. Post and M. Vickers, *The Structure and Conflict in Nigeria, 1960–65* (London: Heinemann, 1973).
31 A. A. Madiebo, *The Nigerian Revolution and the Biafran War* (Enugu: Fourth Dimension Publishing Company, Limited, 1980).
32 J. Ibrahim, "The Political Debate and the Struggle for Democracy in Nigeria," *Review of African Political Economy Journal* 13, no. 37 (1986): 38–48.
33 P. M. Lewis, "Endgame in Nigeria? The Politics of a Failed Democratic Transition," *African Affairs* 93, no. 372 (1994): 323–340.

The military regime of General Abacha, which commenced in 1993, inherited the crisis over the annulment of the "12 June 1993" election. In 1994 the acclaimed winner of that election, Chief M. K. O. Abiola declared himself the legitimate president of Nigeria as there was no sign that the government of Abacha would swear him in as the democratically elected president of Nigeria. Following the declaration, Abiola was arrested and imprisoned on charges of treason. He died on 7 July 1998, the day he was to be released from prison. Meanwhile, General Sani Abacha had died on 8 June 1998, following which the Armed Forces Ruling Council selected General Abdulsalami Abubakar as the new military Head of State. General Abubakar's administration supervised a successful democratic election in 1999 that launched Nigeria's Fourth Republic. The same administration laid the foundation for a new electoral body known as the Independent National Electoral Commission (INEC). The inauguration of the body brought into force the processes that gave birth to the election of Chief Olusegun Obasanjo of the Peoples' Democratic Party (PDP) as president in 1999. Although several political parties registered for the election, only three parties – Alliance for Democracy (AD), All Peoples Party (APP) and Peoples' Democratic Party (PDP) – met the conditions of the electoral body.[34]

Remarkably, after the commencement of the Fourth Republic in 1999, none of the subsequent five elections of this dispensation – 2003, 2007, 2011, 2015 and 2019 – was devoid of incidents of violence and other electoral irregularities, implicating both politicians and officials of the electoral body. As earlier noted, the 1999 election was exceptional for registering fewer incidents of violence. This was attributed to two main factors: the international pressure on the leadership to return power to civilians through a democratic process, and the fear of another annulment that forced politicians to play by the rule.[35]

The 2003 elections, which many viewed as a test of Nigeria's democratic progress, especially coming after four years of civilian administration under Chief Obasanjo, were an abject failure.[36] The Transition Monitoring Group Report,[37] the European Union Observer Mission in Nigeria Report[38] and the

---

[34] O. Robert Dode, "Political Parties and the Prospects of Democratic Consolidation in Nigeria: 1999–2006," *African Journal of Political Science and International Relations*, Volume 4, No 5 (2010): 188–194.
[35] J. S. Omotola, "Elections and Democratic Transition in Nigeria under the Fourth Republic," *Africa Affairs* 109, no. 437 (2010): 535–553.
[36] C. Allbin-Lackey, "Criminal Politics: Violence, 'Godfathers and Corruption' in Nigeria," *Human Rights Watch* 19, No. 16 A (2007): 1–121.
[37] Transition Monitoring Group, "Final Report of the 2003 General Elections in Nigeria," (Abuja: TMG, 2003).

Human Rights Watch Report,[39] all submitted that the 2003 elections were persuasively and openly rigged, and was also very bloody. According to the European Union Observer Mission in Nigeria Final Report on that election, more than a hundred people died in the two weeks of that exercise; several deaths were as a result of political clashes between the contending parties, the Peoples Democratic Party (PDP), the All Nigerian Peoples Party (ANPP), and the Alliance for Democracy (AD). Each tried to weaken other opponents in defence of their political interests. Cross River, Delta, Imo, Kaduna and Rivers States witnessed high incidents of violence more than other states in the federation.[40]

The International Republican Institute (IRI) while evaluating the credibility of the 2003 general election noted that a critical examination of the voting procedure and announced electoral results should be carried out in states like Cross River, Imo and Rivers, and several others where similar cases of electoral fraud were reported by other domestic and international observers.[41] The IRI report confirmed that there were inadequate election administration, a tensed political atmosphere following a violence-wrecked campaign, and numerous deliberate acts of electoral fraud that combined to undermine the foundations for a truly successful electoral process in certain parts of Nigeria. However, these were considered insufficient to doubt the announced electoral results in most of the locations observed by IRI's delegation.[42] Concluding the report, IRI stated that for Nigeria to make democratic progress, a re-examination of the 2003 elections must be conducted and, if necessary, remedial actions taken.[43] But, as it turned out, the 2003 elections became a *'child's play'* when compared with the 2007 elections that followed, which was tagged a "do or die" election by then President Obasanjo.

The 2007 general election was historic, being the first time in the nation's forty-seven years' existence that power would pass from one democratically elected ruler to another. The election, which was a measure of Nigeria's democratic progress, is remembered as one of the worst in Nigeria's electoral history.

---

38 The European Union Observer Mission, *Nigeria Elections Final Report 2003*, http://www.epgencms.europarl.europa.eu/cmsdata/upload/b3b0a3c1-adae-4b32-a670-8a274284e8c9/Nigeria-general-elections_12-&-19-April-03-May-20016_EU-EOM-report.pdf (accessed 20 October 2019).
39 Human Rights Watch, "Nigeria's 2003 Elections: The Unacknowledged Violence," (June 2004), http://www.refworld.org/docid/412ee5b4.html (accessed 18 June 2020).
40 The European Union Observer Mission, *Nigeria Elections*.
41 IRI, "2003 Nigeria Election Observation Report," https://www.iri.org/sites/default/files/fields/field_eo_report/nigerias_2003_presidential_and_national_assembly_elections.pdf (accessed 11 November 2020).
42 IRI, "2003 Nigeria Election Observation Report."
43 IRI, "2003 Nigeria Election Observation Report."

The incumbent president's vow that it would be a "do or die" election unless his party won set the stage for future electoral violence in Nigeria.[44] Little wonder that it became the first election after the return to democratic rule in 1999 that recorded high incidents of political assassinations. Few of the victims were Alhaji Sulaimon Olajokun, a member of the Alliance for Democracy (AD) who was murdered on his way from Ile-Ife in Osun State to Lagos on 15 May 2005; Mr Jesse Aruku, a gubernatorial aspirant of the Advanced Congress of Democrats (ACD), who was abducted and killed near his house in Bassa Local Government Area of Plateau State on 30 June 2006; Chief Funsho Williams (the PDP gubernatorial candidate in 2003 and the most favoured aspirant for the Lagos State gubernatorial candidate in 2007) who was murdered on 27 July 2006; and Chief Ayo Daramola who was to contest against the incumbent governor of Ekiti State, Ayo Fayose, for the PDP ticket in 2007, but was murdered on 14 August 2006.

Despite the assurances from the federal government and security agencies to uncover the perpetrators of these crimes, this has not happened;[45] thus, suggesting the involvement of the government in the assassinations. There were also cases of bomb explosions in the homes of aspiring candidates of the PDP. Victims include Senator Patrick Osakwe of Delta State, whose house was bombed on 24 November 2006, the campaign office belonging to Ndudi Elumelu and the house of Theodora Giwa-Amu, aspirants of the PDP into the House of Representatives, also from Delta State were bombed by unknown persons.[46]

Ekiti, Ondo, Osun and Oyo States were the most volatile, almost following the pattern witnessed in 1964.[47] The spontaneous violent responses in these states resulted in the burning of houses, killings, looting and a general breakdown of law and order. Other states that experienced similar incidents of vio-

---

[44] Ike Okonta, "A Lost Chance," *The Guardian*, 26 April 2007; Kazeem Ugbodaga, "Flashback: How Obasanjo rigged 2007 Presidential Election," *PM News*, 21 January 2019, www.pmnewsnigeria.com/2019/01/21/flashback-how-obasanjo-supervised-a-violent-rigged-2007-poresendential-election/html (accessed 20 June 2020).
[45] Awofeso, "Violence, Security Challenges and Electoral Process in Nigeria," 85–95.
[46] Reuben Abati, "Impeachment, Akume's Lucky Escape and A Democracy of Bombs," *The Guardian Newspaper*, 30 December 2006, 52; Austin Ogwuda, "Nigeria: Fresh Bomb Blast in Asaba, Politicians go into Hiding," *Vanguard*, 1 December 2006, http://allafrica.com/stories/2006/12040983.html (accessed 20 June 2020); Kalu Ogwuda, "Nigeria: Assassinations – Dangers Ahead," *Daily Champion*, 31 December 2006, 22.
[47] J. S. Omotolla, "Challenges, Problems and Prospects of Electoral Reform in Nigeria" (report of a commissioned paper submitted to the South African Institute of International Affairs, Johannesburg, August 2008).

lence were Gombe and Katsina where intimidation and violence became rife.[48] From the report of the International Foundation of Electoral Systems (IFES), in 2007, a total of 967 incidents of violence occurred and 18 deaths occurred in the pre and post-election periods.[49] Irregularities in the conduct of the elections, which invariably engendered electoral violence, were noticeable in the court cases instituted by aggrieved parties as well as the reports of various local and foreign observers, electoral scholars and even in the speech of the elected president.[50]

Indeed, the scale of electoral violence recorded in 2007 was unprecedented that the European Union Election Observers Monitoring (EU-EOM) Group concluded as follows:

> The elections were marred by very poor organization, lack of essential transparency, widespread procedural irregularities, substantial evidence of fraud, widespread voters' disenfranchisement, lack of equal conditions for political parties and candidates and numerous incidents of violence.[51]

Election-Related Violence and Security Challenges: 2011 to 2019

As already mentioned, election-related violence portends serious security challenges in Nigeria. Besides undermining the credibility of an election, it exacerbates political tension and creates an atmosphere of insecurity. It also reinforces ethno-religious pulls, sometimes leading to conflicts and regional sentiments. Bamgbose,[52] Orji and Uzodi[53] link electoral violence to other factors that subvert

---

[48] Human Rights Watch, "Nigeria's General Election Report 2007: Presidential Election Marred by Fraud, Violence," 8 October 2007, https://www.refworld.org/docid/412ee5b4.html (accessed 16 June 2020).

[49] Ugbodaga, "Flashback: How Obasanjo rigged 2007 Presidential Election"

[50] A. S. Adesote and J.O. Abimbola, "Electoral Violence and the Survival of Democracy in Nigeria's Fourth Republic: A Historical Perspective," *Canadian Social Science*, volume 10, No 3 (2014): 140–148.

[51] European Union Election Observation Mission, *Nigeria Elections Final Report on Gubernatorial & State Houses of Assembly Elections April 14 & 21*, 2007, http://eeos.europa.eu/eueom/pdf/mission/nigeria-pdf-2003 (accessed 22 October 2019).

[52] J. A. Bamgbose, "Electoral Violence and Nigeria's 2011 General Elections," *International Review of Social Sciences and Humanities* 4 (2012): 205–219.

[53] O. Orji and N. Uzodi, *The 2011 Post Election Violence in Nigeria* (Abuja: Policy and Legal Advocacy Centre, 2012).

the political system because it has the propensity to polarize the country along ethnic and religious lines, to heighten political tension, and weaken the nation's crisis management capacity. I will now take a closer look at the 2011, 2015 and 2019 elections.

2011

The fourth general election in Nigeria's Fourth Republic was held in 2011. It was generally accepted by local and foreign observers as reasonably fair; yet, the scale of violence it unleashed was high following some deadly attacks that happened three days to the voting in which 800 people died[54] and more than 65,000 were displaced in three days of rioting in 12 northern states, the epicenter of the crisis.[55] The violence resulted from the widespread protest of supporters of the main opposition candidate, Muhammadu Buhari, a northerner and presidential candidate of the Congress for Progressive Change (CPC) party, following the declaration that President Goodluck Jonathan of the PDP, a Christian from the Niger Delta region, South-South geopolitical zone, won the election. The protest degenerated into sectarian killings that saw the massacre of Christians and citizens from southern Nigeria resident in the affected states of Adamawa, Bauchi, Borno, Gombe, Jigawa, Kaduna, Kano, Katsina, Niger, Sokoto, Yobe, and Zamfara.[56] According to a Human Rights Watch report, the election:

> degenerated into sectarian and ethnic bloodletting across the northern states. Muslim rioters targeted and killed Christians and members of ethnic groups from southern Nigeria, who were perceived to have supported the ruling party, burning their churches, shops, and homes. The rioters also attacked police stations and ruling party and electoral commission offices. In predominantly Christian communities in Kaduna State, mobs of Christians retaliated by killing Muslims and burning their mosques and properties.[57]

---

54 Dorina Bekoe, "Nigeria's 2011 Elections: Best Run, But Most Violent" (United States Institute for Peace Brief, 19 August 2011), https://www.usip.org/publication/2011/08/nigerias-2011-elections-best-run-most-violent/html (accessed 22 August 2019).
55 Human Rights Watch, *Nigeria's 2011 Post Election Report: Violence Killed 800* (2011), https://www.hrw.org/news/2011/05/16/nigeriapostelection-violence-killed (accessed 15 October 2019).
56 Human Rights Watch, *Nigeria's 2011 Post Election Report*.
57 Human Rights Watch, *Nigeria's 2011 Post Election Report*.

This post-electoral violence in the northern states claimed the lives of some ten members of the National Youth Service Corps (NYSC) in Bauchi State.[58] The report by Human Rights Watch shows that electoral violence in Nigeria had gone beyond party politics to include ethno-religious violence. The gruesome attacks on Christians in the north led to attacks on Muslims in selected parts of the south, although not in the same magnitude as witnessed in the north. Notwithstanding, the southern state of Akwa Ibom suffered huge infrastructural damages in the violence on 22 March 2011, which was attributed to a fight between supporters of the ruling PDP and the opposition Action Congress of Nigeria (ACN) during a political rally.[59] The key figures in the fracas were the incumbent governor, Godswill Akpabio of the PDP, and John James Akpanudoedehe, the Action Congress of Nigeria's gubernatorial candidate, a former deputy governor of the state under the PDP.[60] According to an eye witness account, about 200 new Peugeot 307 brand cars, 500 new tricycles and over 20 Toyota Hiace brand buses belonging to the PDP and to Governor Godswill Akpabio 2011 Campaign Organization were destroyed along with nine Hilux jeeps belonging to the Government of Akwa Ibom State. Further, properties belonging to Dr Goodluck Jonathan and Vice President Mohammed Namadi Sambo campaign organization were burnt down alongside Fortune International High School owned by Senator Aloysius Etok.[61]

A Presidential Committee of Inquiry led by Sheik Ahmed Lemu was set up to investigate the remote and immediate causes of the violence and recommend ways of averting future political violence in the state. Specifically, the panel was mandated to identify those responsible for the pre-election violence in Akwa Ibom State as well as the incidents in the northern states. Not constituted as a judicial Commission of Enquiry, the panel lacked the authority to indict any individual or group of individuals. Going by its report, released on 10 October 2011, the panel linked the violence to widespread desire for change following

---

[58] G. E. Ezirim and P. O. Mbah, "Electoral process and political violence in Africa: A preview of the 2015 elections in Nigeria," *International Journal of Research in Arts and Social Sciences* 6, no. 3 (2014): 280–295.
[59] VOA, "Election Violence Leaves 12 Dead in Nigerian Akwa Ibom State," https://reliefweb.int/report/nigeria/election-violence-leaves-12-dead-nigerian-akaw-ibom-state/html (accessed 20 November 2020).
[60] VOA, "Election Violence Leaves 12 Dead."
[61] A. Egobueze and C. Ojirika, "Electoral Violence in Nigeria's Fourth Republic: Implications for Political Stability," *Journal of Scientific Research and Reports* 13, no. 2 (2017): 1–11. Also, Sahara Reporters, "Intolerance As Cause of Pre-And-Post Election Violence," 22 June 2011, https://saharareporters.com/2011/06/22/uyo-mayhem-senior-goodlucksambo-campaign-official-finger-akpabio%E2%80%99s-intolerance-cause-pre (accessed 22 November 2020).

failed promises to fix infrastructure, corruption and party zoning policies. Other triggers were ethno-religious competition, rumour-mongering and the individual actions of some political candidates.[62] The panel reported that 943 died in the violence, which mostly occurred in northern Nigeria.[63]

The Presidential Committee report specifically identified the public statements of Muhammadu Buhari, the presidential candidate of the Congress for Progressive Change, as contributing to the violence. One comment credited to the former military leader shortly before the election that voters should 'guard their vote' was misconstrued by many voters to imply recourse to violence. As Lemu put it in his report to the president:

> The first and probably the most important major cause [was] the failure on the part of the previous successive regimes since the military handover of power in 1999 to implement the recommendations of various committees, commissions and panels that had taken place in our nation. That failure facilitated the widespread sense of impunity in the culprits and perpetrators of crimes and violence in the Nigerian society.[64]

The panel recommended that the culprits be prosecuted as well as stringent action taken against corruption, the improvement of general security and changes to school curriculum to inculcate moral values. However, the recommendations of the report were never implemented.

2015

It did not appear that much was learned from the incidents that surrounded the 2011 general election as the 2015 exercise followed almost the same pattern. The events both preceding and succeeding the 2015 elections marked another season of ethnic, religious and regional tensions in Nigeria's democratic history. An important feature of that election season was the political re-alignments along regional and ethnic lines that occurred in 2013 ahead of the contest. This was the first of such political mergers since 1999. An alliance of three opposition political parties – Action Congress of Nigeria (ACN), Congress for Progressive Change (CPC), All Nigerian Peoples Party (ANPP), and a fraction of the All Progressive

---

[62] Federal Government of Nigeria, "Report of the Federal Government Investigation Panel on 2011 Election Violence and Civil Disturbances" (Abuja, September 2011).
[63] Federal Government of Nigeria, "Report of the Federal Government Investigation Panel on 2011 Election Violence and Civil Disturbances."
[64] Lanquart, "Post-election Violence: Lemu Committee Submit Reports; blames Buhari," 11 October 2011, www.nairaland.com/779226/post-election-violence-lemu-committee-submit.

Grand Alliance (APGA), as well as a break-away group from the ruling Peoples' Democratic Party (PDP) known as the New PDP – formed the All Progressives Congress (APC) to challenge the ruling PDP.

The merger into APC culminated into a stiff opposition that exuded marked differences in the depth, trend and magnitude of tension as well as violence across the country. With retired General Muhammadu Buhari, a northern Muslim as the APC presidential flagbearer and Dr Goodluck Ebele Jonathan, a Christian southerner and the incumbent president for the PDP, the country was set for a tough contest. All manner of centrifugal pulls were drawn into the contest. Energized regional militia groups and youth organizations became very vocal, publishing threatening reports and communiqué. The major religious groups, Christians and Muslims, pitched their tent with major candidates based on their religious inclinations. The politicians themselves took to maneuvering the political space, invoking sentiments and propaganda but this time with all kinds of subterfuge in the form of organized crime or deployment of secret cult groups, use of blackmail and violence to promote and defend their interests. In warlike rhetoric, Malam Nasir Elrufai, the gubernatorial candidate of the APC in 2015, while speaking at the "Transformed to Transform" (T2T) Nigerian conference and career fair at the Yar Adua Centre, Abuja, threatened: "the next election would be bloody and many people are likely to die. The only alternative left to get power is to take it by force."[65] Similarly, Asiwaju Bola Ahmed Tinubu, one of the founders of APC, declared: "it is going to be rig and roast, we are not prepared to go to court but drive them (PDP) out."[66] Even the chairman of the Northern Elders Forum, Professor Ango Abdullahi, added his voice to the threats while campaigning against President Jonathan during the build up to the 2015 presidential election. He vowed: "Those who vote for Jonathan and the PDP in 2015 will be considered [enemies] of the North."[67]

In a repeat of what appeared like the 2003 'do or die' politics of President Olusegun Obasanjo, Ayo Fayose, the PDP governor of Ekiti State, who was contesting for a second term, boastfully reiterated the same threat of a 'do or die' election:

> Propaganda would only waste time and attack is the best form of defense [...] the party in general and South West PDP needs to be valiant to face the Tinubus anywhere they are. [...]

---

[65] "SSS detains El Rufai," *Punch*, 28 January 2015.
[66] "Ekiti Osun guber polls," *Vanguard Newspaper*, 24 April 2014.
[67] "2015: We'll regard anyone that vote for PDP as enemy of North – NEF," *Vanguard Newspaper*, 15 October 2014.

> We have control of the Police and the Army and I cannot afford to lose my control on Police and the Army and without Jonathan being the president, we will lose the control.⁶⁸

This statement was made in 27 December 2014 after the PDP South-West geopolitical zone meeting in the Ondo State capital, Akure, in the heat of the electoral campaigns to boost the morale of party supporters to fight for the party and ensure victory at the polls in the election. In a similar manner, the Niger Delta Militants rising from a meeting held at the government house in Bayelsa State declared that they were ready to go to war. One of their leaders, Alhaji Mujadeen Asari Daukubo, was quoted as saying: "For every Goliath, God created a David. For every Pharaoh, there is a Moses. We are going to war. Every one of you should go and fortify yourself."⁶⁹ The magnitude of these threats ahead of the 2015 election informed the following remark by Chief Reuben Fasoranti leader of the pan-Yoruba socio-political group, Afenifere:

> We have in our hands a country that appears to be preparing for a war but almost all are pretending that it is all build-up to the next elections. The saber-rattling going on amongst some major party and political actors are not healthy for the democratic project as most of the noise going on is not even about solving any of the major challenges confronting the country but power mongering.⁷⁰

Despite this warning and the non-violence pact signed by the major political parties, their politicians were not deterred as their hired thugs and irate supporters made good on their threat by unleashing violence on opposition party supporters, and non-indigenes before and during the elections. Violence erupted across all the geopolitical zones prior to the elections. The Nigeria Election Observation Report of 2015 documented that the non-violence pact between the major presidential candidates, President Goodluck Jonathan and his primary rival Muhammadu Buhari did not do much to allay fears of many Nigerians who temporarily relocated to their states of origin prior to the election.⁷¹

---

68 A. Fayose, "Presidential Contest A Do-Or-Die Affair, Advocates Use of police/Army to Win Election," *Sahara Reporters*, 2 January 2015, https://www.saharareporters.com (accessed 22 June 2019).
69 Arodiegwu Eziukwu, "Niger Delta Militants Meets in Yenegoa, Threatens War Should Jonathan Lose Presidential Election," 24 January 2015, https://www.premiumtimesng.com (accessed 22 June 2019).
70 F. Reuben, "Nigeria Preparing for War Not Election," *This Day*, 14 April 2013, http://www.nigerreporters.com/afenifere-nigeria-preparing-for-war-not (accessed 4 July 2019).
71 International Republican Institute (IRI), "Nigeria Election Observation Report: Nigeria National Elections," 28 March 2015, https://www.iri.org/2015/nigeria-election-observation-report/1/assets/basic/html (accessed 4 July 2019).

In February 2015, Nigeria's National Human Rights Commission report documented more than 60 incidents of election-related violence in about 22 states spread across all six geopolitical zones, which left about 58 people dead and many more injured.[72] The report also noted an increase in hate speech in the run-up to the election including those published in the media and during campaign rallies by political party surrogates with an instance where an out-going governor of the PDP, Ibrahim Shema of Katsina State, was caught on video calling on party supporters to "crush" and "kill" "cockroaches," and other alleged incidences of high profile individuals calling for violence against anyone campaigning for change. It is remarkable to note that this vituperations were in reaction to the initial threat for violence from the Katsina State born General and APC Presidential flagbearer, Muhammadu Buhari, that: "If what happened in 2011 (alleged rigging) should happen in 2015, by the grace of God, the dog and baboon will be soaked in blood."[73] A major reason why Jonathan conceded defeat even while results were being collated was to avert what would have been recorded as the worst bloodshed in the history of elections in Nigeria.

The Nigeria Security Tracker (NST) documented 106 election-related deaths; 62 of which happened in the seven months preceding the election and 44 after the election results were announced especially in the first two weeks following the elections.[74] Most of the post-election deaths were accidental self-inflicted deaths by persons revelling over APC victory. States most-affected by the pre- and during-the-election violence were Rivers, Gombe, Adamawa, Yobe, Anambra and Enugu.[75] Bomb blasts at polling units in Gombe killed seven. Regarding the experience of Rivers State, the Federal Ministry of Women Affairs and Social Development report reads:

> Rivers State elections were characterized by a lot of violence, the most the country recorded thus far in the 2015 Gubernatorial and State Assembly elections. The Home of the Commissioner of Women Affairs Mrs Joeba West, in Buguma, Rivers State, was set ablaze along with Registration Area Centres in Kalabari National College (KNC) and a police patrol vehicle at

---

72 National Human Right Commission, *Nigeria Elections 2015: Pre Election Violence*, (Abuja: Human Rights Commission Press, 2015).
73 Rinniyat Luka, "2015 Il be Bloody If... Buhari," *Vanguard* Newspaper, 15 May 2012. https://www.vanguardngr.com/2012/05/2015-Il-be-bloody-if-buhari/.
74 J. Campbell, "Nigeria 2015 Presidential Election: Tracking Election Violence in Nigeria, www.cfr.org/report/election-violence-nigeria/html (accessed 4 July 2019).
75 Campbell, "Nigeria 2015 Presidential Election."

the 24 hours before the Saturday elections by unknown thugs. It was reported that the thugs suspected that election materials were being kept in her residence.[76]

On 8 February 2015, a week before the Presidential and National Assembly Elections, following the advice of the National Security Adviser to the President, INEC announced that it had postponed elections until March 2015. The postponement became necessary after the security chiefs stated that they could not guarantee security on election day due to instability in the North East geopolitical zone and requested six weeks to curb the insurgency. Whatever the real reason might be, it was evident to all that insecurity and tension over the 2015 presidential election was at its peak. The six weeks grace demanded was well utilized and an atmosphere of calm was restored in the troubled zone. The election also ended with a historic outcome, being the first time in Nigeria that an incumbent president accepted defeat from the opposition and also congratulated the winner before the conclusion of vote collation.

2019

The 2019 election was a replica of the 2015 experience, but this time the contestants for the presidential office were both from the northern Fulani Muslims: the incumbent President Muhammadu Buhari (APC) and a former PDP Vice President, Atiku Abubakar (PDP). Atiku Abubakar was among the founding chieftains of the APC before he rejoined the PDP following some disaffection with the APC. The election witnessed all the political maneuvering, chicanery and violence that characterized the 2015 election. There were higher incidents of election-related violence before and during the elections than in the post-election period. There was also a supplementary election just like in 2015. The Nigeria Civil Society Situation Room – a coalition of civil society groups in Nigeria – in their report on the 2019 general election documented that it was marred by violence across the six geopolitical zones of the federation with a record of 626 deaths occurring between the start of party campaigns and the commencement of the general and supplementary elections.[77] The report further listed the number of deaths for each of the six geopolitical zones in the country. The North-West recorded the

---

[76] Federal Ministry of Women Affairs and Social Development, "Election Observation Report on the 2015 General Election in Nigeria," 47–48, https://www.iri.org/2015%20Nigeria%20Election%20Observation%20Report/1/assets/basic-html/page60.html.
[77] Nigeria Civil Society Situation Room, "Report of Nigeria's 2019 General Elections" (Abuja: Situation Room Secretariat, 2019).

highest number of deaths with 172 killed during the elections, while the North-East followed with 146 fatalities. The South-South and North Central had 120 and 111 fatalities respectively. 63 people were killed in the South-West and 14 in the South-East. The states of Benue (North Central), Kaduna (North-West), Rivers (South-South) and Zamfara (North-West) recorded the highest casualties in their respective geopolitical zones.[78] So far, only few perpetrators of violence during the 2019 general election had been arrested by security agencies. With 622 deaths in 2019, that election experience recorded more deaths than the 2015 elections that recorded 106 deaths. In addition to the killings that occurred during the 2019 polls, there were many incidents of ballot box snatching, assaults, abductions and harassment of the opposition.

In evaluating the credibility of the 2019 elections the European Union Election Observation Mission (EU EOM) report of June 2019, published in *Premium Times*, states that the election was marred by violence and intimidation which harm the integrity of the electoral process and may deter future participation.[79] It added that violent killings, political thuggery, rigging and vote buying were prevalent, leading to the low turn-out of voters. The election into federal offices recorded a voter turn-out of 35.6% while the state level election saw an even lower turn out.[80]

Conclusion

There is no doubt that elections in Nigeria since her independence in 1960 have been associated with violence often resulting in deaths and loss of property. Election-related violence disrupts the normal functioning of the country and engenders political instability that subverts governance. The fourth republic elections appear seeped in electoral fraud and violence. Rather than improve on the deficiencies of the first and second republics, the electoral vices of the fourth republic became more intense and recurrent, threatening the very foundations of Nigeria's national security. The ethnic and religious divide also became deepened. With the spate of violence across ethnic and religious lines that was witnessed in some northern states, the country was headed for destruction. The saving grace, however, was the absence of reprisal attacks across ethnic and

---

[78] Nigeria Civil Society Situation Room, "Report of Nigeria's 2019 General Elections."
[79] "EU-EOM Preliminary Report on 2019 Nigeria Elections," *Premium Times*, 30 June 2019. https://www.premiumtimesng.com/news/headlines/343971-626-killed-during-2019-nigeria-elections-report.html.
[80] "EU-EOM Preliminary Report on 2019 Nigeria Elections."

religious lines in the southern part of the country. It is therefore the position of this study that politicians, electoral bodies, law enforcement agencies especially the police, the lead security agency in Nigeria, politicians and other major stakeholders should abide by the rules of elections, and eschew violence to ensure credible, free, fair and violence-free elections in Nigeria. Achieving this goal will both entrench democratic norms and further democracy in Nigeria, rather that truncating it. In addition, the use of the military in elections should be stopped as their presence militarizes the exercise and sends the wrong signals to the opposition as well as the electorate. Finally, negative utterances and rhetoric that can trigger crisis by politicians or their surrogates should be checked by the government using its law enforcement agents regardless of party affiliations, and penalties meted out to offenders according to the law. This would deter potential future offenders.

Fidelis A. E. Paki
The Challenges of Election Security in Nigeria: A Study of the 2019 General Election

Abstract: This chapter examines the challenges that undermined election security in Nigeria during the 2019 general election. Although six successful nationwide general elections were conducted between 1999 and 2019, Nigeria still grapples with insecurity during election seasons. Gory tales of electoral violence in previous elections placed an unmitigated burden on the capacity of the national security architecture to manage the electoral process to ensure free, fair and credible elections. This chapter employs a dense trove of secondary data, deconstructed via the descriptive method, to show that election insecurity is among the major challenges facing Nigeria's democratic experience. Lack of adherence to electoral and security principles and poor financial management were among the main factors undermining the security of elections in Nigeria. Drawing lessons from the 2019 general election, the chapter proposes how best to curb election insecurity during future elections.

Keywords: Nigeria, challenges, election security, election management bodies and security agencies

Introduction

Nigeria's Fourth Republic has witnessed twenty years (1999 to 2019) of uninterrupted democracy, during which six nation-wide general elections were conducted in 1999, 2003, 2007, 2011, 2015 and 2019. Scholars have discussed how each of these elections was characterized by wanton electoral violence, often resulting in loss of lives and properties.[1] Put differently, from 1999 to 2019, issues revolving

---

[1] See Karl Maier, *This House has Fallen: Nigeria in Crisis* (New York: Penguin Books, 2000), 23; Neville Onebamhoi Obakhedo, "Curbing Electoral Violence in Nigeria: The Imperative of Political Education," *African Research Review* 5 no. 5 (2011): 99–110; E. O. Ewa, "Federal Elections in Nigeria, 1959," *The Indian Journal of Political Science* 21, no.2 (1960): 101–113; Anthony Egobueze and Callistus Ojirika, "Electoral Violence in Nigeria's Fourth Republic: Implications for Political Stability," *Journal of Scientific Research and Reports* 13, no. 2 (2017): 1–11; Paul Colier and Pedro

Fidelis A. E. Paki, Niger Delta University

https://doi.org/10.1515/9783110766561-015

around insecurity were major concerns during election periods in Nigeria. Non-securitization of elections has bred both domestic and international worries.[2] When compared to the 2007 and 2011 elections, Nigeria could be said to have conducted relatively peaceful elections in 2019 despite pockets of electoral violence recorded in almost every part of the country.

What then could be responsible for this recurring violence during elections in Nigeria? Can one assert that violent elections are attributes of democratic experimentation in developing countries like Nigeria? Indeed, in attempt to understand electoral violence or election insecurity in Nigeria, scholars have proffered diverse opinions.[3] For instance, a fraction of studies on electoral violence argue that the rate of unemployment that mostly affect young people is a major reason why election insecurity persists since most of the violence that occurred were in actual sense perpetrated by youths under the manipulation of politicians.[4]

Some others argue that one reason alone cannot satisfactorily explain election insecurity in Nigeria. As a matter of fact, violent elections are bound to occur when there are unresolved issues revolving around resource-based competition and social division (between the rich and the poor), among others.[5] The aforementioned premises could not be far from the truth as, all across Nigeria, the problem of violent crime and criminality is on the increase. More so, there is a rising spate of kidnappings, armed robberies, banditry, assassinations, diffusion

---

C. Vicente, "Votes and Violence: Experimental Evidence from a Field Experiment in Nigeria" (Households in Conflict Network (HiCN), Working Paper 50, 2008); John Campbell, "Tracking Election Violence in Nigeria," *Council on Foreign Relations* 15 (2019), https://www.cfr.org/blog/tracking-election-violence-nigeria (accessed 10 November 2020); Richard Bourne, *Nigeria: A New History of a Turbulent Century* (Ibadan: BookKraft, 2016), 183; Samson Adesote and John O. Abimbola, "Electoral Violence and the Survival of Democracy in Nigeria's Fourth Republic: A Historical Perspective," *Canadian Social Science* 10, no.3 (2014): 140–148.

2 Sarah Birch and David Muchlinski, "Electoral Violence Prevention: What Work?" *Democratization* 25, no. 3 (2017): 385–403 and Olowojulo Olakunle, et al, "Trends in Electoral Violence in Nigeria," *Journal of Social Science and Public Policy* 11, no. 1 (2019): 37–52.

3 Lai Olurode, ed., *Election Security in Nigeria: Matter Arising* (Abuja: Friedrich-Ebert Stiftung, 2013), 1–115.

4 Hakeem Onapajo, "Violence and Votes in Nigeria: The Dominance of Incumbents in the Use of Violence to Rig Elections," *African Spectrum* 49, no. 2 (2014): 27–51; Kuro Preye Inokoba and Ebi Agnes Maliki, "Youths, Electoral Violence and Democratic Consolidation in Nigeria: The Bayelsa State Experience," *The Anthropologist* 13, no. 3 (2011): 217–225.

5 Ebere Onwudiwe and Chloe Berwind-Dart, "Breaking the Cycle of Electoral Violence in Nigeria," *Special Report* (Washington, DC: US Institute of Peace, 2010), 1–16.

of illegal arms and their use for prosecuting the aforementioned violent crimes.[6] In addition, roads and waterways are no longer safe. The situation is such that armed robbers wreak havoc even in broad daylight and brazenly attack individuals, homes, banks, markets, hotels and shops. These situations are compounded by the phenomenon of farmers/herders (pastoralists) conflicts affecting a cross-section of the country. These violent scenarios are coming amidst an age-long fault line, where the political landscape is structured along ethno-religious and geopolitical arrangements, forcing a situation where a presidential election, for instance, becomes difficult to win without support from other geopolitical zones of the country. Thus, as the political elites get set for elections, they engender a tensed political atmosphere that exposes the electorates to election insecurity, which in the past resulted in loss of lives and properties

From this perspective, this chapter will explore the non-securitization of Nigeria's election, with focus on the 2019 experience. Some fundamental issues that had affected the security of elections in Nigeria's Fourth Republic will be properly articulated. The chapter largely derives its data from secondary publications; and deconstructs it using the descriptive method. The chapter is divided into seven sections. After the introduction, the second section focuses on the conceptual discourse on election, security and election security. Section three presents the theoretical framework for the study; followed in section four by a discussion of election insecurity in Nigeria. The challenges posed by election security in the 2019 general election in Nigeria are discussed in section five, while the subsidiary security challenges of the 2019 general election are listed in section six. The final section concludes the discourse and recommends ways of improving election security for future elections.

The Conceptual Discourse

Key terms used in this study, such as election, election insecurity and electoral violence, have been defined by scholars. Indeed, these terms enjoy plural definitions and as such are used in a variety of ways depending on how they respectively fit a particular study. Thus, these terms would be conceptualized in a way that would make this study more explicit.

---

[6] Bayo Adekanye and Rachael Iyande, "Security Challenges in Election Management," in Lai Olurode and Attahiru M. Jega (eds.), *Security Challenges of Election Management in Nigeria* (Abuja: Independent National Electoral Commission and Friedrich Ebert Stiftung, 2011), 15–51.

Election, for instance, "is the process by which the members of the community choose one or more persons to exercise authority on their behalf."[7] Heywood defines it as "a device for filling an office through choices made by designated body of people, the electorates."[8] It is the mechanism of election in any democratic setting that ensures that the government exercises its powers with the consent of the governed. They are "institutional procedures for choosing political office holders of a country. Mike Igini posits:

> Election is the fundamental element of modern day representative democracy. It is a means through which the electorates choose their representatives into different positions of governance; it refers to the institutionalized procedures for recruiting political office holders by the electorates of a country or group.[9]

Security, as used in this study, is the state of being free from danger, threat, fear and anxiety. It goes beyond its military connotation to include the absence of threats from hunger, flooding, drought, diseases and pestilence, among others. Succinctly, security entails that political, economic, environmental, health and other forms of threats must be eliminated before human security is attained. In sum, it is a protective condition against external or internal threats.[10] In the context of elections, it establishes an enabling environment that is conducive to holding a democratic poll.[11]

Since election and security have been conceptualized differently, what then is election security? Election security is a form of protection that is intended to guarantee the safety of election materials, electorates, aspirants, election officials and all others during election periods. The aim is to ensure that the activities of actors do not adversely affect the outcome of an election. This definition is in tandem with Jeff Fischer who argues that election security is "the process of

---

[7] Mazi C. C. Mbah, *Foundations of Political Science* (Awka: Rex Charles and Patrick Publications, 2007), 421.
[8] Andrew Heywood, *Politics* (New York: Palgrave Foundations, 2007), 253.
[9] Mike Igini, "Election Security in Theory and Practice: Perspective of a Resident Commissioner," in *Election Security in Nigeria: Matter Arising*, ed. Lai Olurode (Abuja: Friedrich-Ebert Stiftung (FES), 2013), 43.
[10] Ira S. Cohen and Andrew C. Tuttle, *National Security* (New York: Free Press, 1972), 1.
[11] Institute for Democracy and Electoral Assistance (IDEA), *The Electoral Integrity Project: Why Elections Fail and What We Can Do About it* (New York: United Nations Development Program, 2015), 26, https://www.undp.org/content/dam/undp/library/Democratic%20Governance/Electoral%20Systems%20and%20Processes/SAFE.pdf (accessed 29 April 2019).

protecting electoral stakeholders, information, facilities, and events."[12] Election security "means the absence of use of threat or force, harassment and intimidation in all the phases of election."[13]

In Nigeria, for instant, election security is characterized by the increasing concerns over national security to an extent that institutions such are the Ministry of Defense, and the Ministry of Internal Affairs, or the Ministry of Interior are involved in the deployment of security personnel across the country during elections. Constitutionally, security responsibilities during the period of election falls within the domain of the Nigeria Police Force (NPF), which has the primary responsibility of maintaining law and order and by implication carries out election security duties. However, because of constitutional requirements and security peculiarities in the country, the Nigeria Police Force has, in the recent past, received assistance from other security agencies such as the Nigeria Security and Civil Defence Corps (NSCDC). In more intense situations, the military was deployed to aid. This explains the reason why INEC at its meeting of 7 December 2010 approved the establishment of Inter-agency Consultative Committee on Election Security (ICCES), a platform comprising representatives of election managers and security agencies, at the national, state and local government levels in Nigeria. Reacting to the ICCES, Attahiru M. Jega, INEC Chairman during the 2011 and 2015 general elections, observes:

> Election security has been a recurrent challenge to election management bodies in Nigeria over the years. This has spanned several issues including the physical security of election officials, protection of election materials, including results, documents containing election results, ensuring order at polling and collation centres, as well as controlling violence among contending political interests.[14]

Without doubt, the recurring cases of electoral violence or what could be called election insecurity have forced a situation where the Nigerian military are now very close to the ballot box; therefore, almost negating Nigeria's nascent democracy.

---

12 Jeff Fischer, "Electoral Conflict and Violence: A Strategy for Study and Prevention" (IFES White Paper, 2002), http://aceproject.org/ero-en/topics/elections-security/UNPAN019255.pdf/view (accessed 29 April 2019).
13 Lai Olurode, "The Feasibility of Election Security in an Unsecured Global Environment," in *Election Security in Nigeria: Matter Arising*, 1–14.
14 Attahiru M. Jega, "Developing Credible Leaders: The Role of Faith-based Organizations" (Public Lecture organized by Eckanker Nigeria, Abuja, 2010).

Theoretical Underpinning

This study is anchored on the theoretical framework of human security. The theory was birthed by the United Nations General Assembly resolution 66/290. The UN understood insecurity to have gone beyond a mere human threat. Thus, in order to react proportionately to new forms of threat, the notion of human security was coined, which holds that for there to be a comprehensive human security, security must include political, food, environment, economic and finance, among others. Election insecurity is therefore anathema to political security. Ordinarily, election is supposed to be a peaceful contest for votes, but in Nigeria it is characterized by insecurity, which results from widespread violence, destruction of lives and properties, arson, intimidation, thuggery, fraud and rigging. All of these make elections in Nigeria fall short of meeting international best practices. There is need, therefore, to introduce human security concept into Nigerian political terrain in order to avert the recurring spate of election insecurity in Nigeria's democratic experimentation.

The United Nations General Assembly resolution 66/290 has provided the antidote for election insecurity in Nigeria by suggesting that the concept of human security would be an ideal approach towards assisting member-states in identifying and addressing widespread and cross-cutting challenges to the survival, livelihood and dignity of their people.[15] The resolution proposes a "people-oriented, comprehensive, context-specific and prevention-oriented response that would strengthen the protection and empowerment of all people."[16] While adopting the human security approach on the nexus between election and security challenges facing Nigeria, Roger T. Akpan, acknowledges the relevance of the conflict theory, elite theory, functionalist theory and other related theories in election and security studies, but noted their inadequacies in accounting for "the changing realities of the dynamics of election induced insecurity particularly with direct effects on both human existence and the entire social system.[17]

---

15 *"Resolution adopted by the General Assembly 60/1: World Summit Outcome" (United Nations General Assembly, 2005.)*

16 "What is human security?" United Nations Trust Fund for Security, (nd), https://www.un.org/humansecurity/what-is-human-security/ (accessed 27 April 2019).

17 Roger T. Akpan, "Election and Security Challenges in Nigeria: Experience from the Niger Delta (1999–2015)," *International Journal of Political Science* 3, no. 2 (2017): 1–14.

Election Insecurity in Nigeria: A Brief Discourse

Election insecurity is not a new phenomenon in Nigeria. Since her First Republic (1963–1966), Nigeria has recorded election insecurity. Specifically, the 1964 general election was a classic case-in-point.[18] The Second Republic (1979–1983) was equally not devoid of election insecurity, thus constituting part of the reasons the military carried out a putsch on 31 December 1983, as they did on 15 January 1966.[19] Since 1999, when Nigeria returned to civilian rule, there have been series of cut-throat competition among her politicians that resulted in much violence, massive destruction of properties and loss of lives. This is because the stakes are high in every election. In fact, elections under the presidential system of government, which Nigeria adopted, are considered as a zero-sum-game, because the winner takes it all.[20] This makes any election in the country a must win affair for most politicians. Under such circumstances, the issue of providing adequate security becomes not only paramount but also challenging. Nonetheless, elections, as the hallmark of democracy, must be conducted in a manner that it reflects the will of the people. For this to be done, politicians and election managers must ensure that the electorates exercise their constitutional obligations by voting in an atmosphere devoid of fear.

Nothing protects the rights of electorates than the fact that elections are secured so that citizens can cast informed, secret ballot without fear of retributions. In addition, there must be a situation where officials can effectively administer the process; and Civil Society Organizations (CSOs), the media and political parties can engage and observe the election process as well. Similarly, in every election, the authorities take requisite steps to ensure the security of voters, candidates, electoral officials, observers and other stakeholders involved and also ensure that sensitive election materials are kept secure. All of these promote free, fair and credible elections.

Ostensibly, there is different or specific security requirement for every election. For instance, in places such as the NorthEast geopolitical zone where there are on-going conflicts or significant potential for violence, securing an

---

18 Emmanuel Oladipo Ojo, "Leadership Crisis and Political Instability in Nigeria, 1964–1966: The Personalities, the Parties and the Policies," *Global Advanced Research Journal of History, Political Science and International Relation* 1, no.1 (2012): 6–17; Douglas G. Anglin, "Brinkmanship in Nigeria: The Federal Elections of 1964–65," *International Journal* 20, no. 2 (1965): 173–188.
19 Larry Diamond, *Class, Ethnicity and Democracy in Nigeria: The Failure of the First Republic* (New York: Syracuse University Press, 1987), 24–30.
20 Olu Awofeso and Paul A. Irabo, "The Game Theory and the Politics of Cross-Carpeting in Nigeria's Fourth Republic," *Public Policy and Administration Research* 7, no. 7 (2017): 66–72.

election requires addressing a multiplicity of factors and will likely involve deploying relatively large number of security personnel – the police, military and other para-military units – to protect physical locations and individuals.

The security plan for a given election must take into account the implication for deploying armed personnel. Undoubtedly, the deployment of security personnel becomes imperative where the potential for electoral violence is high. Such massive presence dissuades electorates from participating in an election exercise. Again, there is the issue of building citizens' confidence in the electoral process. Ultimately, inputs from Civil Society Organisations in the planning phase can help to ensure that citizens' concerns are more fully considered and that they are informed of the measures in place to ensure their security.

In spite of the benefits of election security, it is, however, noteworthy to state that it requires more comprehensive measures than just the deployment of security forces. After all, as some studies have shown, often these security personnel are compromised when they allow themselves to be used as tools of violence in an election in Nigeria.[21] The roles of security agencies in different segments of Nigeria's democratic experiment are still fresh in the history books. For instance, security agencies were partly responsible for the demise of the first, second and third republics.[22] And, in the current republic, they have been severally used as tools of violence during elections.

The use of violence as a political tool is common in elections in Nigeria. For instance, the 1999 election was marred by violence, intimidation, widespread fraud and rigging.[23] The 2003 election was conducted relatively smoothly in some places, while in others what transpired was a charade where vote-rigging and violent intimidation were commonplace. While in some locations, logistic problems prevented the smooth running of the election, which some parties and candidates took advantage of to falsify the results; in other locations, either election materials never reached the polling stations or election officials never turned up yet results were officially announced from these constituencies.[24]

The Human Rights Watch (HRW) reported that in the Fourth Republic, within a period of eight years from June 2006 to May 2014, there were about 915 cases of election violence in the country, resulting in about 3, 934 deaths. The 2007 polls were widely condemned as the most massively rigged in the country's history

---

[21] Toyin Falola, et al, *Nigeria in the Twentieth Century* (Ibadan: Longman, 1991), 135.
[22] Mike Igini, "Election Security in Theory and Practice: Perspective of a Resident Electoral Commissioner," in *Election Security in Nigeria: Matters arising,* 41–62.
[23] Maier, *This House has fallen,* 23–30.
[24] Akpan, "Election and Security Challenges in Nigeria," 1–14.

amidst widespread violence during the campaign and polling.[25] The 2011 vote was cleaner, but also deadlier as over 800 people died in post-election violence that targeted ethnic and religious minorities in northern Nigeria cities.[26] The 2015 polls were peaceful in comparison but even then, according to the National Human Rights Commission (NHRC), at least 108 people were killed, 58 in pre-election violence and 50 on election day and afterwards, as a result of fights that broke out between the supporters of major parties in nine states.[27] In 2019, going by reports obtained by the Nigerian Civil Society Situation Room (NCSSR), 58 persons died as a result of electoral violence, with Rivers State accounting for 28 of these election victims.[28] The report also stated that since 2011, Rivers State has been a major theatre of violence.[29] Therefore, there is need to identify Conflict Early Warning Signs (CEWS) in order to take adequate preventive measures and address rumours concerning potential or actual incidents of violence. There is also need to institute potential violence mitigating measures. The significance of election security, therefore, cannot be over emphasized because it damages the democratic experience of Nigerians.

Challenges Posed by Election Insecurity During the 2019 General Election

As already noted, the elections conducted during Nigeria's Fourth Republic were characterized by wanton election insecurity. In other words, there were many challenges with election security in Nigeria. The underlisted factors undermined the 2019 general election:

---

[25] "Nigeria: Polls Marred by Violence, Fraud," *Human Rights Watch*, 7 April 2007, https://reliefweb.int/report/nigeria/nigeria-polls-marred-violence-fraud (accessed 15 April 2019).
[26] "Nigeria: Post-election Violence Killed 800," *Human Rights Watch*, 17 April 2007, https://reliefweb.int/report/nigeria/nigeria-polls-marred-violence-fraud (accessed 15 April 2019).
[27] ICG, "Nigeria's 2019 Election: Six States to Watch."
[28] Friday Olokor, "58 Nigerians Killed in 2019 Elections – Situation Room," *Punch Newspaper*, 10 March 2019, https://punchng.com/58-nigerians-killed-in-2019-elections-situation-room/ (accessed 15 April 2019).
[29] Olokor, "58 Nigerians Killed in 2019 Elections."

Lack of Adherence to Election Principles

Ordinarily, an election is a contest for legitimate power; it is a non-violent competition, keenly contested among aspirants with the aim to acquire or retain power. Nonetheless, in this process, confrontation is inevitable. There is, therefore, the need to realize that election security should focus on containment and management of the process based on electoral principles. The organization and conduct of credible elections demand adherence to principles and rights that define democratic elections. Thus, election entails that the following election principles, which are quite challenging to election stakeholders, be observed:

a) Transparency: This requires that steps involved in the electoral process be made well known to all members of the society. Where the electoral process is shrouded in obscurity, there is the likelihood of mistrust among the electorate and the candidates.

b) Compliance with national laws: This requires that elections must be held not only within immutable timeframes, but also in accordance with the electoral laws of the country. In a situation where an election is not compliant with extant laws, it ultimately generates a legitimacy crisis. That is to say, where the national election laws are suspected to have been amended to favour any section or party, it could lead to wrangling within the political class.

c) Freedom of speech and association: This denotes that Nigerians are guaranteed their social, political, economic and legal rights. Where citizens' fundamental human rights are trampled upon arbitrarily, it generates distrust for legitimately elected authority that is supposed to protect such rights.

d) Impartially: The institutions responsible for the administration and security of an election must carry out their constitutional mandates without favouring any particular political competitor. In line with this submission, Lopez-Pastor observed that a democratic election implies "freedom from coercion and fairness as the correlate of impartiality."[30] Laus A. Jinadu[31] also states that the notion of impartiality as applied to electoral governance involves a paradox; the requirement of the institutionalization of procedural certainty

---

[30] Rafael López-Pintor, "Electoral Management Bodies as Institutions of Governance," *An IFES Research Paper* (2000), 103, http://www.eods.eu/library/UNDP.Electoral%20Management%20Bodies%20as%20Institutions%20of%20Governance.pdf (accessed 15 April 2019).

[31] Liasu Adele Jinadu, "Comparative Analysis of Security Challenges of Elections in Nigeria," in *Security Challenges of Election Management in Nigeria*, eds. Lai Olurode and Attahiru Jega (Abuja: The Independence National Electoral Commission and Friedrich Ebert Stiftung, 2011), 53.

to secure the substantive uncertainty of electoral outcomes, or what is sometimes described as the "strategic dilemma of establishing democracy as a system of organized uncertainty."[32]

e) Inclusiveness: This means that the involvement of the citizens at every level of the process should not be restricted. Similarly, election security should be an inclusive affair.

f) Competitive or non-competitiveness: This requires that elections offer the electorates a genuine choice of both candidates and parties. In other words, public offices ought to be effectively filled through an appropriate nomination process.[33]

From the above provisions, it is pertinent to note that some members of the Nigerian political class, the government and its agencies very often undermine election principles in the process of conducting election. Lack of adherence to electoral principles is indeed a major challenge to election security in Nigeria. This is because it leads to lack of confidence in the electoral processes of the country. For instance, there were reports that most countries in the Global North refused to send representatives to the inauguration ceremony of President Muhammadu Buhari for a second term in office, after the 2019 general election, because of the flawed nature of that election, which did not observe basic democratic tenets. The United States of America followed up on this and issued travel bans on Nigerian politicians found culpable of undermining democratic principles and human rights during the 2019 election.[34]

Lack of Adherence to Security Principles

For security operatives to effectively discharge their functions during an election, they must be guided by their own rules of engagement. Other necessary guidelines would include:

a) Equitable and rights-based election security: This requires that contestants and the electorate must be treated in an equitable manner by both security

---

[32] Shaheen Mozaffar, "Patterns of Electoral Governance in Africa's Emergent Democracies," *International Political Science Review* 23, no. 1 (2002), 85–101.

[33] Heywood, *Politics*, 261.

[34] Samuel Ogundipe, "U.S Bans Nigerians Who 'Undermined Democracy' during 2019 Election," *Premium Times*, 24 July 2019, https://www.premiumtimesng.com/news/headlines/342595-u-s-bans-nigerians-who-undermined-democracy-during-2019-election.html (accessed 10 November 2020).

forces and electoral officials. The actions of security forces must not be determined by political factors. They must bear in mind that an election provides opportunity for the people to exercise their civic and human rights. Any security that does not consider and acknowledge this fact is defective. Undoubtedly, the people whose rights are infringed on have the prerogative to challenge whoever causes such infringement in a court of law. Hence, security must be exercised in equitable and rights-based manner.

b) National ownership: There should be awareness that elections are a sovereign process. Similarly, security in a country is an aspect of the sovereign processes of that nation. Thus, security and elections are processes that must be guided by the ownership and control of a national authority to reflect sovereignty. This will make election security avoid allegations of international interference, but regulated by the laws of the land. The security forces must bear this in mind and adhere strictly to national cultural practices.

c) Strategic Planning: Elections are planned affairs. Ordinarily, elections are planned within a period of about 18 to 24 months before the polling day and occur as a widely dispersed exercise requiring significant planning and preparatory activities.[35] Often the security forces (police and/or military) hardly possess sufficient standing personnel and resources to secure an election, and simultaneously carry out their regular duties. For this purpose, integrated strategic planning by the electoral and security institutions is essential in order to allocate and coordinate available resources. Hence, senior security managers must adhere to strategic plans made for an election.

d) Flexible and efficient: The electoral process should be amenable to changes in order to be efficient. The amendments should be in the areas of accommodating legal, operational or political conditions that arise. Thus, the need for security planning requires a range of contingency plans and resources to ensure flexibility. Alternatively, clearly defined constraints on security capabilities and resources based on efficient planning should be available to inform decision makers on the range of options that are feasible to accommodate.

e) Transparent and accountable: This ensures that election security operations are carried out in the public interest. A disclosure of operational security policies to parties involved in a transparent manner increases public confidence on security operations. Transparency requires that there must be wide consultation in the election project. Necessary information should be shared

---

35 "The Electoral Integrity Project: Why Elections Fail and What We Can Do About It."

and the defined roles of security forces well understood. This will make security forces on election duties accountable for their actions and inactions.

Lack of Adherence to Election Plan

It is said that failure to plan is an indication of a plan to fail. Planning affects human beings as well as institutions in their polities. In every election, there must be plans put in place by the authorities to secure, transfer and store sensitive election materials. Therefore, planning an election is important for the successful conduct of polls, even when it might sometimes prove challenging. There are many on-going violent conflicts already in Nigeria that could trigger violence during election periods also. Conflict comes from political, economic and social dimensions of a given society. Therefore, the identification of flashpoints is very important. Also, there is the need to put in place effective violence mitigation plans. This often involves identifying early warning signs, mobilizing citizen monitoring and mitigation efforts, dispatching properly trained security forces, coordinating among government agencies and educating the public, among other things.

The matter of election planning also involves identifying the institutions that are involved in election. Ultimately, multiple institutions, like election management bodies (EMB), INEC, the Ministries of Interior, and Defense, among others, may be involved in creating a secure election environment. These institutions work to develop, implement and review security measures throughout the electoral process. The Civil Society Organizations, the media, trade unions, religious, traditional and opinion leaders, also play important roles in creating a secure electoral environment by mediating, building intolerance for violence and enhancing public confidence in experiencing secure electoral participation.

The INEC Manual, which states the regulations and guidelines for the conduct of the 2019 general elections, identifies the number of persons allowed to carry out election duties. Section 48(1–6) of the manual reads:

The following shall be allowed access to the electoral material distribution centres, polling units, polling stations and collation centres:
a) Voters (at polling units only);
b) INEC officials on election duty;
c) Security agents;
d) Candidates or their accredited polling agents;
e) Accredited journalists/media; and

f) Accredited domestic and foreign observers.[36]

In section 51(1–8), the manual lists the role of security agents as follows: Security agents on election duty shall:

a) Provide security at the polling units/polling stations and collation centres to ensure that the polling units, counting of ballots, collation and declaration of results are conducted without any disturbance;
b) Take necessary measures to prevent violence or any activity that can threaten to disrupt the elections;
c) Comply with any lawful directive(s) issued by or under the authority of INEC;
d) Ensure the safety and security of all election personnel and materials by escorting and guarding the materials at all levels as appropriate;
e) Arrest on the instruction of the presiding officer or other INEC officials, any person(s) causing any disturbance or preventing the smooth conduct of proceedings at polling units/stations and collation centres;
f) On the instruction of the presiding officer, stand at the end of the queue of voters at the polling unit at the official close of poll to prevent any person joining in;
g) Escort the presiding officer and other election officials to deliver the election results, ballot boxes and other election materials safely to the RA/ward collation centre; and
h) Escort collation officers to deliver election results to the returning officer and subsequently to the Resident Electoral Commissioner or Electoral Officer, as the case may be, for the submission of election materials and results.[37]

The effect of lack of adherence to election plan made INEC to postpone the 2019 general election by one week, giving as reason logistic problems and sabotage. The Presidential and National Assembly (NASS) election originally scheduled for 16 February 2019 was moved to 23 February 2019 while the gubernatorial, State Houses of Assembly and Federal Capital Territory Area Council election expected to hold on 2 March 2019 eventually held on 9 March 2019. It was for similar reasons that the 2015 general election was postponed by several weeks so that instead of commencing on 14 February 2015 as planned, it was held on 28 March 2015. With the postponement of the 2015 and 2019 general elections in Nigeria, it seemed that elections would likely be arbitrarily postponed in the future, which is a matter of security concern to election managers and the general electorate.

---

36 INEC, *Regulations and Guidelines*, 31.
37 INEC, *Regulations and Guidelines*, 30.

Faulty Financial Arrangements for Election Security

The 1999 Constitution of the Federal Republic of Nigeria (as amended), section 222–229 provides rules and regulations on the operations of political parties. Sections 225 and 226, affirm the powers of INEC to inquire and assess campaign finances and a party's source of fund and its management. Section 228 expressly provides sanctions with regard to party finance and campaign finance based on powers from the National Assembly. The best the National Assembly had ever done in this regard, however, has been the enactment and review of the Electoral Acts to guide the conduct of elections in Nigeria, notably the Electoral Acts of 2002, 2006 and 2010.[38]

Reuben Abati documents that the amended 2010 Electoral Act caps spending limits as follows: Presidential (1 billion naira), Governorship (200 million naira), Senatorial (40 million naira), House of Representatives (20 million naira) and State House of Assembly (10 million naira). Section 92 (3) of this enabling law also requires every political party to submit an audited revenue and expenditure report of the party six months after every election, failing which penalties apply.[39] Political parties in Nigeria, especially the dominant ones, notably engage in corrupt practices during elections.[40] There is, however, no sufficient evidence to show that political parties have complied with the financial aspect of the electoral law. Similarly, there is no evidence of diligent prosecution of defaulting political parties and their candidates. Thus, the subject of corrupt campaign and election financing is a big challenge to election security and the survival of democracy in Nigeria.

When the opposition candidate, General Muhammadu Buhari of the All Progressive Congress (APC), won the 2015 presidential election, his administration investigated the campaign finances of the Peoples' Democratic Party (PDP) and discovered monumental corruption. Some of the key actors received campaign funds worth billions of naira to help the re-election drive of the former president, Dr. Goodluck Jonathan. Surprisingly, the party (PDP) was made to refund the looted funds, while some key actors like Colonel Sambo Dasuki (rtd), former National Security Adviser to President Goodluck Jonathan, Chief Femi

---

[38] Reuben Abati, "2019 and the Politics of Campaign Finance," *The Eagle*, 15 May 2018, https://www.theeagleonline.com.ng/2019-and-the-politics-of-campaign-finance-by-reuben-abati/ (accessed 10 November 2020).
[39] Abati, "2019 and the Politics of Campaign Finance."
[40] Hassan A. Saliu, "Introduction," in *Political Parties and Electoral Process in Nigeria: Exploring the Missing Links*, eds., Ibrahim A. Shuaibu, Hassan A. Saliu and Aloysius-Michaels Okolie (eds.), (Keffi: Nigerian Political Science Association, 2018), 4.

Fani-Kayode, former Minister of Culture and Tourism, former Minister of Aviation and the Director of Publicity of former President Goodluck Jonathan Campaign Organization, Chief Olisa Metuh, National Publicity Secretary of the PDP, Senator Esther Nenadi Usman, former Minister of State for Finance, among others, were called to give account of funds they received during the 2015 election. Yet, the sources of campaign funds of the APC in the 2015 general elections have not been investigated. Similarly, nothing has been heard about the investigation into the sources of campaign funds of political parties in the 2019 general elections in Nigeria.

Related to the above is the matter of INEC's election budget and the corruption scandals that surrounds it. Both constitute a major challenge to election security in Nigeria. For instance, in order to fund INEC's budget for the 2019 general election, President Muhammadu Buhari, in July 2018, wrote a letter to the National Assembly for virement of 242 billion naira from the 2018 budget. The money was meant largely for the conduct of the 2019 general election. The breakdown of the budget shows that the sum of 89.21 billion naira was earmarked for INEC, 4.3 billion naira for the Office of the National Security Adviser (ONSA), 12.21 billion naira for the Department of State Security (DSS) and 3.6 billion naira for the Nigeria Security and Civil Defence Corps. The Nigerian Police Force was allocated 30.5 billion naira in the budget while 32.6 billion naira was earmarked for the Nigeria Immigration Service (NIS). Specifically, President Muhammadu Buhari requested that 164.10bn of the total funds proposed for the elections be funded from the 578.31 billion naira inserted into the 2018 budget by the National Assembly.[41]

After much deliberation, the National Assembly approved a total sum of 189, 207,544,893 billion naira as expenditures for the conduct of the 2019 general election, which was proposed by INEC. 45 billion naira was provided for INEC under statutory transfer, bringing the total to 234 billion naira. The National Assembly also invited heads of other beneficiary institutions such as the Inspector General of Police (IGP), National Security Adviser (NSA), Director of DSS, Comptroller-General of NIS and Commandant of the NSCDC, to defend their estimates. Thereafter, it approved the following sums: ONSA (9,481,500,000 billion naira); DSS (10,213,282,455 billion naira); NSCDC (3,573,534,500 billion naira); NPF (27,341,317,433 billion naira); and NIS (2,628,143,320 billion naira), totalling

---

[41] Jide Ojo, "Controversial N242 Billion Budget for 2019 Election," *Punch Newspaper*, 26 Jul 2018.

242,245,050,100 billion naira.⁴² These were to be funded through transfers from MDAs.

The above amounts would likely double or triple when the sums spent by the 36 states in organizing local government council elections were added to it. Meanwhile, if the same amount is judiciously spent, there would be positive improvement in the living condition of Nigerians. A 2018 world data showing extreme poverty ranking, compiled by the World Poverty Clock for the Bookings Institute, stipulates that out of more than 643 million people across the world living in extreme poverty, Nigeria emerged the country with the largest number of people living in extreme poverty. It was estimated that 87 million Nigerians, about half of the country's population, live on less than $1.90 a day.⁴³ This earned Nigeria the epitaph: 'poverty capital of the world.'⁴⁴ Funds that would have been otherwise spent to improve the standard of living of the citizens were wasted on two days election.

It is apt to also mention that security agencies in Nigeria, in addition to receiving election finances, have their annual budgetary appropriation for their normal security duties that sums up to billions of naira. There is no doubt that some of the funds for providing election security and election management are mismanaged. Therefore, the huge amount of money spent on elections in Nigeria is a great security threat to the survival of democracy in the country.

Security Challenges During the 2019 General Election

Critical and in-depth assessment of the 2019 general election in Nigeria reveals serious security breaches that include:
a) Widespread undemocratic manifestation during party primaries resulting in many pre-election court cases;

---

42 Abati, "2019 and the Politics."
43 Bukola Adebayo, "Nigeria Overtakes India in Extreme Poverty Ranking," *Cable News Network (CNN)*, 26 Jun 2018, https://edition.cnn.com/2018/06/26/africa/nigeria-overtakes-india-extreme-poverty-intl/index.html (accessed 10 November 2020).
44 *World Bank, World Development Report (New York: Oxford University Press, 2018)*. The 2018 extreme world poverty ranking listed Nigeria as 156th poorest country among 177 countries in the world.

b) Pervasive manipulations of INEC officials by national office holders and state governors especially in the selection of electoral officials and ad hoc staff for election duty;
c) Several forms of collaboration between INEC officials, security operatives, major political parties and their candidates to subvert the popular will of the people in that election;
d) Widespread irregularities and electoral fraud led to the conduct of supplementary elections in 14 states of the federation, covering 7 senatorial districts and 24 federal constituencies. Elections in these areas were disrupted by acts of violence, ballot box snatching and stuffing, abduction of INEC officials and over voting (where number of votes announced exceeded number of voters accredited. For instance, in the presidential election, nearly three million votes were cancelled. In Rivers State, for example, the number of cancelled votes exceeded votes cast by nearly 300,000 votes);
e) Inconclusive elections also led to re-run elections in Adamawa, Bauchi, Benue, Kano, Plateau and Sokoto States;
f) Failure of political parties, candidates, security agents and some electorates to adhere to INEC regulations and guidelines;
g) Supplementary National Assembly elections were conducted alongside Governorship and State Houses of Assembly elections;
h) Smart Card Readers (SCRs), used for authenticating the Permanent Voters Card (PVC) of accredited voters and match voter biometrics with the INEC database, were dogged by glitches, mainly related to reading and matching of fingerprints of voters;
i) In some locations, INEC electoral officials deliberately refused to use the Smart Card Readers and relied instead on manual voting. This occurred in Kazawa Ward of Kano Central Senatorial District and Unwanar Ganji Open Space Ward in Rimi Gado of Kano North Senatorial District, areas favourable to the ruling party;
j) Voter turnout was higher across Nigeria for the presidential election than the state gubernatorial and House of Assembly elections;
k) Threats or actual violence kept many voters from coming out to vote on polling day;
l) Armed bandits and Boko Haram attacks occurred on the Presidential Election Day in Katsina and Adamawa States;
m) Harassment, intimidation and assault of voters were reported during the elections;
n) Weapons were used to undermine free and fair election and in the abduction of INEC staff and ad hoc staff in Akwa Ibom, Benue, Imo, Katsina, Kogi and

Rivers States. For instance, Katsina States recorded 20 cases of abduction of INEC electoral officials;
o) Vote buying and selling prevailed despite voter education and warning by INEC, security agencies, the anti-corruption agencies and Civil Society Organisations;
p) Underage voting was reported in Kano, Bauchi and Plateau States;
q) Late commencement of collation was reported in many states;
r) Inadequate training of ad hoc staff by INEC resulted in inefficient performance of such staff during the election;

Concluding Remarks

This chapter illustrates that Nigeria's electoral process is still fraught with massive election insecurity using evidence from the 2019 general election. It has been noted that the country has witnessed twenty years of uninterrupted democracy, within which it has conducted six national elections between 1999 and 2019. Yet, a dense drove of data suggests that these elections were undermined by election insecurity. This shows that steps taken by the Nigerian government to avert such issues are inadequate, namely the deployment of para-military agencies and, in extreme cases, the military to aid the police in ensuring peaceful elections throughout the country.

The difficulty in ensuring election security in Nigeria hinges, as noted, on lack of adherence to election principles and lack of adherence to security requirements. The postponement of the 2019 general election shows that the Nigerian electoral system does not adhere to election plans. Also, repeated faulty financial arrangements that lead to corrupt campaign and election, financing of political parties and INEC, constitutes a major challenge to election security and the survival of democracy in Nigeria. Thus, to improve future elections in Nigeria, the following should be integrated:
a) Strict adherence to transparency, compliance with national laws, freedom of speech and association, impartiality, inclusiveness in competitive and non-competitive elections;
b) Strict adherence to security requirements, and ensuring a secure electoral environment;
c) Adhering strictly to election plan;
d) Moderating party finances and national electoral budget.

These will deepen and consolidate democracy in Nigeria.

Uche S. Odozor, Olasupo O. Thompson, Scholastica N. Atata and Stanislaus O. Okonkwo

Beyond the 2019 General Election: Critical Lessons for Nigeria's Democratic Experiment

Abstract: With the high level of violence and fraud recorded during different elections held in 2019, Nigeria may have consolidated her image abroad as being incapable of conducting free and credible polls, despite twenty years of uninterrupted civil rule. This culture of electoral fraud is traceable to the actions and inactions of all cadres of stakeholders in the polity. Politicians have assumed office after willfully subverting the wishes of voters. Most electorates, like in past elections, voted along ethnic and religious lines after receiving pittances. It is plausible to say that the Independent National Electoral Commission (INEC) remains under the stranglehold of politicians. Above all, the Nigerian Constitution continues unruffled in its calculated assault against democracy and social progress. Everything continues as usual; yet hope for change rises even higher. Using data from a variety of published and unpublished sources, this chapter is a critical exposition of Nigeria's 2019 general election. It discusses especially the lessons that were not learned in twenty years of democratic experience, for which reason credible elections and democratic consolidation have been a mirage and an international embarrassment to Nigeria.

Keywords: Nigeria, democracy, election, politics, violence

Introduction

This chapter explores Nigeria's most recent electoral process of 2019 using the methods of critical and content analysis. It surveys and examines the factors that hindered credible elections in the country for the past two decades, beginning from 1999. The long-awaited 2019 elections have come and gone. The current dispensation had barely begun before the same electorate that voted it into office resumed their litany of complaints over bad governance. Yet, as this chapter makes clear, majority of the citizens and their leaders have learned little or nothing from previous electoral engagements in the country; critical lessons

Uche S. Odozor, Olasupo O. Thompson, Ngozi S. Atata and Stanislaus O. Okonkwo, Federal University of Agriculture Abeokuta, Nigeria

with which to keep in check the policies and actions of emerging leaders, who, as political aspirants, would promise good governance and sterling leadership. What are these perennial problems that marred Nigeria's polls all over again in 2019? How can the lessons therein be used to interrogate Nigeria's democratic experience and inform her aspirations to social development, as it currently stands, and to improve the electoral process for future engagements?

In stating the problem of the 2019 elections in Nigeria, attention is drawn to a recent study suggesting that the Not-Too-Young-To-Rule (NTYTR) Bill signed into law by the Federal Government of Nigeria shortly before the elections, elicited higher youth political interest and participation in the 2019 elections than in all the elections since 1999.[1] Projecting into the future, the author had claimed thus:

> The Not-Too-Young-to-Run Act will encourage more youth participation in future elections. It is evident that youths are now prepared to take part in the political administration of the country. This is because most political parties have reviewed their ideologies in favour of the youths with more dialogues, debates, seminars to sensitise them. The effect this will have on future elections is that more youths are now encouraged with minimal or no electoral violence (sic). Election rigging and vote buying will also be reduced since the youths are not likely to sell their votes again. The implication of all this is that after the 2019 general elections, the governance of Nigeria will witness a new era, an era where more youths will become more refined.[2]

Optimism is unarguably a good thing, as it gives meaning to life. However, evidence shows that election-related fraud, violence, and deaths are rather on the increase with each round of election in Nigeria.[3] A 2019 editorial makes the following observation:

> The integrity of virtually all elections conducted since 2015 have been suspect with voter intimidation, despicable violence and sometimes, open falsification of results at collation centres [as] the major hallmark of these elections. As attested to by numerous election monitoring teams, Nigeria has taken several steps backward in the conduct of credible elections.[4]

---

[1] Aliyu M. Kolawole, "2019 General Elections in Nigeria and the New Dimension of Youth Involvement in Osun State," *Global Journal of Human Social Science* 19, no.2 (2019): 37–46.
[2] Kolawole, "2019 General Elections in Nigeria," 44.
[3] Olugbemiga Afolabi, "The Police and Electoral Process in Nigeria," *African Journal of Public Affairs* 10, no. 3 (2018): 155–169; Nigeria Civil Society Situation Room, *Niger Delta Watch 2019: A Civil Society Report on the Conduct of the Nigerian Elections* (Port Harcourt, Nigeria: Nigeria Civil Society Situation Room and Stakeholder Democracy Network, 2019), vii–46.
[4] "Mr. President, This is not 1985," *Business Day*, 13 December 2019, 12.

Events in Bayelsa and Kogi States, both of which held their respective governorship elections in November 2019 are a clear indication that the NTYTR is anything but a panacea to electoral violence and fraud that have assumed the status of culture in Nigeria. For example, not only was vote buying widespread, an INEC official was reportedly abducted in Bayelsa State. In Kogi, a boy was shot in the leg when suspected thugs invaded a polling area to snatch the ballot boxes used for the exercise.[5] Also Mrs. Salome Acheju Abuh, a political leader of the Peoples Democratic Party (PDP), the major opposition party, was burnt alive inside her family home.[6] It is estimated that about ten people lost their lives in Kogi State, not counting the severely wounded. At an Abuja public presentation of election findings, the chairman of the Board of INEC Institute, Soyebi Adedeji, summarily noted that "the number of bullets flying in Kogi State were more than ballot papers."[7] Yet, about 35,000 police were presumed to be in Kogi to ensure a violence-free exercise, while 31,000, including 87 gunboats, were deployed to Bayelsa for the same purpose.[8] Meanwhile, a few days before the election, the federal government released N10 billion to the Kogi State Government claiming it was money it owed the state, which was needed to offset the backlog of salaries of state civil servants in the several months leading to the election.[9] Even if this were true, it is curious that such a huge amount of money should be released to a state government only on the eve of an election in which it has a stake. Experience has amply confirmed that the privileges of incumbency are readily abused in Nigerian politics, suggesting that so much money at the disposal of state political actors at an election period would likely fuel even more violence, not to mention being deployed for vote buying.

The problems besieging the conduct of credible elections in Nigeria are represented in the 2019 Elections Factbook as follows:

> Elections in Nigeria are a critical part of her budding democratic process; however, just like most aspects of Nigeria's democracy, the electioneering process is still being blurred by specs of debris from several years of colonial rule followed by the military influence span-

---

5 "Sporadic Violence Greets Bayelsa, Kogi Gov. Elections," *Punch*, 16 November 2019.
6 Ibrahim Mustapha, "The Kogi and Bayelsa Elections," *Thisday*, 26 November 2019, https://www.thisdaylive.com/index.php/2019/11/26/the-kogi-and-bayelsa-elections (accessed 9 December 2019).
7 Matthew Ogune and Azimazi Momoh Jimoh, "Kogi, Bayelsa Elections were marred by Violence, Vote Buying, INEC Admits," *The Guardian*, 5 December 2019.
8 "Sporadic Violence Greets Bayelsa, Kogi Gov. Elections."
9 Jide Ojo, "The Controversial N10bn Refund to Kogi State ahead of November 16 Election." *Thisday*, 20 October 2019, https://www.pressreader.com/nigeria/thisday/20191022/282480005573847 (accessed 7 December 2019).

ning about three decades and a dose of an aggressive political elite unwilling to relinquish her hold to what has become a lucrative business for most. The history of elections in Nigerian has been characterized by threats to statehood based on the manipulation of ethnicity as a divisive mechanism for the acquisition of political power by political actors, the fragile nature of political cum democratic institutions is acquainted with poor democratic culture among Nigerian citizens.[10]

The report notes that elections have consistently served as the only thing that brings the Nigerian electorate and their politicians together once every four years. As a result, the ruling elite carefully keeps questions of good governance and social progress out of focus. The Factbook expresses regret that both the electorate and politicians seem to have resolved to let the issue of lack-lustre governance continue unaddressed, in spite of the crippling poverty in the land:

> Elections in Nigeria from 1999 to date have continued to recycle in vicious violence and unimaginable manipulation especially from the political elites [...] The violence, coupled with the glaring disorganised manual election process, has discouraged a sizeable number of citizens from participating [...] Many citizens' faith in the integrity of the electoral process has [...] waned over the previous years due to the incessant stories of rigging. The number of registered votes is always significantly more than the actual votes cast and these numbers have significantly dwindled in the past years.[11]

Furthermore, in its January 2019 pre-election security assessment report, CLEEN Foundation notes that the 2019 elections were already compromised by various degrees of security threats. Twenty-two states were dubbed the "red zone," meaning that they were volatile for the eruption of violence; and eleven had slightly less security concerns. Only five, namely Katsina, Jigawa, Kebbi, Niger and Abuja, the Federal Capital Territory (FCT), were expected to have relatively peaceful exercises.[12]

It is often presumed that Nigeria's electoral problems are mere 'mistakes' that can simply be improved upon in subsequent elections. However, a mistake is something that presumably happens once due to oversight and human limitation. It is never intended; and there is genuine resolution, effort, and vigilance to ensure that it does not repeat itself. Although INEC keeps promising to learn

---

10 2019 Elections Factbook, *What's at Stake? An Elections Voter's Guide*, (Lagos: Budgit, 2019), 1, https://yourbudgit.com/wp-content/uploads/2019/02/factbook-1.pdf (accessed 11 December 2019).
11 2019 Elections Factbook, *What's at Stake?*, 1–2.
12 CLEEN Foundation, "2019 Election Security Threat Assessment of Nigeria," https://cleen.org/wp-content/uploads/2019/02/2019-Election-Security-Threat-Assessment-of-NigeriaJanuary-2019.pdf (accessed 11 December 2019).

from its mistakes and to do better in future elections, it simply keeps repeating these mistakes in subsequent elections, as though Nigeria is doomed to remain in this state of impasse.[13] Without realising the nexus between credible elections; social peace and progress; and a firm resolve backed by conscientious effort to do things differently, starting from undertaking the necessary electoral reforms, to the reorientation of INEC officials and the electorate, Nigeria will never escape the vicious cycle of fraudulent elections producing poor and ineffective leadership.[14]

The Gaps in Nigeria's Electoral System

Major factors hindering credible elections and democratic consolidation in Nigeria, as well as the lessons which different stakeholders have consistently failed to learn, could be summarised as follows:

Campaigns of calumny rather than of issues: For the past twenty years (1999 – 2019), electioneering campaigns in Nigeria were used mostly for hurling the worst kinds of defamation at opponents, rather than for demonstrating real grasp of national issues or articulating strategies for meeting the challenges, if elected.[15] These campaigns were specifically designed to throw political opponents in bad light and create distrust against them in the minds of voters, often with outright use of threats and crafty appeals to ethnic and religious sentiments. Because ethnicity and religion are placed ahead of other considerations in Nigeria, this strategy frequently works for the unscrupulous politician bent on realising his political ambition. It is a two-pronged ploy used to distract the electorate from real issues of governance and national development and to conceal the aspirant's lack of vision and proper understanding of national issues. Regrettably, the media, many of which are either privately owned by politicians or con-

---

[13] Chucks Okocha, "INEC to Correct General Election Mistakes with Bayelsa, Kogi Polls," *Thisday*, 23 October 2019, https://www.thisdaylive.com/index.php/2019/10/23/inec-to-correct-general-election-mistakes-with-bayelsa-kogi-polls/ (accessed 11 December 2019).
[14] Nigeria Civil Society Situation Room, "Kogi State Governorship Election 2019: Socio-Political Context" (Abuja: Nigeria 2011 Civil Society Situation Room, 2019), 1–27.
[15] Mohammed Ademilokun and Rotimi Taiwo, "Discursive Strategies in Newspaper Campaign Advertisements for Nigeria's Elections," *Discourse & Communication* 7, no.4 (2013): 435–455; Afolabi, "The Police and Electoral Process," 156.

trolled by them, sometimes lend themselves to this mischief.¹⁶ In stark display of mediocrity, they mislead the electorate who look up to them for reliable information on candidates seeking election or re-election. They collaborate with politicians who wield state power and influence, while denigrating those in the opposition who have neither money to dole out nor political office to brandish. Carel and Gamez describe this phenomenon as "postmodern corruption,"[17] which erodes social progress and development. They note that:

> In an era of [...] massive advertising budgets for political campaigns, it is no longer the credibility of an idea or its philosophical value that counts, but the extent to which it has been effectively branded. The 'weightiest' ideas are those that have been most advertised and the political party with them gets elected.[18]

The underlying attitude seems to be that if politicians can carry out much more heinous crimes, such as the appropriation of public funds, vote buying, and thug violence at elections, as well as the assassination of those perceived as threats to their ambitions, then calumny against an opponent during campaigns would be trivial. However, people do not simply sit around and watch their names being dragged in the mud. As Afolabi appositely observed, "the politicians' indecorous and vulgar disposition in the use of language naturally produces hate [and incites] their followers into an orgy of violence."[19] Another deeply entrenched facet of this problem is the reckless boycott of presidential election debates set up by the media and civil society organisations. This behaviour was perpetrated by the candidates of Nigeria's ruling political parties, PDP and APC, first by President Goodluck Jonathan in 2011 and by President Muhammad Buhari in 2019. Both used the advantage of incumbency to gloss over such blatant violation of public trust.[20]

---

[16] Fidelis Chuka Aghamelu, "The Role of the Mass Media in the Nigerian Electoral Process," *Unizik Journal of Arts and Humanities* 14, no.2 (2013): 154–172; Tsegyu Santas and John Dogara Ogoshi, "An Appraisal of Mass Media Role in Consolidating Democracy in Nigeria," *African Research Review: International Multidisciplinary Journal* 10, no. 1 (2016): 73–86; Raphael Ojebuyi Babatunde and Salawu Abiodun, "Partisanship and Selective Reporting in Nigerian Newspapers' Coverage of Elections," *African Renaissance* 15, no.4 (2018): 75–98.
[17] Havi Carel and David Gamez, *What Philosophy Is: Contemporary Philosophy in Action* (London: Continuum, 2004), 9.
[18] Carel and Gamez, *What Philosophy Is*, 9.
[19] Afolabi, "The Police and Electoral Process," 158.
[20] "Nigeria Election: Jonathan Rivals pull out of TV Debate," *BBC News*, 25 March 2011, https://www.bbc.com/news/world-africa-12859073 (accessed 11 December 2019). Emmanuel Aziken, Joseph Erunke, Omezia Ajayi and Dirisu Yakubu, "Drama at Presidential Debate: Buhari absent, says he is busy; Atiku walks away from Debate," *Vanguard*, 20 January 2019.

Sheer lack of moral and political will to amend the relevant sections of the Constitution: Perhaps, the central reason Nigeria's electoral problems may not be readily taken as mere 'mistakes' is that Nigeria has, in the past twenty years, been governed with a constitution that is antithetical in many respects to the fundamental principles of democratic governance; and there is no indication on the horizon that the situation is about to change. For example, how could Nigeria make democratic progress with a constitution that vests public officers – especially the executive – with so much power and for no apparent reason? Under what conceivable circumstance could a constitution endowing the president with the sole prerogative of choosing the national electoral umpire produce a free and fair election? Such a chief electoral officer would only end up as an errand boy of the one who put him in office. This problem evidently conduces to electoral fraud. Beyond politics, it is simply immoral and antagonistic to public interest. In the later part of 2018, the Eighth Senate, under Bukola Saraki, sent an electoral amendment bill to President Muhammadu Buhari for ratification as required by law.[21] According to analysts, the bill was designed to address many critical issues of electoral reform and overhaul Nigeria's electoral system. The president refused assent to the bill, citing as reason the nearness of the 2019 elections, which would apparently make it difficult for the demands of the bill to be met in such a short time.[22] Two years after the elections, and with Buhari no longer eligible to contest in future presidential elections, the bill is yet to receive presidential endorsement, even as Nigerians continue to clamour.

Unavailability of reliable data on national population: The last official census in Nigeria took place in 2006 during the Olusegun Obasanjo administration.[23] Ever since, even with the controversies trailing the exercise, no subsequent administration has deemed it necessary to revisit this absolutely indispensable ingredient of national planning and development. This raises the critical question: What kind of development do Nigerian leaders hope to achieve without requisite population data, the integral parts of which are elections, governance, policy development and implementation? How could the many problems besetting the country be resolved in the absence of vital knowledge architecture that administrators need to comprehend the intricacies of national challenges in order to plan for

---

[21] Henry Umoru, "NASS Sends Electoral Act Bill to Buhari for Assent," *Vanguard*, 16 November 2018.
[22] John Alechenu, Olusola Fabiyi, Eniola Akinkuotu, Leke Baiyewu and Ade Adesomoju, "Again, Buhari Refuses to Sign Electoral Bill," *Punch*, 4 September 2018.
[23] Okechukwu Eme and Adeline Nnenna Idike, "Census Politics in Nigeria: An Examination of 2006 Population Census," *Journal of Policy and Development Studies* 9, no.3 (2015): 47–72.

appropriate solutions? Owing to this lacuna, Nigerian policymakers and researchers rely on estimated figures when referring to national population and for planning and capacity building. Granted that data could be acquired through voter registration exercises, it should be noted that such data do not provide much insight about the comprehensive population of the country. Apart from the problems of multiple and underage voter registrations, data from voter registration depends on the availability of the electorate during the registration exercise. This means that the data cannot be relied upon for other aspects of national planning, such as the arduous task of governance that lies beyond politics and elections.

Unwillingness of politicians to emulate democratically advanced societies: Besides entrenched constitutional and other systemic hindrances to credible polls, the electoral fraud in Nigeria is largely caused by the actions and inactions of the political class, the direct beneficiaries of the anarchy. No polity can be progressive if its politicians are utterly self-centred. Nigeria's political class is educated enough to perceive the world of difference between the Western world, for instance, and Nigeria, in terms of social development and progress. They travel around the world from time to time; attend every eligible international summit where current global challenges are deliberated upon, and also pay whatever it costs to bring in world-renowned experts as resource persons for periodic local summits. These exposures and encounters are needed opportunities to get them acquainted with governance in advanced cultures and societies, and to see how things are properly done in civilized societies. Many of them know precisely why things are working in developed countries and what needs to be done to successfully parallel Nigeria with the rest of the world. But, instead of bringing the relevant lessons and experiences to bear on the Nigerian situation, they conveniently set these lessons aside, while recycling electoral malpractices and violence, vote buying and other illegal activities, unchallenged by the law.[24] So, a lot of activities go on without much actually being accomplished to bring about the desired development. As Schwarz aptly observes in his apt distinction between busyness and accomplishment:

> Doing is not the same as being 'active'. In films, for instance, or at political conferences, a great deal goes on without anything being done [or] achieved. [...] The elements and characteristics of 'doing' are intention, planning, taking risks, and responsibility, and making things.[25]

---

24 Nigeria Civil Society Situation Room, "Kogi State Governorship Election 2019," 2.
25 Oswald Schwarz, *The Psychology of Sex* (London: Penguin, 1956), 169.

Non-enforcement of the extant electoral laws: One of the most powerful factors empowering electoral fraud in Nigeria is the near absence of consequences for the crime, as culprits customarily go unscathed, even after their culpability has been duly established in a court of law. On many occasions, nobody gets arrested or arraigned in court. Thus, despite the crippling deficiencies in Nigeria's current electoral law, there are still some basic provisions that could go a long way in stemming the tide of electoral crimes if duly and conscientiously implemented. The main challenge, in this regard, is abysmal law enforcement coupled with the unprofessional conduct of some security agencies during elections. In typical colonial fashion, and as obtains in many parts of Africa, Nigerian law enforcement agents generally pander to the whims of those in power because of the money, power and influence they wield. Rather than serve as agents of the law during elections, law enforcement officers are routinely used by politicians to intimidate the voting public and to carry out other kinds of antisocial activities at elections.[26] It is fairly reasonable to suppose that most of the crimes committed by politicians against the citizenry are actually executed by the security and law enforcement agents who seem to be empowered by the arms they bear and also because the law is too ineffective to rein in official misconduct. Yet, political thugs can carry out their onslaught at polling centres only if the security agents do nothing. Reports of the military becoming the real menace at polling centres they have been assigned to secure were rampant.[27] On several occasions, these security agents failed in their most basic responsibility of protecting voters from hoodlums. This was already buttressed in the Bayelsa and Kogi States' experience in 2019 mentioned earlier. What may be worth mentioning here is that the thousands of police personnel on election duty in these states were not remunerated. Hence, within one month of the elections, those drafted to Kogi for the polls went on a protest to demand their duty allowances.[28] In the end, bad governance inevitably takes its toll even on those who fail to safeguard due process.

---

26 Afolabi, "The Police and Electoral Process," 156–157.

27 Segun Olaniyi, Kanayo Umeh and Chido Okafor, "Fresh Outrage at Use of Soldiers for Election," *The Guardian*, 7 March 2019; "Global Concerns Mount over Army Interference in Election," *Thisday*, 11 March 2019, https://www.thisdaylive.com/index.php/2019/03/11/global-concerns-mount-over-army-interference-in-election (accessed 10 December 2019).

28 Emmanuel Ani, "Kogi Election: Police Protest Alleged Non-payment of Allowances in Ekiti," *Daily Post*, 12 December 2019, https://dailypost.ng/2019/12/12/kogi-election-police-protest-alleged-non-payment-of-allowances-in-ekiti/ (accessed 5 December 2019); Yomi Ayeleso, "Kogi 2019: Ekiti Police Protest Alleged Non-payment of Allowances," *Nigerian Tribune*, 12 December 2019; Abiodun Nejo, "Policemen Protest Non-payment of Election Duty Allowance," *Punch*, 13 December 2019.

Inability of the electorate to be ethno-religiously neutral: Many Nigerians of voting age see and identify themselves first as members of their ethnic or religious enclaves before and above any nationalistic considerations. Apparently owing to the traditional African communal system of life, ethnic loyalty and consciousness have evolved as rather strong traits among the populace. And unscrupulous politicians tactfully latch onto this situation to actualise their political ambitions by emphasising ethnic and religious cleavages of the citizenry. Nigerian electorates are well acquainted with the beauty of the democratic process at elections, as well as the need for good governance and democratic consolidation; however, they basically pay lip service to these notions and easily get swayed by politicians to vote otherwise during elections. For that reason, citizens vote along ethnic and religious lines in every election following the embers of ethnic and religious hatred fanned by party leaders who refuse to promote good governance, especially when it is manifestly found in a different party or ethnicity.

Lack of internal democracy among political parties: Democracy is not just a political theory or ideology that may be waved at will. More fundamentally, and even prior to politics, it is a way of life.[29] This means that democracy as a way of life is antecedent to democracy as a political theory and operating principle. The latter emanates from the former, which is its nurturing ground. Thus, for democracy to grow and flourish in any polity, it must first be internalised as an attitude of the mind and a philosophy of life.[30] But, on account of greed and inordinate ambitions, political parties consistently fail to imbibe the principles of true democracy starting from their most basic level of existence in Nigeria's rural communities. In this regard, the 2019 general elections did not fare any differently from earlier elections in Nigeria, where political parties are basically run like private businesses of their founders, financiers, and their most politically influential members. Contrary to laid down party constitutions and operating policies, strong party leaders operating as god-fathers impose candidates on other members during primary elections. Since the candidate in question does not emerge legitimately, the political god-fathers use every means at their disposal to manip-

---

[29] J. Hans Kohn, "Democracy," *Encyclopedia Britannica*, vol. 7 (Chicago: University of Chicago, 1944), 182–187.
[30] Uche S. Odozor and Emmanuel O. Akintona, "Re-evaluating the Political Philosophies of Plato and Wiredu for the Maximisation of Democracy in Nigeria," *Journal of Research in National Development* 16, no. 2 (2018): 64–71.

ulate the electoral process and push the pre-selected candidate into office.[31] In the few instances where the plot fails despite everything, this 'do-or-die' attitude ultimately leads to the rejection of duly certified election result, even when it is obvious that the electorate clearly voted for a different candidate. This leads to divisions within the party, culminating in rancour and acrimony of the most savage kind; and, sometimes, even to political assassinations. This raises the question: how can anyone who does not respect and practice the basic tenets of democracy in his home front possibly be relied upon to champion democracy when he or she gets into public office? In the end, the real problem is that many Nigerian politicians do not attach much meaning to the notion that power belongs to the people, or that aspiration to public office is neither by force nor for personal aggrandizement, but a matter of humble service to the community. The most debilitating aspect of this problem is that the handpicked candidate automatically loses the power to take the necessary critical decisions of the office he occupies, because his authority is hijacked and controlled by the god-father who sponsored him, who equally determines the people he must work with. If this happens at the state-level, all appointments and revenue allocations are squarely determined by the god-father.

Ignorance of the distinction between politics and governance: While politics is about what people do and say to win elections, governance is what they do in office if elected. Politics and governance converge when an elected official is delivering good governance, on the basis of which the electorate may vote him or her for another term of office.[32] In the Nigerian setting, actual governance is calculatedly swamped by politicking and partisanship. A political party is supposed to be merely a platform for political aspiration, but elected officials often speak and behave as if their responsibilities were to their parties rather than to the electorate. The majority of Nigerian politicians fail to realise that there is a fine line of distinction between politics and governance. The citizens, who are used to the arrogance of politicians, forget this distinction as well, thereby emboldening politicians to exploit this anomaly to the fullest possible extent. Rather than deliver good governance on assumption of office, they play politics with serious national issues and waste entire tenures and resources on frivolous activities that include flamboyant wedding and birthday ceremonies, partying, while blaming

---

31 Ibrahim Mustapha, "The Kogi and Bayelsa Elections," *Thisday*, 26 November 2019, https://www.thisdaylive.com/index.php/2019/11/26/the-kogi-and-bayelsa-elections (accessed 10 December 2019); Nigeria Civil Society Situation Room, *Kogi State Governorship Election 2019*, 11.
32 Tamara Cofman Wittes, *Politics, Governance, and State-Society Relations* (Washington: Atlantic Council, 2016), 6–7.

past administrations for their own lacklustre performance. They lie to the citizens at every turn to maintain good image of themselves and spend whatever remains of their tenure asking for another four years of misrule. Sometimes, this is done on their behalf by their patrons, supporters and admirers, who, owing to factors ranging from sycophancy, partisanship, sympathy to tribal affiliations, do not consider that, as members of the society, neither their admiration nor their support is potent enough to render them and their families impervious to the effects of bad governance. During the election campaigns for the recent Kogi election, both the wife of President Buhari, Mrs Aisha Buhari, and the Kaduna State Governor, Mallam Nasir El-Rufai, pleaded with the Kogi electorate to forgive "the sins" of the incumbent governor, Yahaya Bello, and elect him for a second term, knowing that Bello had performed woefully in the first term.[33] At the end of the elections, Bello was declared winner of the Kogi polls. It remains to be seen whether Kogi State is better off than before the election. However, what is clear at the moment is that the same governor, whose record of poor leadership is decried across the country, has already declared his presidential ambition for 2023.

Government aversion to criticism: When a government views criticism as an assault, it would be difficult for it to grasp the need to improve on its short-comings, which, in the Nigerian case, include poor governance and overseeing elections that are totally lacking in credibility. The current Nigerian government has repeatedly interpreted criticism as a salvo from the enemy – and routinely responded with resentment, impudence and threats – instead of as opportunity for self-appraisal for better performance. These misgivings lead these public officials to wallow in odious self-praise, coupled with misplaced praise singing from their sycophantic supporters, causing them to talk down on the citizens with abject contempt. Even the best-intentioned criticism is wont to be sanctioned as 'hate speech', especially if it comes from the opposition, or from people outside the government.[34] Supporters of the current APC administration have coined the nickname of 'hailers' for themselves, and carefully refrained from

---

[33] Kunle Sanni, "KogiDecides: Forgive Yahaya Bello His 'Sins', Aisha Buhari, El-Rufai Beg Voters," *Premium Times*, 15 November 2019, https://www.premiumtimesng.com/news/headlines/363080-kogidecides-forgive-yahaya-bello-his-sins-aisha-buhari-el-rufai-beg-voters.html (accessed 13 December 2020).

[34] Seun Bakare, "Nigeria: Bills on Hate Speech and Social Media are Dangerous attacks on Freedom of Expression," *Amnesty International Nigeria*, 4 December 2019, https://www.amnesty.org/en/latest/news/2019/12/nigeria-bills-on-hate-speech-and-social-media-are-dangerous-attacks-on-freedom-of-expression/ (accessed 15 December 2020).

speaking the truth to power. It appears that their liking for those in power has skewed their sense of judgment, including when their heroes and heroines are performing far below expectation. Taking a cue from public officials, they denigrate their fellow citizens who do not share their sentiments with the corresponding title of 'wailers.'[35] The social media platforms are awash with a war of words between hailers and wailers over the abysmal state of Nigeria's post-2015 democracy. The present Nigerian government's aversion to criticism has strongly alienated it from the citizenry. It is foreseen that this would cause strong negative impulses that could engender more bloody violence in future elections.

Apathy of the electorate: J. S. Mill, the British utilitarian philosopher, is credited with the adroit remark that "Bad men need nothing more to compass their ends than that good men should look on and do nothing."[36] Most enlightened, eligible Nigerian voters refrain from participating in elections partly due to the violence with which these elections have inevitably and increasingly become associated. Many would joke that they prefer to sit at home and watch cable television during elections,[37] ironically waiting on the unenlightened members of society to bring about the coveted change in the polity. Be that as it may, it is not unreasonable to suppose that their unwillingness to join politics or, at the very least, to come out on election days and exercise their most fundamental civic duty, amounts to the entrenchment of electoral fraud, mediocre leadership and bad governance in Nigeria. Democratic politics is a game of numbers. If there is an influx of noble people willing to stand their ground and blatantly refuse to be intimidated, or be taken in by the antics of politicians on election days, then political thugs can hardly overwhelm them, and they can easily sway the outcome of any election in the desired direction. As do all criminal activities, electoral fraud thrives on secrecy – the secrecy inadvertently provided by Nigerians who boycott the polls; for these crimes are indirectly empowered by low turnout of voters. The influx of determined voters would, at least, gradually flush miscreants from the system until sanity prevails. The quintessential question, however, is: are Nigerian citizens determined and ready for such an onerous undertaking?

---

[35] Raymond Oise-Oghaede, "The Politics of Hailers, Haters and Wailers," *The Guardian*, 12 August 2019; Mohammed Adamu "'Wailers' vs 'Hailers'," *Vanguard*, 26 October 2017.
[36] Cited in Kenneth R. Westphal, "Back to the 3 R's: Rights, Responsibilities and Reasoning," *SATS: Northern European Journal of Philosophy* 17, no.1 (2016): 39.
[37] Simon Kolawole, "Thou Shall Not Underrate Atiku," *The Cable*, 10 December 2017, https://www.thecable.ng/thou-shall-not-underrate-atiku (accessed 5 December 2019).

Reckless and unguarded utterances by politicians: It is not only during election campaigns and rallies that Nigerian politicians use irresponsible and inflammatory language. Many issue volatile statements before, during and after elections. Such was attributed to the Kaduna State Governor, Nasir El-Rufai, who threatened that foreign election observers would be sent back to their respective countries in body bags if they interfered with the 2019 electoral process.[38] El-Rufai's outcry had seemed gratuitous at the time; however, given the supposed tacit interference of the US government, under Barack Obama, which enhanced the chances of the APC party in the 2015 elections against the incumbent, President Goodluck Jonathan of the PDP,[39] it shows that El-Rufai apparently knew exactly what he was talking about. Naturally, the utterance sparked widespread outrage from local and international critics who considered such comments from highly placed agents of government a disservice to Nigeria whose image was already battered by the *Boko Haram* and cattle herders crises.[40] Long before this time, in the 2007 campaign season, the then President Olusegun Obasanjo had stated that the electoral victory of his party, the PDP, was "a do-or-die affair."[41] This set a dangerous precedence that has been a reference point for Nigerians and their sly politicians. Although subsequent politicians have carefully refrained from using Chief Obasanjo's exact phraseology and even publicly denounced it in strong terms, and although the former president has retracted the statement on occasions, it is evident that the phrase has been the underlying philosophy discernible from the actual behaviour and attitude of Nigeria's political class especially during campaigns, inclusive of the 2019 general election.

Porous national frontiers: To a considerable extent, Nigeria has some relatively well guarded borders in the southern part of the country, though some illegal exit and entry points also exist there. Comparatively, the story is decidedly different at the northern fringes where, admittedly, a 2000-mile stretch of frontiers lies poorly guarded and unprotected, such that there is free infiltration of people and

---

[38] .Igho Akeregha, Emeka Nwachukwu, Joseph Wantu and Abdulganiyu Alabi, "Outrage as El-Rufai threatens foreigners over Elections," *The Guardian*, 7 February 2019.

[39] Chris Ewokor, "Nigeria ex-President Goodluck Jonathan on 'Obama Interference' In 2015 Election Bid," *BBC News*, 30 November 2018, https://www.bbc.com/news/av/world-africa-46387779 (accessed 11 December 2020); Ezinne Ukoha, "How the Obama Administration Destroyed Nigeria's Path to Progression," 21 March 2018, https://nilegirl.medium.com/how-the-obama-administration-destroyed-nigerias-path-to-progression-13c0ce8bb708 (accessed 11 December 2020).

[40] Dapo Adegboye, "Rant Here: El-Rufai's Body-bag Comment," *Punch*, 17 February 2019.

[41] Kolade Olarewaju, "Nigeria: Obasanjo Explodes – April Polls Do or Die Affair for PDP," *Vanguard*, 11 February 2007, 1.

goods from nearby countries namely Niger, Mali and Chad.[42] This situation facilitates the proliferation of small arms and light weapons before, during and after elections.[43] In addition, migrants from these countries are believed by experts to be strategically used to bloat northern population figures during elections and censuses. Mention must be made of the perennial security challenges coming from the northern borders, including the *Boko Haram* insurgency, the recent spike in cross-border armed banditry, as well as foreign marauding herdsmen, all of which have led to massive loss of Nigerian lives.

Militarisation of electoral space: Across the world, there is a tacit consensus that the job of the military in a well-ordered society is to ward off external aggression. In the United States, for example, this principle is so ingrained that military action is seen only in rare moments of heightened threat to national security such as that of Pearl Harbor. Even the dastardly attacks of 11 September 2001 did not have the streets of New York or the suburbs of Pennsylvania taken over, or overrun, by the American military, despite the Pentagon being a potential target of the terrorists.[44] This is neither because of American bureaucracy nor because of the complacency of her political leaders, but because security is essentially a matter of intelligence gathering, not of wielding dangerous arms in crude intimidation of civilian members of the society. Most American military engagements take place abroad, far away from the home front.[45] The police and other homeland civil security agencies are groomed and equipped to control anti-pacifist activities. In Nigeria, on the other hand, perhaps due to the many years of military incursion into politics, the military are used for almost every conceivable task ranging from fighting Islamic insurgency to providing casual

---

[42] Daniel E. Agbiboa, "Borders That Continue to Bother Us: The Politics of Cross-border Security Cooperation in Africa's Lake Chad Basin," *Commonwealth & Comparative Politics*, 55, no.4 (2017): 403–425; Leena Koni Hoffmann and Paul Melly, *Nigeria's Booming Borders: The Drivers and Consequences of Unrecorded Trade* (London: The Royal Institute of International Affairs, 2015); Joseph K. Ukwayi and Bassey E. Anam, "Cross-border Crimes and Security Challenges in Nigeria," *International Journal of Scientific Research in Humanities, Legal Studies & International Relations*, 4, no.1 (2019), 103–114.
[43] Ibrahim Mustapha, "The Kogi and Bayelsa Elections," Thisday, 26 November 2019, https://www.thisdaylive.com/index.php/2019/11/26/the-kogi-and-bayelsa-elections.
[44] Janet A. McDonnell, *The National Park Service: Responding to the September 11 Terrorist Attacks* (New York: National Center for Cultural Resources, 2004), 5; Kim R. Holmes, "What Is National Security?" in *2015 Index of US Military Strength*, ed. D.L. Wood (Washington D.C.: Heritage Foundation, 2015), 17–26.
[45] Holmes, "What Is National Security?", 18.

security during elections.⁴⁶ The military have also been used for roles as demeaning as debt recovery, sometimes ending in the tragic death of the debtor, who, unable to repay, is beaten to a pulp.⁴⁷ It has repeatedly happened that the military are sent to polling centres in the belief that their presence would deter trouble mongers. A typical election day in Nigeria is, thus, characterised by military deployment, in spite of heavy police presence, not excluding other agencies, such as the Nigerian Navy (in Niger Delta elections) and the Nigerian Security and Civil Defense Corps (NSCDC). This scenario is popularly regarded as the 'militarisation of the political space' because election days in Nigeria feel as if the country were at war. Proponents of this practice argue that the military are a necessity in the supervision of elections in Nigerian due to the volatile nature of these exercises. However, the very idea of 'militarisation' readily presupposes that this claim is clearly untenable and that the military are not at all a necessity in civil, democratic activities like elections. In any case, the mere presence of the military at polling centres constitutes a potential source of intimidation to voters and an obvious threat to democratic consolidation. So far, the militarisation project has not produced the desired result; nor has it automatically translated to peaceful and incident-free elections as expected. Rather, electoral malpractices have spun out of control in Nigeria with the alleged complicity of some military personnel.⁴⁸

Inefficiency of the Independent National Electoral Commission (INEC): The Independent National Electoral Commission (INEC) is Nigeria's constitutionally empowered electoral body. As already noted, it has certain in-built constitutional encumbrances; for example, there is no constitutional backing for electronic voting. Also, the electoral body is only independent in designation. In practice, the president of Nigeria unilaterally determines the chief electoral officer, while the executive arm of government funds the commission. But INEC has other factors inhibiting its positive impact such as malfunctioning electronic card readers and the willful violence perpetrated by greedy politicians and their thugs with no consequences. Many of the perennial problems in Nigeria's elections are inherent

---

46 "Why We're Involved in Elections – Military," *Premium Times*, 8 March 2019, https://www.premiumtimesng.com/news/top-news/318531-why-were-involved-in-elections-military.html (accessed 10 December 2019).
47 Matthew Omonigho, "Soldiers Allegedly Torture 43-Year-old Man to Death in Warri over N1.5 m Debt," *Daily Post*, 13 May 2017, https://dailypost.ng/2017/05/13/soldiers-allegedly-torture-43-year-old-man-death-warri-n1-5m-debt/ (accessed 7 December 2019); Ade Adesomoju, "Army to Pay N50 m for Beating Father of Three to Death," *Punch*, 19 December 2019.
48 Nigeria Civil Society Situation Room, *Niger Delta Watch 2019*, 15.

in the inefficiencies of INEC. Since 1999, the commission has routinely promised to use forthcoming elections to remedy the shortfalls of previously concluded ones. However, with each promise of improvement and assurance of readiness for every upcoming election come monumental failures that jeopardize democracy and erode the basis for the very existence of INEC. Avoidable logistical issues, such as late arrival of electoral officials and sensitive election materials to polling centres, and the poor handling of these materials even after the exercise, are commonplace. The 2019 elections were cancelled the morning they were scheduled to commence, causing Nigeria and her citizens untold losses in cash and kind.[49] Even when elections hold in Nigeria, delays and the poor public relations of some INEC officials are partly responsible for the low level of voting. Further, some highly placed members of the commission have been indicted for rigging elections, by switching the figures that originally came in from polling centres, with no disciplinary action taken against them.[50] Notably, INEC would declare people the winners of elections they did not contest for, or which have been manifestly marred by unprecedented levels of violence and fraud, and declare other election results inconclusive for flimsy reasons.[51] During the presidential election petition tribunal hearing in the aftermath of the 2019 general election, INEC shocked the public with the declaration that it had no online server for storing its data, thereby raising basic questions about the authenticity of its purported official election results and about how the hundreds of billions of naira it received for each round of elections were spent.[52] In a 2019 statement issued in Abuja, Mr Clement Nwankwo, the Nigeria Civil Society Situation Room convener, regretted that INEC had, over the years, demonstrated stark inability even to stand up to politicians at the state level, who used incumbency to manipulate elections in flagrant violation of clearly stipulated electoral guidelines.[53] Ulti-

---

[49] "Nigeria Election 2019: Poll Halted in Last-minute Drama," *BBC News*, 16 February 2019, https://www.bbc.com/news/world-africa-47263122 (accessed 21 December 2019).

[50] Davidson Iriekpen, Shola Oyeyipo and Udora Orizu, "NBA Accuses INEC Officials of Aiding Election Rigging," *Thisday*, 27 February 2019, https://www.thisdaylive.com/index.php/2019/02/27/nba-accuses-inec-officials-of-aiding-election-rigging (accessed 17 December 2019).

[51] "PDP Alleges Fraud as INEC Declares Six States' Governorship Poll Inconclusive," *Punch*, 12 March 2019).

[52] "2019 Elections: Buhari Requests Senate's Approval of N242bn for INEC, DSS, Others," *Punch*, 17 July 2018; Halimah Yahaya, "We Don't Have a Server, INEC Replies Atiku at Tribunal," *Premium Times*, 13 June 2019, https://www.premiumtimesng.com/news/headlines/334976-we-dont-have-a-server-inec-replies-atiku-at-tribunal.html (accessed 10 December 2019).

[53] Onyebuchi Ezigbo, "INEC Lacks Courage to Check State Interference, Says Situation Room," *Thisday*, 30 December 2019, https://www.thisdaylive.com/index.php/2019/12/30/inec-lacks-courage-to-check-state-interference-says-situation-room (accessed 31 December 2019).

mately, few elections conducted by INEC have been credible in the period under discussion.

Conclusion

This chapter identified and analysed the critical factors inhibiting credible elections and democratic consolidation in Nigeria after twenty years of uninterrupted civil rule. The importance of credible elections is emphasised in pedestrian and scholarly discourses, but many people do not truly appreciate the depth of its pragmatic importance for good governance, social stability and national development. Given the issues raised in this chapter, it is no wonder that Nigeria appears to be in a slow, uncertain and torturous journey towards becoming a well-ordered nation. Nigeria is akin to the proverbial individual who expects change and progress while deliberately doing things in the same unproductive way. Democracy begins from fair and credible elections where the citizens exercise their civic office of voting the candidate of their choice without interference and intimidation. For this reason, according to CLEEN Foundation, credible elections are the hallmark of legitimacy for every democratic government. Ensuring that elections are peaceful and free is, thus, imperative and vital to the survival and entrenchment of democracy and in building strong and effective institutions.[54]

As this study has established, setbacks to the success of Nigeria's electoral exercises come from all cadres of the nation's citizenry. For this reason, the solution must be a well-coordinated and joint effort. Since the country's constitution reposes so much responsibility on political leaders, they cannot afford to lower their integrity and esteem – on which the legitimacy of government heavily relies – by appearing to encourage electoral crimes. To achieve credible polls, the government must play its overarching role in a transparent and responsible manner. Its specific roles in this regard range from spearheading the electoral reform process and timely release of funds, to granting INEC adequate leeway for its operations, while ensuring that all electoral offenders are duly prosecuted, irrespective of their social standing or political leaning. The proposed electoral amendment suspended by President Buhari should be revisited on the basis of more recent developments. In this way, the government would be fully exonerated even if electoral malpractices persist thereafter.

---

54 CLEEN Foundation, *2019 Election Security Threat Assessment of Nigeria*, 1.

INEC should ensure that it is ready for elections not merely in principle but by making timely and adequate provision for the necessary materials and personnel. It must be transparent and accountable to the general public and impartial to all election contestants by boldly exercising its powers of sanctioning electoral offenders, including politicians and errant staff members of the commission as duly enshrined in the national constitution.[55] In this regard, security agencies such as the police and the National Security and Civil Defense Corps are absolutely indispensable and must be appropriately trained in intelligence gathering and sufficiently equipped to control troubling situations before and during elections. To heighten their morale, their remuneration must be reasonably adequate and timely paid. Above all, the hierarchies of these agencies should undergo ethical re-orientation to enable them come to terms with the full consequences of bad governance.

Starting from the establishment of the principle of internal democracy, political parties need to orientate their members to understand that playing the game by the rules of engagement would endear them to the voting public and still produce the desired result. On the contrary, circumventing the due process only attracts public odium and disaffection. Even when party representatives are elected, they should humbly keep in mind that power is as much a trust as it is transient; that when they leave public office, they will return to live among the people. This means that they must cherish their tenure in office and use it to establish enduring policies and legacies that will make their administration memorable. For their part, the citizenry should acquire sufficient political enlightenment to appreciate the fact that the progress and development of Nigeria squarely rest on the enduring exercise of their franchise at elections. The media should also realise that election periods in Nigeria are volatile, meaning that the slightest mismanagement of information can spark full-scale violence. Thus, they must conscientiously abide by their professional ethics and ensure timely and accurate reportage of events during elections, while avoiding tendencies towards partisanship, fake news and half-truths that derail social stability and peace. In all, transparency and sincerity of purpose should be the guiding principles of all segments of the society so that the perennial problems hindering credible elections in Nigeria would be comprehensively resolved. This would give way to social development and credible elections, the indispensable ingredients of the nation-building process Nigerians have yearned for in the twenty years of the current democratic experiment.

---

[55] CLEEN Foundation, *2019 Election Security Threat Assessment of Nigeria*, 1.

Appendix: Timetable and Schedule of Activities for 2019 General Elections

Independent National Electoral Commission

Time Table and Schedule of Activities for 2019 General Elections

By virtue of the provisions of the Constitution of the Federal Republic of Nigeria, 1999 (as amended), tenure of the President, Vice President, Governors and Deputy Governors of States of the Federation (except **Anambra, Bayelsa, Kogi, Edo, Ondo, Ekiti,** and **Osun States**) will expire on the 28th day of May, 2019 while Membership of the National and State Assemblies will stand dissolved on the 8th day of June, 2019.

Pursuant to Sections 76 (2), 116 (2), 132 (2) and 178 (2) of the Constitution of the Federal Republic of Nigeria, 1999 (as amended) and Section 25 of the Electoral Act, 2010 (as amended), elections to the said offices shall hold **not earlier than One Hundred and Fifty (150) days** and **not later than Thirty (30) days** before the expiration of the term of office of the last holder of that office. The Commission is empowered by Section 30(1) of the Electoral Act 2010 (as amended) to issue Notice for the elections not later than Ninety (90) days before the date of the elections.

In exercise of the powers conferred on the Independent National Electoral Commission (hereinafter referred to as "the Commission") by the Constitution of the Federal Republic of Nigeria, 1999 (as amended) and the Electoral Act (as amended) and of all other powers enabling it in that behalf, the Commission hereby issues this Time Table and Schedule of Activities for 2019 General Elections:

S/N	Activity	Date	Remark
1	Notice of election	17th August, 2018	Section 30(1) of the Electoral Act, 2010 (as amended) provides not later than 90 days before the election.
2	Collection of Forms **for all elections** by Political Parties at INEC Headquarters.	17th – 24th August, 2018	For Political Parties to issue to their candidates.
3	Conduct of Party Primaries including resolution of dis-	Commencement date 18th August, 2018 End	To enable Political Parties democratically nominate candidates for the election

Continued

S/N	Activity	Date	Remark
	putes arising from the Primaries.	7th October, 2018	as required by Section 87 of the Electoral Act, 2010 (as amended).
4	Commencement of campaign by Political Parties.	Presidential & National Assembly – 18th November, 2018 Governorship & State House of Assembly – 1st December, 2018	Section 99(1) of the Electoral Act, 2010 (as amended) provides 90 days before polling day.
5	Last day for submission of Forms CF001 and CF002 at the INEC Headquarters **(for all elections)**.	Presidential & National Assembly – 18th October, 2018 Governorship & State House of Assembly – 2nd November, 2018	Section 31(1) of the Electoral Act, 2010 (as amended) provides for not later than 60 days before the election.
6	Publication of Personal Particulars of candidates (CF001) **(for all elections)**.	Presidential & National Assembly – 25th October, 2018 Governorship & State House of Assembly – 9th November, 2018	Section 31(3) of the Electoral Act, 2010 (as amended) provides for publication within 7 days of the receipt of the form CF001.
7	Last day for withdrawal by candidate(s)/replacement of withdrawn candidate(s) by Political Parties	Presidential & National Assembly – 17th November, 2018 Governorship & State House of Assembly – 1st December, 2018	Section 35 of the Electoral Act, 2010 (as amended) provides for not later than 45 days before the election.
8	Last day for the submission of Nomination forms by Political Parties.	Presidential & National Assembly – 3^{d} December, 2018 Governorship & State House of Assembly – 17th December, 2018	Sections 32, 37, 38 and 39 of the Electoral Act, 2010 (as amended). (Commission to appoint time for submission).
9	Publication of official Register of voters for the election.	7th January, 2019	Section 20 of the Electoral Act, 2010 (as amended) provides not later than 30 days before the election.
10	Publication of list of nominated candidates.	Presidential & National Assembly – 17th January, 2019	Section 34 of the Electoral Act, 2010 (as amended)

Continued

S/N	Activity	Date	Remark
		Governorship & State House of Assembly – 31st January, 2019	provides at least 30 days before the day of election.
11	Publication of Notice of Poll **(for all elections).**	2nd January, 2019	Section 46 of the Electoral Act, 2010 (as amended) provides not later than 14 days before the election.
12	Submission of names of Party Agents for the Election to the Electoral Officer of the Local Government Areas or Area Councils.	Presidential & National Assembly – 1st February, 2019 Governorship & State House of Assembly – 16th February, 2019	Section 45 of the Electoral Act, 2010 (as amended) provides not later than 14 days before the election.
13	Last day for campaigns.	Presidential & National Assembly – 14th February, 2019 Governorship & State House of Assembly – 28th February, 2019	Section 99(1) of the Electoral Act, 2010 (as amended) prohibits Advertisements or broadcasts of campaigns 24 hours prior to the day of election.
14	**Dates of Elections** National Assembly/Presidential Governorship/State House of Assembly.	Presidential & National Assembly – 16th February, 2019 Governorship & State House of Assembly – 2nd March, 2019	Section 25 of the Electoral Act, 2010 (as amended), empowers the Commission to appoint date not earlier than 150 days but not not later than 30 days before the expiration of the term of office of the last holder of that office.

Note: (i) Run-off election to the office of President or Governor of a State (if any) will be held within 7 days after the announcement of the result of the election in accordance with the Constitution of the Federal Republic of Nigeria, 1999 (as amended).

Dated this 9th day of January, 2018.

Mrs. Augusta C. Ogakwu
Secretary to the Commission

List of Authors

Chikaodili Arinze Orakwue is a Researcher with the Institute for Peace and Conflict Resolution Abuja, a NUFFIC Alumni and Orange Knowledge Programme Fellow. Her interests include conflict resolution, peacebuilding, climate change and gender studies.

David O. Gogo attended the Universities of Port Harcourt and Calabar. He is currently a Senior Lecturer in the Department of Political Science, Niger Delta University.

Egodi Uchendu is a Professor of History at the University of Nigeria. She leads the African Humanities Research and Development Circle (AHRDC) and the Centre for Policy Studies and Research at her university.

Faeren M. Agaigbe holds a PhD in Political Science from Benue State University where she currently lectures.

Fidelis A. E. Paki graduated from the Universities of Jos (1998) and Ibadan (2001), specializing in International Relations.

Isa Mohammed is with the Department of Political Science and International Relations at Taraba State University, Nigeria.

John Tsuwa is a Professor and specialist in peace and conflict studies at Benue State University. His second PhD in Defense and Strategic Studies is from the Nigerian Defence Academy, Kaduna. He has served as the Chairman, Benue State Independent Electoral Commission.

Nsemba Edward Lenshie is with the Department of Political Science and International Relations at the Taraba State University, Jalingo, in North-East Nigeria. He is concluding his PhD at the University of Nigeria, Nsukka

Obinna Ukaeje is Research Fellow II at the Centre for Strategic Research and Studies (CSRS), National Defence College, Abuja-Nigeria.

Olasupo O. Thompson taught International Relations at the Olabisi Onabanjo University Consultancy Services before moving to Federal University of Agriculture Abeokuta, Nigeria.

Olawari D. J. Egbe (PhD) is a scholar in International Relations. His interests are in environment and aboriginal peoples, military and strategic studies, international political economy (IPE) and transnational organisations.

Patience Jacob Kondu is with the Department of Political Science and International Relations at the Taraba State University, Nigeria.

Patrick Agbedejobi is a Nigerian in the diaspora. His research interests include democracy, populism, political communication, Nigerian and European politics, and socio-legal studies.

Patrick Chukwudike Okpalaeke holds the B.A. and M.A. degrees in History and International Studies from the University of Uyo. He is now working on his doctoral dissertation.

Scholastica N. Atata is a lecturer at the Department of Communication and General Studies, Federal University of Agriculture, Abeokuta, Ogun State, Nigeria.

Stanislaus O. Okonkwo graduated from the Universities of Ibadan and Lagos, both in Nigeria. He is currently working on his Ph.D.

Tony Johnson Ekpo is concluding his PhD in international relations at the Department of History & International Studies, University of Uyo.

Tunde Agara is a Professor of Comparative Politics and Strategic Studies in Ambrose Alli University, Ekpoma, but presently on sabbatical leave at Igbinedion University, Okada, Nigeria's first private university where he is serving as the Dean of Dr. Goodluck Ebele Jonathan College of Arts and Social Sciences.

Uche S. Odozor is a senior lecturer in the Department of Communication and General Studies, Federal University of Agriculture, Abeokuta (FUNAAB), Nigeria.

www.ingramcontent.com/pod-product-compliance
Lightning Source LLC
Chambersburg PA
CBHW050521170426
43201CB00013B/2040